CLOSE UP

IRANIAN CINEMA, PAST, PRESENT AND FUTURE

HAMID DABASHI

VERSO

London · New York

First published by Verso 2001
© Hamid Dabashi 2001
All rights reserved
The moral rights of the author have been asserted

Verso
UK: 6 Meard Street, London W1F 0EG
USA: 180 Varick Street, New York, NY 10014–4606
www.versobooks.com

Verso is the imprint of New Left Books

ISBN 1–85984–332–8 (paperback)
ISBN 1–85984–626–2 (hardback)

British Library Catologuing in Publication Data
A catalogue record for this book is available from the British Library

Library of Congress Cataloging-in-Publication Data
A catalog record for this book is available from the Library of Congress

Typeset by The Running Head Limited, www.therunninghead.com
Printed and bound in England by Bath Press Ltd, Avon

for goli

CONTENTS

ILLUSTRATIONS

. . . not to forget in dreams the present world
but to change it by the strength of an image.
Theodor W. Adorno

to make a long story short:
the heart
in this barren desert
wishes for a different vision.
Ahmad Shamlu

INTRODUCTION

In the city of my childhood, Ahvaz, there were six movie houses. Two of them were located on Pahlavi Avenue. Every major city's Main Street was named after the reigning monarch in those days. Now they are mostly called Imam Khomeini Avenue. Cinema Iran showed mostly Iranian films. Cinema Pars showed mostly Hollywood productions and Indian musicals. There was a third movie house, Cinema Sahel, on the banks of the Karun River, which split the city into two parts. Cinema Sahel featured what today we might call art-house films. Another theater, the name of which I no longer remember, was in the old part of the city, on Si Metri Avenue, and specialized in more costly Hollywood productions, films like *The Guns of Navarone*, *Ben Hur*, and *The Ten Commandments*. Years later, when I was about to graduate from high school and leave for Tehran to attend college, two other movie houses were built in Ahvaz, with state-of-the-art equipment, including a stereo sound system, in one of which I remember we saw *Paint Your Wagon* starring Lee Marvin, as well as Franco Zeffirelli's *Romeo and Juliet*. I remember everyone's utter astonishment when Lee Marvin began singing "I was born under a wandering star," and the sounds came from all over the theater.

All movie houses in those days were divided into three sections, according to ticket price. The cheapest was 10 rials (about a dime in the early 1950s). This was the section closest to the screen and had long benches on which about four or five kids could sit. The next section, further from the screen, cost 15 rials and consisted of four or five rows of wooden chairs. Finally, the best section, furthest from the screen, where you could enjoy your movie on comfortable, leather-covered armchairs, cost 20 rials. The balcony was also 20 rials. In addition to the main theaters, all movie houses had an open-air section for summer. In Ahvaz the summer days were long and monotonous, but because of the breeze from the Karun river, the evenings were extraordinarily cool and pleasant. Very few pleasures in the world could compare with watching an Indian musical on a cool summer evening in an open-air theater. People living in the adjacent apartments, if they were lucky, could actually see the screen and hear the soundtrack in the privacy of their own homes. Television had not yet come to the Ahvaz of my child-hood, and these big screen miracles could quadruple the price of a house. Even those who were too far away to see the screen but close enough to hear the sound-track considered themselves fortunate. The breeze would carry the sound of an Indian musical into the furthest reaches of town. All you had to do was see a film once and then listen to its soundtrack and songs from the top of your roof for night after night. Women in some neighborhoods would have impromptu parties on their roofs, as they were laying out the bedding for their family (we slept on the rooftops during the summer), listening to the soundtrack of *Sangam*, particularly the songs sung by Nargess and Raj Kapour. Cinema Sahel had slightly more adventurous possibilities during the summer. The street adjacent to its open-air theater had a row of trees, from the top of which one had a splendid view of the screen. We would climb those trees hours before the show began (because we had to hide from the nasty police officers at the station nearby), and watch the film from the privacy of a well-covered branch. The more enterprising youngsters would spread themselves over two or three well-located branches and then "sell" those branches for about a penny or so to the latecomers.

From a penny to about a quarter, the price of a ticket in my hometown repre-sented the political economy of cinema, by far the most popular art form in Iran. Ahvaz was not much different from the rest of the country in terms of its socio-economic disposition. Then a city of about a million, Ahvaz, the provincial capital of the southern, oil-rich province Khuzestan, was overwhelmingly populated by a petty-bourgeois class of shopkeepers and artisans providing goods and services to civil servants, military personnel, and, most significantly, the employees of the booming oil industry. The national railroad that went from Khorramshahr to

Amir Naderi's *The Runner* was filmed near Ahvaz, where I grew up. In the lead character, Amiru, the director captures the essence of every young boy's dream of escaping an inevitable fate

Mashhad had a major station in Ahvaz, and around it a bustling urbanity had emerged. Workers at this railroad station, my father being one of them, as well as those of the oil industry, were by far the most politically conscious group of the population. In the 1940s, the Tudeh Party was chiefly responsible for organizing and politicizing these workers in Ahvaz, Abadan, Khorramshahr, and other smaller cities in Khuzestan province.

From colonized India to colonizing Hollywood, the world of cinema was our window to a modernity we experienced only vicariously. The intersection of art and modernity has made aspects of Iranian cinema signify something beyond itself. In particular, Iranian cinema of the 1980s and 1990s has had a significance in the public culture matched only by the modernist Persian poetry of the 1950s through the 1970s. Two crucial distinctions make Iranian cinema far more important in the range and endurance of its effects. First, its reception by millions of Iranians inside and outside the country (an audience that modernist poetry could never boast), and, second, its critical celebration by a global audience (an achievement inherently barred to Persian poetry because of the language barrier). As a quintessentially verbal culture, we exploded into a visuality that made our cinema a particularly powerful art. During the course of the twentieth century, fiction and poetry were the principal forms of cultural articulation in Iran. Although the origin of cinema in Iran goes back to the earliest years of the twentieth century, it was not until the early 1960s that it emerged as a serious art form. Partaking in the achievements of Persian poetry and fiction, this cinema became the focal point of an entirely new generation of hopes and anxieties, attracting an audience that, aware of the modernity of its condition, crowded the theaters, whether for momentary entertainment and escapism, or for enduring reflection on their predicament.

This audience consisted of young Iranians restless with a volatile combination of expectation and denial. The population of Iran in the early 1950s was about forty million. The decline in the infant mortality rate without a corresponding increase in life expectancy had made the population overwhelmingly young, more than 50 percent being under the age of twenty-five. High schools were the most populous centers of the younger generation, far more so than the colleges. The Iranian universities could not absorb more than 10 percent of the annual high school graduates, ten thousand out of a hundred thousand in 1970, when I graduated from Doctor Hesabi High School in Ahvaz (in the 1990s the numbers jumped to 250 thousand out of almost three million applicants). The brutal formality characteristic of Pahlavi state-controlled public education had made the curriculum a particularly painful experience. Years later, Abbas Kiarostami's *Homework* (1990) would give a glimpse of the cruelty of this education. The daily activities of our high school were routine reminders of the military discipline with which Reza Shah had envisioned and Mohammad Reza Shah had implemented the very idea of public education. We would be marched in rows and columns early every morning into the barren courtyard of our school according to grade, and then ceremoniously led in prayer to God Almighty for the creation of the universe, thanking the glorious Pahlavi dynasty for our peace and prosperity, and then expressing our ample gratitude to our teachers and parents for the gift of life, liberty, and the pursuit of happiness which we were afforded that day. We were then herded into the dark cloisters of our dimly lit classrooms where a barely breathable air awaited us. Our teachers, God Almighty incarnate, would then arrive with a solemnity that would scare the living daylights out of us and banish any iota of intelligence we might have been able to muster on a stomach full of bread, cheese, and sweetened tea (the Iranian national breakfast of all ages, ranks, and classes). Standing in front of the room, respectfully welcoming the teacher, was the *mobser* (literally, "the observer"), usually one of the best students, who was appointed to help the teacher take attendance and do other chores. "*Bar Pa!*" the *mobser* would yell at the top of his adolescent voice, and we would all rise. "*Bar ja!*" the teacher would mumble, and we would, scared witless, sit down. It is impossible to describe the suffocating atmosphere of power and obedience in our classrooms. The classroom was the picture-perfect image of the nation at large: the teacher was God Almighty, His Imperial Majesty, the guide, the father, the policeman on the street, every real and imagined figure of power summoned in one man. We were the subjects, with no rights, unsure of our responsibilities, totally at the mercy of a system that did not exist except in the tyranny of a figurative constitution of power.

From the sixth to the ninth grade we would usually endure our stupefying classroom routine with numbing obedience and maddening boredom. But beginning with the ninth and through the twelfth grade, in my case from 1967 to 1970, our hormones would inspire more rebellious agitations. A band of rabble-rousers would inevitably emerge in every high school, and, with varying degrees of success, would rebel against the systemic mendacity of our entire educational program. When I was in the tenth grade, during the academic year 1968–69, I was the *mobser* of my class. Though a moderately good student, I preferred the company of my tougher and less studious classmates. In the heat of a particularly hot spring day, a band of rebels and I decided that we had had enough fear and intimidation. Before Mr. Al-e Usfur, our professor of Persian literature, arrived, I, now representing the band of rebels, announced that the following day we were going to cancel class and all go to see Mas'ud Kimiya'i's *Qeysar* (1969), which had just been released, and that if anybody failed to join us in this act of defiance, and reported to class, there would be severe consequences. The following day, I actually took the class roll to the cinema, stood in front of the first row, and took attendance right there and then. More than twenty, out of a class of 100 or so, had joined us for a memorable screening of Kimiya'i's pioneering film. The following day we were all summarily punished. I was deposed from my illustrious position, and Yadollah Zardi Dehno, my chief rival, was duly appointed the next *mobser*.

Going to the cinema was an act of defiance. I had a classmate, Ahmad Badakhshan, who, as the only son of a rich and extremely devout merchant in our hometown, was forbidden to set foot in a movie theater, lest he lower the dignity of his family. He practically lived in movie houses. He would skip school regularly, buy a ticket for an early matinee, and then hide in the toilet about ten minutes before the film ended in order to return for the next show. (He never saw the ending of films and we had to fill him in later.) There was something exhilarating, transgressive, even dangerous, about cinema. In the heat of the Islamic revolution of 1979, the Cinema Rex in the city of Abadan was set on fire, and hundreds of people were burned alive. (I used to visit my older brother regularly in Abadan and attended this cinema on many occasions.) Before and after that tragic incident, many movie theaters were bombed in symbolic protest against Pahlavi corruption. There was something palpably political about the cinema, even in its most innocent and entertaining moments. The Shah used the cinema as the most effective form of propaganda. At the beginning of every screening, the audience was forced to rise and stand to attention while the national anthem was played and pictures of the glories of the Pahlavi regime were paraded on the screen. When a rumor suddenly spread that Crown Prince Reza Pahlavi was dumb, a short documentary was made about a day in the life of his majesty the king and the crown prince, in the course of which they both talked. But movie theaters were also transgressive spaces, where in the dark palpitation of our youthful intimations we held the hands of those we loved, stole our first kisses, and dared the authorities by not rising when the national anthem in praise of the monarchy was played. There was something extraordinarily new, inviting, forbidden, unexpected about the cinema.

I think much of the positive response that we see today among peoples of different cultures to Iranian cinema is due precisely to our having watched and assimilated the world through its own self-representations in our movie houses. Iranian cinema is now reflecting back to the world what we have seen, adding our own cultural color. Indian and Egyptian musicals, the American Western, the European avant-garde, Russian social realism—the spectrum of our cinematic cosmovision was global, urbane, emancipatory. Iranian cinema took the world by surprise simply because the world got a glimpse of our cinema only after it had decided the character of our culture through the prism of the Islamic revolution. These disabling circumstances and our liberating vision did not quite add up. So the world wondered. But we were not surprised by the world. We watched and internalized, assimilated its vast and vociferous voices and visions from our own angle and then projected them back. There was something extraordinarily liberating about the vast open-endedness of a white screen suddenly darkened, and then illuminated with colorful im/possibilities. In the cinema, we were re-born as global citizens in defiance of the tyranny of the time and the isolation of the space that sought to confine us. In cinema, everything was possible, and in that possibility we defied our paralyzing limitations. The cinema revealed our hidden hopes as a nation. With all the political and religious censorship that brutally limited our visual pleasures and experiences, we reveled in the rainbow of images that colored our cinematic daydreams.

From the cinema, a critical awareness of modernity and all its consequences penetrated the streets and back alleys of our physical surroundings. When we could not put together enough money to see a film, we gladly opted for the next best thing: a lively, animated, and memorable account of every film was offered by those with a natural gift for storytelling. Invariably, you would see a crowd of five to ten kids gathering around a young narrator who had just seen a film, and who, for one-tenth the price of the cheapest ticket, would bring you right to the foot of its poster outside the theater, and then, from the national anthem to "The End" would narrate for you the story of the movie. The centuries-old Persian art of storytelling, the performative traditions of *Naqqali*, *Pardeh-dari*, *Ta'ziyeh*, *Ro-hozi*, etc., would all be summoned to serve the most imaginative expectations of the young audience. You would vicariously participate in the film, visualize it, phantasmagorially summon the images from that dark room beyond the thick walls guarded by a pricey ticket and imagine the hero and his entourage in the neighborhood. Every adventure film had to have, at the very least, the following indispensable figures: the *artisteh*, the *dokhtareh*, the *jimi-ye*, and the *ra'is dozda*. The *artisteh* (literally, "the artist") was the hero, the protagonist—Burt Lancaster, Gary Cooper, and Kirk Douglas being the examplars. The *dokhtareh* (literally, "the girl") was his sweetheart, the object of his affection, with Elizabeth Taylor, Gina Lollobrigida, Sylvana Mangano, Claudia Cardinale, and Sophia Loren at the top of the list. The *jimi-ye* (literally, "the Jim") was the sidekick of the hero, probably deriving from a certain Jim in one film whose persona was then categorically extended to all other sidekicks. The *ra'is dozda* (literally, "the leader of the thieves") was the chief villain, the bad guy, the nemesis of the hero. With these typical characters magnified to mythical proportions, the street-corner storyteller recounted to his small band the trials and tribulations of the hero.

From the dark temptation of movie theaters these characters thus moved into the public space of our streets and then into the privacy of our homes. As children, we collected in our *dafter film* ("film booklet") pairs of matching slides of our favorite scenes from popular movies. A pair of close-ups of Steve Reeves pulling two chariots against a blue sky in a scene from *Hercules* would cost about the monthly allowance of a teenager. We would collect and trade these pairs of slides pretty much as American kids did baseball cards, except that procuring them was far more of an adventure than simply paying a visit to a local store. We found hours of pleasure in just sitting and viewing these slides against sunlight or a lamp. Once in my early adolescence I became quite creative and adventurous with these slides. I got an old shoebox and made two round holes on its opposite ends. Then I put a slide inside a paper frame and taped it in front of one of the holes inside the box. Next I placed a magnifying glass horizontal to the slide and aligned with the hole. Then I closed the shoebox and called it my "projector." I took the box to the middle of the stairway that connected our courtyard to the roof. When the door to the roof was shut, the stairway was dark even during the day. I then commissioned my kid brother, Aziz, to go and stand on the roof, holding a mirror to reflect the sun's rays through a crack in the door that opened to the roof. After some instructions from behind the closed door I could guide Aziz to reflect the sunlight with his mirror exactly into the back hole in alignment with the front hole of my projector. Thus, the sunlight was guided by the mirror into the crack of the closed door, from there to the shoebox and then through the first hole, through the slide and the magnifying glass, and then through the second hole, projecting an image on the white wall of the stairway. Suddenly, Steve Reeves' magnificently burnt face against a blue sky blazed on the 5×5 foot wall in the complete privacy of our stairway. Glory Hallelujah: a home-made slide projector.

The trick worked and before long I could sell "tickets" to my buddies in the neighborhood, seat them in the "amphitheater" of our stairway, and show them one slide after another, with my own narration. The profits, even after what I had to pay my kid brother for his indispensable and grueling task (especially in the July and August heat of Ahvaz), were quite substantial. Soon this spectacular success gave me another idea that almost burnt down our house. I thought I could relieve my poor kid brother from his arduous task of standing on the rooftop in 40° Celsius holding a mirror to reflect the sun through the crack of the door, by placing a light bulb right inside the shoe box in front of the slide. Then it occurred to me that if I could only find a way of actually unrolling film through the shoebox at the speed of sixteen (or was it thirty-two? I forget now) frames per second, I could make the figures move on the screen, instead of just standing still. (The idea had come to me from a friend who used to draw pictures of a horse on the upper corners of the pages of his textbook and then flip them fast to see the horse actually gallop through the pages.) I recruited the help of my cousin Jamshid and the two of us went to our living room and began to assemble the apparatus. We darkened the room and turned on the current to the light bulb, and I placed the fateful role of film inside the little opening I had cut into the top of the shoebox. The two halves of a beautiful black-and-white frame appeared on our yellowish wall. A chilling thrill ran through my belly and even in the dark I could see Jamshid's grin. I thought the moment of truth was now upon us and all that I had to do was unroll the film through the box as Jamshid held it. As soon as I jolted the film roll it suddenly caught fire, and as a red flame flashed out of the box, the roll began to unravel in a fiery track emitting smoke as if it were a fuse burning on its way to explode dynamite in a John Wayne Western. By some miracle the fire died out, but a smoke of hellfire thickness had already filled our tiny living room. We could hardly breathe. I was too scared to open the door for fear that my mother, busy in the courtyard, would notice the mischief. But the smoke itself had already given us away. Noticing the thick cloud seeping from under the door, my mother rushed into the room screaming for Jamshid and me.

We survived that little escapade with minor smoke inhalation discomfort and some major damage to our carpet. No extreme punishment was meted out by my mother either. Jamshid was quite dear to our family because he and his twin brothers and elder sister had just lost their mother, my mother's sister, to cancer. They were told that their mother had been sent abroad for treatment until they grew a little older, and the sad news could be given to them. So everyone, especially my mother, was on pins and needles to make sure that my young aunt's spirit was not unduly disturbed.

Disturbed, though, was the creative cast of our imagination, not just Jamshid's or mine, but that of our nation at large. There was always something dangerous about the cinema, something unexpected, inviting, unforeseen. For us, the cinema soon became a room full of creative explosion, fire, smoke, and sedition, transforming our small and secure living room. We could no longer breathe in that room without opening the door and letting the world notice the hazards of our situation, nor could the world ignore the curious smoke that was already escaping the dark dungeon through our creative crack.

In this book I have peered back through that crack and given an account of what I believe animates this cinema the most. The result is at once a tribute to and a reading of Iranian cinema. I have thought and written myself in and out of Iranian cinema for the insider that I am and the global audience that now watches it. There is much wonder and magic in these films. The bewildered journalism that has so far attended them cannot afford to trace their perils and promises. A much richer audience now awaits. From international film festivals to university campuses, from museums of modern art to neighborhood theaters, Iranian cinema has now emerged as the staple of a cultural currency that defies the logic of nativism and challenges the problems of globalization. In this reading of Iranian cinema, I have tried to remain true to that nativity, warn against the dangers and yet celebrate the emancipatory possibilities of that globalism.

After an examination of the rise of Iranian cinema in the context of modernity, I focus on a number of key filmmakers, some of whom have received substantial international attention, and others rather less. As one observant critic of Iranian cinema put it, Abbas Kiarostami is like a locomotive that has pulled the train of Iranian cinema into the global arena. But long before the world took note of Kiarostami, he was busy carefully crafting the precision of his vision. Beginning with an account of the Iranian encounter with the project of modernity, I have paid particular attention to the role of cinema. In the context of the Iranian social and cultural history that informs the work of Kiarostami, I have given an account of his creative persistence in dialogue with the Persian poetic imagination. My interview with Mohsen Makhmalbaf intends to give an account of the most significant postrevolutionary director, while my chapter on Beiza'i outlines the defining moment of a major prerevolutionary visionary who has persistently probed the enduring leitmotifs of Iranian culture. When I interviewed Bahman Farmanara, I was not fully conscious of the intergenerational continuity of Iranian cinema that he represents. The chapter on the predicament of women in Iranian cinema traces the origin of a corrective insight into the history of the Iranian encounter with modernity. In my concluding chapter, I have reflected on the challenges of a new generation of Iranian filmmakers.

It is in the concluding chapter that much of my concern about the future of Iranian cinema is set against the backdrop of its increasing globalization. Here I have tried to articulate the benefits that Iranian cinema has reaped from its much-deserved global audience. But I have also sought to delineate the undue influence that international film festivals and, subsequently, distribution companies have on the commerce and politics of artistic creation. A handful of major film festivals and a comparable number of distribution companies have an inordinate amount of power over and influence on what happens in the best of world cinema. The rather lucrative business of producers and distributors is predicated on the creative effervescence that seeks to communicate the insurrectionary disposition of an aesthetic shattering of the real. Whether that promise is ultimately fulfilled or not depends on the ability of art to transcend the all-too-human limitations of its creators, the all-too-prosaic banalities of its financial beneficiaries. Iranian cinema has much to offer its immediate and distant audiences: it has emerged from the painful memories of a modernity denied, a future delayed, to become the rising hope of a people restored to their dignity, the immediate aspirations of a nation dreamt for the world.

ONE

ON MODERNITY AND THE MAKING
OF A NATIONAL CINEMA

On 18 August 1900, for the first time an Iranian looked at the world through a camera. The camera was a Gaumont, purchased in Paris a few weeks earlier. The filmmaker was Mirza Ebrahim Khan Akkasbashi, the official court photographer. The location was Ostend, Belgium. The sequence involved a royal visit and a flower parade. The principal actor was His Royal Majesty Muzaffar al-Din Shah. In the same momentous year, a public cinema was opened in Iran. Soli Cinema was founded in Tabriz by Roman Catholic missionaries to spread the Good Word and further the glory of the Lord Jesus Christ. Between God, the King, and the Everlasting Kingdom of Heaven on Earth, has the fate of Iranian cinema been narrated ever since.[1]

The story of Iranian cinema is concomitant with the project of modernity as an extended arm of colonialism, itself necessitated by the rise of competing national bourgeoisie (the British and the French in particular), the Industrial Revolution, and ultimately the commencement of the Enlightenment. After almost 200 years of Iranian exposure to the project of modernity, the historical experiment ultimately failed for a number of crucial reasons, among them the colonial prevention of the formation of a self-conscious national bourgeoisie and the catastrophic consequences of the economic placement of Iran in a disadvantageous position in the productive logic of global capitalism. But equally important in the contour of this failure was the moral collapse of any successful formation of individual subjectivity. The history of modern Iranian art, and, in this case, cinema, is as much a record of that failure as a wish list for its successes. At its best, this cinema has succeeded in resubjecting the Iranian self where the project of modernity has failed.

THE COMMENCEMENT OF MODERNITY

As one of the most crucial texts in the history and theory of the Enlightenment, Kant's *Grounding for the Metaphysics of Morals*, published in 1785, proposes the principle of the "categorical imperative" as the guiding force behind a morality no longer biblical. The Kantian proposition of the "categorical imperative" holds that one should "act only according to that maxim whereby you can at the same time will that it should become a universal law."[2] In the history of the Enlightenment, this proposition represents Kant's attempt to define a mode of subjectivity that rests on individual responsibility to a morality no longer predicated on any sacred certitude or biblical commandment. The plight of the project of modernity in Iran may indeed be seen as a prolonged history of failure to generate and sustain the kind of subjectivity that is conducive to the assumption of "categorical imperatives." The history of Iranian art in modernity can be read at times as a jeremiad of that defeat, and at others as a joyous wish for its victory.

Since the early nineteenth century, looking at the world through a camera has been a critical component of the project of modernity in Iran. While the political and religious custodians of law and order sought to adopt and adapt the new visual invention for their respective purposes, Iranian cinema proper began to develop on the margin of these central sacred certitudes, piloted by various social minorities. The Armenians, the Jews, and the Zoroastrians, most of them Iranians of deep nationalist proclivities and yet outside the dominion of Islamic authority, were principally responsible for introducing cinema to the public from the remissive corners of its cultural inhibitions. The first two Iranian films (both silent) were made by an Armenian, Avanes Oganians. While his *Abi and Rabi* (1930) was a comic depiction of the adventures of two men, one tall and the other short, his *Haji Aqa, the Movie Actor* (1932) narrated the story of a religious authority who has a radical change of heart, turning from a staunch anti-cinema fanatic into a movie actor. Already evident in *Haji Aqa* is the transformative power of cinema, turning religious orthodoxy into creative artistry. Haji Aqa, played by Habibollah Morad, an acting student from Oganians's own school, is lured by his daughter (played by Asia Qestanian) and son-in-law (Abbas Khan Tahbaz) to various locations in the city and filmed. Finally, he is taken to a screening of his own acting debut and becomes a loyal supporter of cinema.[3] An active dialogue with the religious and political authorities of the culture thus became a crucial component of Iranian cinema from its very inception. But the fact that religious minorities were left to initiate its earliest stages is an indication of the oblique angle from which Iranian cinema found its way. Moving from a mere potentiality to an actuality, both the moral and the aesthetic subjectivity underpinning this cinema have had a peripheral vision of reality, both unwilling and unable to confront the abyss of fear when a comfortable poetics of being must yield to a new and terrifying alternative.

Religious opposition to the cinema was immediate and emphatic. The earliest efforts to introduce cinema to Iran "drew strong opposition from the Muslim fanatics who despised the idea of recreating the human face and human body on the screen."[4] The opposition to cinema, however, is a much more serious doctrinal issue and cannot be dismissed simply as "Muslim fanatics" objecting to an aspect of modernity. At least four major philosophical and doctrinal objections to any mode of visual representation have been made by Muslim theologians, some of which in fact are drawn directly from Platonic influences on Islamic philosophy. The first objection is the supposition that through any kind of creative visual representation the imaginative faculties will overcome one's reason.[5] The second objection is based on the assumption that sustained reflection on visual representations of real things prevents us from examining the realities they represent. The third objection stems from the historical opposition of the Prophet of Islam to idolatry. Finally, the fourth objection is based on the belief that any act of creation which simulates the original creation by God is blasphemous. Islamic theology, in both its juridical and philosophical aspects, ultimately failed to adapt to the project of modernity, in either its doctrinal beliefs or theoretical speculations. Its passive-aggressive opposition to cinema in fact became a token of its more universal failure to account for the Enlightenment.

A WINDOW UNTO THE WORLD

By late 1904, a certain Ebrahim Khan Sahhafbashi Tehrani, who was also the first to import European films into the country, established the first commercial movie house in Tehran. The introduction of foreign films opened up a whole new window to the world outside. The visual possibility of seeing the historical person (as opposed to the eternal Qur'anic man) on the screen is arguably the single most important event allowing Iranians access to modernity. The Qur'anic conception of *insan* ("man") was coterminous with that of God. Man was as quintessential a proposition as God was: pre-eternal (*qadim*), post-eternal (*azali*), and omnipresent (*qayyum*). In the entire spectrum of Persian visual arts that commenced and predicated itself on the Qur'anic conception of man, mankind was kept outside history, safely sinful in the Garden of Eden. With the introduction of newer forms of visual representation, the picture began to change. Still photography was the first shock. But its history in Iran, which dates back to the middle of the nineteenth century and the interest of Naser al-Din Shah Qajar in the art, remained much isolated in the royal court. In its representation of life, it was also inherently limited to freezing moments of the human presence in the world. The historical antecedent of these pictorial representations of frozen realities was Persian court painting, and the narrative miniatures that illustrated the classics of Persian prose and poetry, especially the *Shah-nameh*. The initial religious objection to still photography, voiced by such prominent philosophers of the nineteenth century as Mulla Hadi Sabzavari, obviously noted the *creative* effervescence that it exudes, and the mobile mirror that it places in front of the created world.

Cinema, however, had a much wider audience. Its closest ancestor was the coffee house narrative paintings, which, along with *Naqqali* (public storytelling), constituted the audiovisual antecedent of cinema in popular culture. The visual observation of a historical (as opposed to a biblical/Qur'anic) person made the mere potentiality of "Iranian" subjectivity possible. But from the very beginning, these collective gazings at the historical person were a stolen look, a forbidden glance, mediated by the remissive corners that religious minorities had long occupied. The darkness of the movie houses were thus the increasingly transgressive spaces where Iranian subjectivity had to negotiate an extraordinarily precarious and borrowed presence for itself. In a culture in which even painting and still photography were forbidden, the translucent representation of reality was dangerously sacrilegious. This anxiety made the nascent formation of individual subjectivity in modernity even more precarious. Be that as it may, the very proposition of an Iranian subjectivity was made possible precisely via these flickering images. As an art form, the cinema could not be limited by the colonial conditions through which it had reached Iran. It had unanticipated consequences that trespassed those conditions. Its medium was far too unpredictable, its audience far too many, for any single colonial or patriarchal mandate to control.

THE CONSTITUTIONAL REVOLUTION

The early 1900s were not ordinary years in the life of Iran as a culture in the throes of the colonial consequences of modernity. From 1906 to 1911, the Constitutional revolution rocked Iran to its foundations. More than a century of exposure to new ideas from the outside world—from colonized India, China, and Japan, from the emancipated peasantry in Russia, and from the European age of Enlightenment—as well as the changing economic and political circumstances inside the country, had ultimately led to a "bourgeois revolution" with the most widespread implications. The ancien régime was falling, a new revolutionary elite was assuming power, the colonial forces were competing for Iranian resources and markets, a corrupt aristocracy was falling to pieces, the religious authorities were in disarray, and the colonially militated project of modernity was in full swing. By 1911, a medieval absolutist monarchy had yielded reluctantly to a constitutional government. Under these circumstances, "Iran" as a national consciousness was at least a century and a half behind the active formation of any mode of moral subjectivity that was willing and able to leave the Garden of Eden for good. Kant had theorized a mode of enlightenment for the European age of modernity.[6] But receiving the influence of the Enlightenment through the intermediary of colonialism, the Iranian individual subjectivity was in effect confronting the project of modernity through enduring Qur'anic modes of objectivity, whereby "man" was still an essentialist counterpart of "God," with no moral duties stemming from his own historical presence in the world. Thus, as far as material conditions were concerned, Iran was exposed to the project of modernity via its colonial agency, and as far as its cultural conditions permitted, it could not but face that modernity with medieval morality. Art, however, was not to be contained within these material and cultural boundaries.

The possibilities of slipping through the gates of the Garden of Eden were quite evident from the early nineteenth century. In 1907, a certain Mehdi Khan-the-Russian established a movie house in Tehran. Because of his pro-monarchical tendencies and Russian connections (his father was British, his mother Russian) he was rather successful in his business. But his movie house was constantly under attack and occupied by the opposing forces during the constitutional period.[7] As the Revolution gradually collapsed, its high hopes for the formation of a national bourgeoisie falling into the trap of colonial rivalries, the discovery of oil in Masjid Soleiman in 1908 marked the heightening of an intense imperialist interest in the material resources of the country, undermining the goals of the revolution. By 1912, the Anglo-Persian Oil Company is formed and begins to produce oil. Two years later, in 1914, at the outbreak of World War I, the Allied forces occupy Iran, with Russia in control of the north and Britain in virtual possession of the south. The country is divided into two spheres of influence, the Qajar dynasty is corrupt and inept, and the colonialist superpowers plunder the country's natural resources. Popular discontent is rising. The promises of the constitutional revolution are all but forgotten. The religious establishment continues to play an active role in leading popular discontent. But the nationalism of the Constitutional period is still alive and well. By 1921, the Iranian Communist Party has been founded. The result of all this upheaval is Iran's forced entrance into the age of global capitalism, both economically and culturally, through a colonizing presence. As the first two decades of the twentieth century draw to their close, Iran is ruled by a weak constitutional monarchy; the colonialist powers, the British and the Russians, in particular, are in outright competition; a self-conscious national bourgeoisie is nowhere in sight; and the comprador bourgeoisie is increasingly dependent on the colonial economy.

In the world of art, however, it is a time of high promise. Poetry in particular is beginning to articulate the terms of a national emancipation from this tangled state of affairs. Through the poetry of the Constitutional period in particular, the very idea of "the nation" assumes legitimacy and currency. A "national con-sciousness" is engendered, albeit primarily by a group of inorganic intellectuals who have just "heard" of the ideas of enlightenment and modernity, and thus cannot articulate them in a particularly compelling way, as necessitated by the material conditions. Equally significant developments are evident in the emerg-ing works of fiction. In 1922, Mohammad Ali Jamalzadeh's *Once upon a Time*, the first Iranian novel, is published in Berlin. In the same year, in Tehran, Nima Yushij publishes *Afsaneh*, and thus is born the modernist movement in poetry. Between them, Jamalzadeh and Nima define the aesthetic space in which the fate of Iranian literary and poetic modernity will be narrated. In poetry and in fiction, the Iranian project of modernity begins to find aesthetic spaces in which the colonial mediation of the project cannot fully control the outcome. Art begins to define a location for itself beyond the colonially conditioned moder-nity and clerically militated anti-modernity. Beyond colonially dependent poli-tics, yet extraordinarily political, bypassing the dogmatic traditionalism of religion, but palpably ethical in its own terms, modern Iranian art begins to delineate for itself its vital presence in the material history of its time.

When Reza Shah ascended the Pahlavi throne in 1926, a new era in the history of Iranian modernity commenced. It is fortuitous that two years before Reza Shah came to power, the multi-volume history of Persian literature by the British Orientalist E. G. Browne was completed and published. As Reza Shah sought to construct a political apparatus for the Iranian national identity, Browne gave that identity a literary narrative. When, in 1927, the construction of the trans-Iranian railroad was completed, that identity began to assume a traceable geographic framework. "Iran" now became the official designation of a territorial integrity, transhistorically presumed to be continuous from the time of the Elamites to that of the Pahlavis. Conceptions of "the Persians," "the Iranians" as a branch of "the Aryan race," and other such powerful and at times dangerous fictions, began to be narrated in compelling terms. As the dictatorial reign of Reza Shah began to appropriate the Iranian project of modernity, artists and the literati had to nego-tiate a place for themselves, one that always hovered on the outskirts of central power. That paralyzing fear of power would remain the defining factor in the critical formation of an active subjectivity. Reza Shah became "the father" of modern Iran and ruled his children with an iron hand. Infantilism once again became the condition of arrested maturity that defined Iranian subjects. Colonialism was rampant, the global market for oil adding fuel to the fire. Reza Shah was no match for the giants of colonial expansion, Britain and Russia. The weaker he was vis-à-vis the colonialists, the more brutal he became toward his own subjects. No dignity could be presumed in being an "Iranian."

No dignity, except that cultivated in the creative imagination of Iranian artists, searching the world and their souls for a noble presence in their history. By 1930, Sadeq Hedayat had returned to Iran from Europe to craft modern Persian fiction in extraordinarily enduring terms. In the same year the first Iranian silent motion picture was shown: Based on a Danish model, Avanes Oganians's *Abi and Rabi* (1930) reached for the comic force of the motion picture and its prelude in the Iranian visual culture. By 1929, Ebrahim Moradi had established a film studio by the Caspian shore of northern Iran in Bandar Anzali. It was here, in 1931, that he made his *The Brother's Revenge*, also known as *The Body and the Soul*. A melodramatic story of two brothers in love with the same girl, it was never completed, but he managed to do a patchwork screening of it.[8] Moradi made another melodrama in 1934, *Rapacious*, about a young peasant who abandons his wife for a woman of the city. What these early attempts at a national cinema indicate is the growing awareness of an emerging bourgeoisie that needed modes of entertainment beyond the earlier varieties of performing arts. The process of urbanization, labor migration from rural areas to the cities, and the transformation of medieval ethics into bourgeois morality are among the themes of the emerging Iranian cinema. The movie houses are filled with city-dwellers, young revolutionary intellectuals, merchant capitalists, petty bourgeoisie, civil servants, military personnel, and a modicum of women who dare to venture into the open.

As these first innocent steps are taken in Iranian cinema, violent events were in the offing. In 1931 Reza Shah banned the Iranian Communist Party and commenced a reign of terror. His jails became notorious for their brutal conditions. In the same year Reza Shah banned the traditional Iranian performing art, *Ta'ziyeh*. As a theater of protest, *Ta'ziyeh* was doubly intolerable for Reza Shah: it harbored much symbolic possibility of Shiite revolt, and its violent features (such as extreme forms of self-flagellation) were not palatable to his modernist proclivities. *Ta'ziyeh* went underground until it was once again freed from restriction. But its temporary eclipse coincided with the rise of cinema. In 1932, a year after the banning of *Ta'ziyeh*, the first Persian-language sound newsreel was shown. In it, the Iranian prime minister Mohammad Ali Foroughi, and Kemal Ataturk appeared live to the astonishment of the Iranian audience. Two years later, Abdolhossein Sepanta directed *Ferdowsi* (1934), an adaptation of the life of the Iranian national poet for the screen. The banning of *Ta'ziyeh*, the first appearance of an Iranian talkie, and the adaptation of the life of the Iranian epic poet all point at once to the rapid changes driving Iran, willing or not, to embrace the modern world. The forced modernism of Reza Shah could not but translate into either an artificial acceptance by the emerging bourgeoisie or rejection by the clerical establishment, always speaking on behalf of the old merchant capitalists. Be that as it may, the emerging Iranian cinema began to attract an audience and entertain them in a way that affected their moral and political consciousness beyond anything they had ever experienced before.

Thus, when Ardeshir Irani's *The Lor Girl* is made in 1933, Iran is in the midst of a rampant period of forced and colonially militated modernization. Tehran University is founded in 1934, giving rise to the most significant institution of higher learning in the country, with far-reaching implications for the nation's political and cultural development. The establishment of Tehran University marks the active formation of the Iranian bourgeoisie, a significant increase in the number of urban intellectuals, and the successful institutionalization of secular learning. In the same year, Sadeq Hedayat publishes his version of *The Ballads of Khayyam*, which resuscitates the medieval skeptic for a whole new generation of modernist intellectuals.

To consolidate the emerging state's new image, Reza Shah changed the official name of the country to "Iran" in 1935. His dictatorial policies (in 1939, he brutally tortured and then executed Farrokhi Yazdi, a leading dissident poet) caused popular resistance in parts of the country, such as the short-lived uprising in Mashhad, but to no avail. In the same year that the *The Lor Girl* was released (1936), Reza Shah banned the wearing of the chador by women. The coincidence marked the parallel fate of modernity and Iranian cinema. The unveiling of women thus became a major feature of the newly imported art. Not until the advent of the Islamic Revolution, and the active "Islamization" of the cinema, did women appear veiled in motion pictures unless it was required of the role they were playing. Cinema thus played an extraordinarily significant role in the emancipation of Iranian women. The very idea that women could appear in motion pictures, despite the fact that the first Iranian actresses were drawn from religious minorities, was a very positive step toward their release from patriarchally mandated seclusion. But even more important, the few women in the audiences could see women without veils and appearing in public. This had an indelible mark on the history of Iranian modernity.

The Lor Girl, directed by Ardeshir Irani in India from a script by Abdolhossein Sepanta, depicted a love affair between Jafar and Golnar under threat from a group of bandits. The film, which was also called *The Iran of Yesterday and the Iran of Today*, ultimately served as propaganda for Reza Shah and his centralized administration. *Shirin and Farhad* (1934) was another production of the Sepanta and Irani team for the Imperial Film Company in India. A cinematic adaptation of the classical poem by Nezami Ganjavi, *Shirin and Farhad*, was one of the earliest attempts to tailor the new art form to familiar themes in classical Persian poetry. In *The Dark Eyes* (1936), Sepanta tackled the thorny issue of Nader Shah's invasion of India in the seventeenth century, and against this background narrated the love story of Homa and Homayoun. In *Leila and Majnun* (1937), also produced by the East India Company in Calcutta, Sepanta turned to another story by Nezami. These first few decades of Iranian cinema indicate an active adaptation of the new art form to the Iranian context. Its principal task at this time was to entertain an emergent middle class. Themes were drawn from the classics of Persian poetry, and the promise of a modernized society was localized for an Iranian audience. The earliest phases of Iranian cinema thus coincide with the project of state-sponsored modernization. A poster advertising *The Lor Girl* reads as follows:

> *The Lor Girl*, or *The Iran of Yesterday and the Iran of Today*, The first Iranian Talkie and Musical, produced at the Iranian Film Studio in the Imperial Film Company of Bombay, directed by Ardeshir Irani, with the participation of Iranian actors, will soon be shown in Tehran. In this film you will see and compare the condition of Iran as it used to be and the rapid progress of the country under the reign of the Just and Capable Shahanshah, His Majesty Pahlavi . . .[9]

The outbreak of World War II and the Allied occupation of Iran in 1941 resulted in the abdication of Reza Shah and the coming to power of his son Mohammad

Reza Shah, who reigned from 1941 until his downfall in 1979 in the course of the Islamic Revolution. The establishment of the Tudeh Party as Allied forces occupied the country heralded the most significant event in the political and social history of the country. It was also in 1941 that Sadeq Hedayat published his seminal novel *The Blind Owl*. Thus commenced a decade of unprecedented freedom in the social and cultural life of a nation fully cognizant of its collective identity.

When in 1942 the American military forces landed in Iran, a new social and political awareness of the United States entered the consciousness of Iranian intellectuals. American propaganda documentaries began to flood Iranian theaters. Meanwhile the Soviets were equally active in supporting the Tudeh Party and its political ambitions. In 1945, the Soviet-backed republics of Kurdestan and Azerbaijan pushed the country to the brink of territorial disintegration. The religious forces began to assert themselves politically and in 1946 assassinated Ahmad Kasravi, a leading social reformer. It was in the midst of these tumultuous events that Esma'il Kushan directed *The Tempest of Life* (1948), the first Persian language film produced inside Iran. One year later, Kushan directed *The Prince's Prisoner*, one of the earliest forays into historical drama. In the story of Borzu, the protagonist falls in love with the prince's daughter and helps her restore her deposed father to power. The postwar era in Iran was marked by an increased attention to its geopolitical significance by the Soviet Union and the United States, the two superpowers that were to dominate the region from the 1940s to the 1980s. This era, however, ushered in much political freedom as well. The Iranian intelligentsia took full advantage of the opportunities brought about by the Allied occupation. It was under these circumstances that the Tudeh Party transformed the very nature of the Iranian political culture. Powerful progressive forces were set in motion. A vanguard revolutionary elite began to organize the working class and educate them in their collective interests. A rudimentary democracy started to operate in the Iranian parliament. The bourgeoisie, though still comprador in its disposition, became more self-conscious. Hedayat's *The Blind Owl* is a dark and powerful portrayal of the decadence of a society failing to achieve its own modernity. Though there is much despair in Hedayat's masterpiece, it harbors an acute awareness of literary modernism, proclaiming an aesthetic self-confidence never before achieved in the modern Iranian creative imagination.

This decade of political and cultural effervescence came to an abrupt end in 1949 with the attempted assassination of Mohammad Reza Shah, which led to the banning of the Tudeh Party. As the Tudeh Party went underground, the religious forces intensified their activities, and in 1951 the so-called Devotees of Islam assassinated Prime Minister Razmara. These radical political incidents were marked by a tragic literary event: in 1951, Sadeq Hedayat committed suicide in Paris. The coming to power of Prime Minister Mohammad Mosaddiq that same year marked a dramatic democratic development that once again offered an opportunity for representative democracy. Mosaddiq nationalized the Iranian oil industry, and, by 1953, his insistence on parliamentary limitations on the Shah's power forced the monarch to leave the country. A CIA-engineered coup toppled Mosaddiq's government and restored the Shah to power, inaugurating the period of American involvement in Iranian affairs. A decline in the social presence of secular forces, a bitter experience with liberal democracy, the continued treacheries of the superpowers, and a pervasive sense of betrayal were the legacy of the Mosaddiq period. The Tudeh Party failed miserably to support Mosaddiq, and he in return could not sustain his power in the face of American and Soviet opposition. The stage was set for a far more bitter experience in the decades to come.

The post-Mosaddeq era was a period of brutal dictatorship that intermittently plagued Iranian intellectual and artistic life. The Shah returned to power determined to suppress any form of political or cultural opposition to his rule. The publication of Ahmad Shamlu's *Fresh Air* in 1957 marked the introduction of a literary style at once lyrical, political, and metaphoric. The establishment of the Shah's dreaded secret police, SAVAK, in 1958 consolidated one of the most brutal totalitarian states in modern history. The publication of Jalal Al-e Ahmad's *School Principal* in the same year was one of the critical indications of social realism in modern Persian fiction, which lasted well into the late 1970s. By 1960, Nima Yushij, the founder of modernist Persian poetry, was dead, and the legacy of his poetic genius well on its way to revolutionizing the millennium-old authority of a rich and proud tradition. A year later, Ali Mohammad Afghani published *Ahu Khanom's Husband*, one of the most successful novels in modern Persian fiction, a crucial turning point in literary imagination.

With the Shah back in power with full American support, Iran is entirely at the service of US imperialism. With the banning of the Tudeh Party, the Soviets are effectively eliminated as a force. An almost complete despair reigns among the intellectuals and literati. Nima Yushij, Ahmad Shamlu, and Mehdi Akhavan-e Sales are the three major voices in poetic modernism. And, most significantly, Iran is drawn fully into the bosom of a global market that needs its oil and courts its expanding commercial possibilities.

The emergent comprador bourgeoisie serving that market begin to be tantalized by the alternative moralities that find their way into such melodramatic films as Esma'il Kushan's *Intoxicating Love* (1951), a daring and imaginative story of a ménage à trois of a woman and two men. *The White Glove* (1951), directed by Parviz Khatibi, engages a similar relationship, this time between a father and a son and their mutual object of desire. While these films lack the substance to give them an enduring significance, they do, as early as the 1950s, represent an awareness of a middle-class urban life beyond the common preoccupation of most Iranian films with the petty bourgeoisie. Depicting the life of the educated middle-class and urban intellectuals would prove to be, by far, the most difficult challenge of Iranian cinema, a task that would remain for Bahram Beiza'i and Daryush Mehrju'i to tackle a few decades later.

Since the constitutional revolution of 1906–11, a nationalism conducive to anti-colonial politics had been a major force in the political culture. In the early 1950s and probably as a reaction to the intervention of the Allied Forces during World War II, nationalism as a theme entered Iranian cinema. Gholamhossein Naqshineh, whose *The Nationalist* (1953) was based on a script written by Lieutenant Mohammad Derambakhsh, was among the first to develop this theme. Similar nationalist subjects and sentiments were also explored in such historical melodramas as Ali Kasma'i's *Ya'qub Layth Saffari* (1957), in which historical anti-Arab feelings surfaced. The cinema of the postwar era thus continued to cater to the tastes of a growing middle class, while also trumpeting nationalist themes. Ideas of "the homeland," "the national heritage," "the foreigner," and "the enemy" were leading sentiments of this cinema, but all of them almost exclusively subservient to the Pahlavi monarchy.

In the mid 1950s, cinema is still an entirely commercial enterprise. The number of productions per annum increases sharply. Movie houses are built throughout the country. Foreign films, the Hollywood Western and the Indian musical in particular, are as, if not more, popular than *Filmfarsi*, as the native melodramatic films would soon be called, with a certain indignant air. Cinema is yet to emerge as a serious art form. Short stories and novels, but most important of all, poetry, are the preferred cultural modes of production. Poets and novelists are the national icons of modernity, progress, and political opposition. Sadeq Hedayat in fiction, Nima Yushij in poetry, and Jalal Al-e Ahmad in social criticism are the leading public intellectuals. Not a single filmmaker yet appears among these cultural heroes.

In the early 1960s stirred the beginnings of a tumultuous decade. Iran recognized the state of Israel in 1960 and thus actively separated itself from the other Muslim and Arab states with which it shared a cultural heritage. A year later a major crisis of leadership shook the Iranian Shiite establishment, as the Grand Ayatollah Boroujerdi's death left a power vacuum. The event occasioned a major conference of the leading clerical authorities in Qum, where the question of the supremacy of Shiite authority in a rapidly changing world was discussed. In 1962, while the Shiite clerics were busy discussing the fate of believers, Jalal Al-e Ahmad published his highly influential essay "Westoxication," in which he outlined the principal symptoms of the "disease" he detected among Iranian secular intellectuals. A doctrine of "authenticity" was at the root of Al-e Ahmad's diagnosis. Having failed to perceive the project of modernity through the intermediary of colonialism, Al-e Ahmad viewed modern Iranian history as one of increasing "Westernization." A result of this topsy-turvy view of modern history was the emergence of such notoriously reactionary figures as Sheykh Fazlollah Nuri, the adamant anticonstitutionalist, as the hero of Al-e Ahmad's essay.

An air of fervent expectation was perfectly evident when, in 1962, the Pahlavi regime enacted a major land reform and then in 1963 launched its "White Revolution." This was meant to initiate a series of reforms in the agricultural and industrial segments of society that would preempt any grass-roots revolutionary outbursts. In partial opposition to the "White Revolution," and taking full advantage of the popular discontent that had been swelling against the Pahlavi regime since the coup of 1953, Ayatollah Khomeini led a major uprising in June 1963. The revolt was brutally crushed by the military and Khomeini was exiled, first to Turkey and then to Iraq. The Shah, however, was determined to match the bonanza he had found in oil money with a cosmetic modernity. In 1967, he implemented a "family protection law" whereby he tried to limit the freedom of Shiite men to divorce their wives, practice polygyny, or contract temporary marriages. These remnants of medieval Shiite jurisprudence did not suit the rapid modernization the monarch now felt on a mission to accomplish. Along the same lines, women were recruited into the Literacy Corps in 1968, and dispatched to the remote corners of the country to teach young peasants how to read and write His Majesty's praises. These were paradoxical developments that, while initiated as part of a larger program of state-sponsored modernization, did not significantly contribute to the formation of a self-conscious national bourgeoisie.

While the formation of a middle class was thus thwarted by both domestic and international forces, the most wretched strains of Persian patriarchy found their cinematic expression in the genre *film jaheli*. The production of *Kolah-Makhmali* (1962), directed by the veteran of Iranian cinema, Esma'il Kushan, in the early 1960s began a long series of *film jaheli* in which the character of a particular kind of lumpen proletarian, or "lumpen petty bourgeois," was at once explored and celebrated. *Jahel* (literally, "ignorant") referred to a type of lumpen who embodied the most sordid traits of patriarchy. A caricature of the medieval practice of *futuwwat* ("chivalry"), the *jahel* represented the basest manifestations of male chauvinism in which masculine "honor" was vested in the chastity of men's female relatives. The *jahels* themselves, however, frequented the bordellos and prided themselves in pederasty. The phenomenon of *film jaheli* plagued the Iranian cinema of the 1960s. In *Ebram in Paris* (1964), Esma'il Kushan turned his attention to the active awareness of cultural differences between "Iranians" and "Europeans," and who should represent the "Iranian" but a *jahel*, in this case played by the veteran actor of *film jaheli*, Naser Malak Moti'i.

But such catastrophes were not to define the Iranian cinema of the 1960s. By then, the country was already exposed to the best of world cinema. Frequent trips to international film festivals added to the momentum generated by the influx of art films into the country, and a group of young filmmakers began to cast a whole new gaze at Iranian society. Forough Farrokhzad's *Khaneh Siyah Ast* ("*The House Is Black*," 1962) must be considered by far the most significant film of the early 1960s, a film that with its poetic treatment of leprosy anticipated

In Daryush Mehrju'i's *The Cow* Ezzatolah Entezami's masterful portrayal of the metempsychoses of a man turned into his dead cow is a landmark in Iranian cinema

much that was to follow in Iranian cinema of the 1980s and 1990s. Equally important was *Shab-e Guzi* (*"The Night of the Hunchback,"* 1964) by Farrokh Ghaffari, which may very well be considered a turning point in Iranian cinema. Adapting a story from *The Thousand and One Nights*, Ghaffari managed, with a minimum of technical resources, to produce a film far beyond the expectations of his contemporaries. Ebrahim Golestan's *Khesht va Ayeneh* (*"The Brick and the Mirror,"* 1965), and Fereydun Rahnema's *Seyavash dar Takht-e Jamshid* (*"Seyavash in Persepolis,"* 1967) are among other major cinematic events of the 1960s. By the end of the decade, Daryush Mehrju'i's *Gav* (*"The Cow,"* 1969) was to transform the very definition of Iranian cinema. Based on a story by Gholamhossein Sa'edi,

The Cow became the touchstone of every major cinematic event since. The study of a man's relationship with his cow, the simplicity of Mehrju'i's narration gradually evolves into a rich examination of the nature of the animality of man, far beyond anything achieved in his generation.

The world of fiction and poetry was equally productive. The publication of Forough Farrokhzad's *Another Birth* in 1964 is a milestone in modern Persian poetry. Farrokhzad became the paramount voice of generations of Iranian women suppressed and denied by a brutally patriarchal culture. Far more important than a brilliant and courageous voice, Farrokhzad became the iconic representation of the suffocated sensibilities of a feminine presence in the Iranian poetic imagination. Her untimely and tragic death in 1967 cut brutally short the career of the most eloquent female author in the history of Persian literature. The publication of three major novels in the late 1960s illuminated the rich effervescence of the creative imagination of this decade: Sadeq Chubak's *Patient Stone* (1966), Houshang Golshiri's *The Prince Ehtejab* (1968) and Simin Daneshvar's *Savushun* (1969). These works revolutionized the Iranian aesthetic and poetic sensibilities. Farrokhzad and Daneshvar made the feminine voice an essential presence in the Iranian cultural modernity. Sadeq Chubak, Mahmoud Dolatabadi, and Houshang Golshiri, among many others, pushed the boundaries of literary modernity into uncharted regions. They spoke of hope, of possibilities, of a better tomorrow, while their fiction and poetry were firmly grounded in the soil of the present day.

The formation of the Association of Writers in 1968 reflected the heightened awareness of a political presence for the Iranian literati. The death of Samad Behrangi in 1968, who drowned in the Aras river in Azerbaijan, coincided with a particularly acute moment of anxiety among Iranian intellectuals, one soon to be even more debilitating with the death of Jalal Al-e Ahmad from a heart attack in 1969. The Pahlavi monarchy was in full control of a state-sponsored modernization. As an economy, Iran was in the grip of a global capitalism that needed its oil and did not mind exploiting its expanding consumer market. Under these circumstances, secular intellectuals were limited mainly to the educated classes of the major cities, Tehran in particular. Though demographically confined and categorically inorganic, the Iranian intellectuals managed to generate a language of engagement with the dominant issues of modernity that, at least in its anticolonial tone and rhetoric, could sustain a revolutionary posture.

The 1970s was a decade of hope and courage. When, in 1971, the Siyahkal guerrilla movement was brutally suppressed by the Shah's army, the news, instead of creating an atmosphere of despair, in fact sparked a new and heightened political awareness of the susceptibility of the Pahlavi dictatorship. Tehran University in particular became the scene of courageous confrontations with the police. Similar encounters between student activists and the police were rampant throughout the country. The underground publications of the Fada'ian-e Khalq guerrilla organization boasted of their valiant resistance against the regime. Hamid Ashraf, Ashraf Dehqan, Amir Parviz Pouyan, and Bizhan Jazani emerged as the leaders of a revolutionary movement against the Pahlavi government.

In the realm of art, no less groundbreaking events were in the offing. Amir Naderi's *Tangsir* (1973) was the cinematic adaptation of a novel by Sadeq Chubak that gave further momentum to anti-establishment sentiments. The central character of *Tangsir*, Zar Mammad, takes revenge on the religious and political authorities who had robbed him of his life savings. The audience that knew about the heroic efforts of the Siyahkal uprising would read far and further into the implications of Naderi's film. This audience, mostly university students in the major cities, did not need such overt celebrations of revolt. Ever simpler incidents were pregnant with suggestion. Sohrab Shahid Sales' *Yek Ettefaq-e Sadeh* ("*One Simple Incident*," 1973), soon to be followed by his *Tabi'at-e Bijan* ("*Still Life*," 1975), introduced a whole new way of looking at reality. It was with this pioneering film that an almost passive documentation of reality became the hallmark of a new form of realism. The lucid narration, the unmasking of the real by a deliberate emphasis on the material endurance of the present, became the key operating force of Shahid Sales' cinema, soon to have an enduring effect on much of the best in the work of both Kiarostami and Makhmalbaf in the 1980s and 1990s.

With Bahram Beiza'i's *Gharibeh va Meh* ("*The Stranger and the Fog*," 1974) something altogether different from the tactual realism of Sohrab Shahid Sales began to appear in the cinema. Beiza'i's principal engagement throughout his long and illustrious career has been an active mythologization of Iranian culture, tracing what he considered to be its contemporary ailments back to their mythical origins and treating them in and with a language appropriate to their character. Two things then occur simultaneously: first, the roots of these ailments are detected in the mythological layers of the collective consciousness, and, second, their subversive derailments are equally sought in mythological counterattacks. One unfortunate result of this kind of cinema has been that most of Beiza'i's Iranian critics have considered him too complicated and obscure for his audience. But the enduring legacy of Beiza'i's cinema is that he is arguably the most visually literate Iranian filmmaker, if one is permitted that oxymoron. Beiza'i's fablization of Iranian culture, most evident in such masterpieces as *The Stranger and the Fog* (1974) and *Cherikeh-ye Tara* ("*The Ballad of Tara*," 1978), has resulted in the most effective challenge to messianism and patriarchy ever mounted in Iranian contemporary art. Beiza'i's epic cinema, overtly influenced by his admiration for Akira Kurosawa, renders the enduring challenge of the divergent traits of Iranian patriarchy in their own terms. If one is able to follow Beiza'i's allegorical narrative, there is nothing particularly obscure or obtrusive about his work. His ocularcentricism has gone a long way in teaching contemporary Iranians how to see, effecting the transformation of a quintessentially aural culture. In its substitution of the *mythos* for the *logos*, and the eye for the ear, Beiza'i's cinema launched a strategically crucial move that he deemed necessary to challenge the lasting effects of a self-delusional culture.

As these active negotiations with the enduring forces of Persian patriarchy were underway, the material elements of that culture continued to strengthen themselves in the Pahlavi monarchy. The Arab oil embargo of 1973, in which the Shah did not participate, put His Imperial Majesty in a fantastically lucrative position to sell the natural resources of the country and make a bundle of money not just to fill the royal family's Swiss bank coffers, but also to fund outlandish domestic projects intended to make Iran "the Japan of the Middle East." The Shah's suppression of political and cultural activities increased exponentially in the mid 1970s. The incarceration of Gholamhossein Sa'edi in 1973 and the execution of Khosrow Golsorkhi in 1974 marked one of the most brutal periods in the Pahlavi dictatorship. By 1976, the Shah was ready to move faster and more aggressively in his megalomaniacal self-aggrandizement. "The Imperial Calendar," which he instituted in this year, was meant to put center stage his dynasty and his own rule in particular. He celebrated the 2500th anniversary of the establishment of the Persian monarchy, inviting heads of state from all over the world to come to Persepolis to hear him tell the ghost of Cyrus the Great to "Sleep peacefully, because we are awake." Monarchs the world over would have difficulty competing with the decadence that inundated this celebration.

These effronteries to human dignity could not go unchallenged. The death of Ali Shariati (1933–1977) in Britain brought to a climax more than a decade of an active ideological buildup against the Pahlavi regime. The leading Iranian dissident intellectuals participated in the ten nights of poetry organized by the Goethe Institute. By 1978, the anti-Pahlavi demonstrations had reached a critical strength in both the capital and the provincial cities. Gradually, Ayatollah Khomeini emerged as the leader of the movement. One of the most tragic incidents of the revolutionary period was the massacre of more than 300 people in the Rex Theater in the southern city of Abadan, where they burned to death in a brutal act of arson. The audience was watching Mas'ud Kimiya'i's *The Deer*.

Early in 1979, the Shah left the country and Ayatollah Khomeini returned in triumph. The American Embassy was seized by a group of radical Muslim students in November 1979 and the diplomatic staff were taken hostage. Thus began an ordeal which lasted for 444 days, and linked the last tumultuous year of the Carter administration to the inaugural podium of Ronald Reagan. One of the most significant consequences of the American hostage crisis was the rapid ratification of the constitution of the Islamic Republic. By early 1980, the US–Iran confrontation had reached deadlock and all diplomatic ties were severed. The outbreak of the Iran–Iraq war in 1980 plunged both countries into one of the most devastating conflicts in modern warfare. Under extraordinary wartime circumstances, repressive measures were taken by the ideologues of the Islamic Republic to eliminate all alternatives to theocracy. The universities were closed, and professors and students whose ideas were unacceptable to the custodians of the sacred were summarily dismissed. Newspapers were shut down, demonstrations were banned, and the most repressive regulations were implemented against women. Secular intellectuals were put under severe pressure, some forced into silence or imprisoned, while others were made to acquiesce to the indignity of exile.

The death of Sohrab Sepehri in London in 1980 marked the symbolic end of an era. The execution of Sa'id Sultanpour in 1981 brought to national attention the lengths to which the officials of the Islamic Republic would go in eradicating any hint of secular resistance to their reign of terror. When, in 1982, the leading Iranian playwright, Gholamhossein Sa'edi (d. 1985), fled from Iran to Paris, where he resumed the publication of his literary journal *Alefba*, it was clear that the intimidation and persecution of secular intellectuals had become the order of the day. In 1985 the death of Sa'edi, who effectively drank himself to death, symbolized the extinction of an entire literary culture. Esma'il Fasih's *Sorayya in Coma* (1983) examines the rise of a forceful Iranian dissident intellectual community abroad, effectively cut off from their homeland. The death of Ayatollah Khomeini in 1989 concluded a revolutionary decade that had transformed much more than the ideological foundation of the state apparatus.

The development of Iranian cinema came to a standstill immediately after the revolution. The organs of the Islamic Republic actively used the medium for their own propaganda purposes. The state poured millions of dollars into films that supported and consolidated the revolution. The most gifted Iranian film directors were prevented from working. But the fire smoldering under layers of ash was not to be extinguished. Bahram Beiza'i, Abbas Kiarostami, and Daryush Mehrju'i, among the old masters, were soon joined by Mohsen Makhmalbaf and Rakhshan Bani-Etemad, and thus dawned the light of a new day on the saga of Iran's encounter with modernity and the crucial function of art within it.

TWO

THE MAKING OF AN IRANIAN FILMMAKER: ABBAS KIAROSTAMI

A year before Abbas Kiarostami was born on 22 June 1940, a prominent Iranian poet, Farrokhi Yazdi, was brutally murdered in one of Reza Shah's prisons. The strong-willed Reza Shah had ascended the peacock throne in 1926 and subsequently inaugurated a brutal campaign of state-sponsored "modernization" that had no room for liberal, let alone radical, dissent. Just a year after Kiarostami was born, Iran was invaded and occupied by the Allied powers, who were wary of the old patriarch's flirtation with the Nazis. Reza Shah was forced to abdicate in favor of his young son Mohammad Reza Shah in 1941, and in the confusion of the Allied occupation, the Tudeh (Communist) party was founded, and a decade of unprecedented freedom in Iranian polity commenced. Foreign powers had occupied the land, the old monarch had abdicated, the young king was powerless and inexperienced, and there was no effective government. Published also a year after Kiarostami's birth was Sadeq Hedayat's *The Blind Owl*, by far the most brilliant indication that Persian literary modernism had commenced in earnest.

Kiarostami was born in the glorious age of modernist Persian poetry and grew up to wed that poetry to the best in Iranian cinema. The cinematic career of this Iranian filmmaker is the history of one festive celebration of artistic modernity giving ebullience and energy to another, the chronicle of the Persian poetic imagination giving rise to a visual attendance on reality.

Kiarostami was a child of postwar Iran, an Iran temporarily occupied by the Allied forces, an Iran abandoned by an old dictator and yet to be effectively ruled

Abbas Kiarostami, with the Lumière camera, making a one-minute short
on the hundredth anniversary of cinema

by his successor, an Iran of the new Tudeh Party, where the daily details of the political culture were charged with a new force of anxiety and expectation. Kiarostami was a child of the Mosaddiq era, a time of temporary relief from the frightful claws of absolutist monarchy, an era in which the active memories of the constitutional revolution of 1906–11 had once again come to color the hope for a tolerant society and a democratic state. When Kiarostami was born, the generation of his parents and his teachers could still vividly remember the revolutionary euphoria that at the turn of the century had mobilized a huge orchestra of sentiments, power, and ideology to awaken an ancient land to the realities of its colonially militated modernity. The revolution of 1906–11 had resulted in at least the theoretical changing of an absolutist monarchy into a constitutional democracy. The constitution had been drafted by a generation of Iranian liberal humanists, firmly grounded in both their traditional learning and their European education. It stipulated to limit radically the power of the monarch, establish a parliament with sole power to legislate, enable the forma-tion of political parties, put a prime minister in charge of the administrative apparatus of the state, and create an autonomous judiciary system to interpret the laws. Kiarostami's parents were among the first generation of Iranians who could recognize themselves as "citizens" of a modern nation-state, and not "sub-jects" (*ra'iyyat*) of a monarch.

The discovery of oil in the north and south of the country soon intensified the colonial rivalries between the Russians, the French, and the British, and the out-break of World War I (1914–18) brushed aside every illusion of liberal democ-racy latent in the nascent nation-state. The civil and political maturity of the new country became evident in 1921 with the formation of the Iranian Communist Party, while the publication of Mohammad Ali Jamalzadeh's *Once upon a Time* in 1922 marked the birth of modern Persian fiction. In the same year, Nima Yushij had published his long narrative poem *Afsaneh*, revolutioniz-ing Persian poetics and aesthetics. Kiarostami was thus born into a nation-state that had become conscious of its political and cultural identity through a century-long process of secularization of its political culture, a semibourgeois revolution, a foreign occupation, the bloom of literary and poetic self-awareness, and a series of catastrophic and debilitating colonial interventions.

Two years before Reza Shah came to power, we witness the completion of one of the greatest achievements of European Orientalism, the magisterial *A Literary History of Persia* by E. G. Browne. Whatever Reza Shah lacked in the literary and cultural symbolics of nation building, Browne's *A Literary History of Persia* provided in full detail. Fascinated by Mustafa Kemal of Turkey (as he later was by Hitler), Reza Shah presided over a massive and brutal program of "modernization." But his project was interrupted in the late 1930s by the Allied occupation and his forced abdication and replacement by his son. The occupation of Iran during the war ended Reza Shah's dictatorial reign. The Tudeh Party was established in this period, and scores of Iranian intellectuals joined the progressive movement. Mohammad Reza Shah became the Iranian monarch in 1941, and throughout the 1940s exercised only a nominal rule over the country. Much political and cultural development occurred in the 1940s that the monarchy was in no position to oppose.

There was not much of a cinematic industry in the Iran of Kiarostami's childhood. During the war, Iran could not enjoy the luxury of film production. Whatever was available was along the lines of Allied propaganda documentaries. From 1945 onward, a pioneer in Iranian cinema, Esma'il Kushan, began to introduce European and American films into Iran. He dubbed these films in Turkey and Egypt and screened them in Iran. They were well received in Tehran. This success prompted Kushan to make his first film, *The Tempest of Life* (1948), which ended up a commercial failure.[1] Kushan's next two films, one of which, *The Prince's Prisoner* (1948), had a pro-monarchy theme, also failed at the box office.

As much as the Iranian cinema of Kiarostami's childhood was poor and primitive, the poetry of the time was rich and revolutionary. Rooted in its ancient tradition, modernist poetry had begun, as early as during the constitutional revolution of 1906–11, to respond swiftly and effectively to cultural modernity. But the publication of *Qesseh-ye Rang-e Parideh* ("*The Story of the Paled Color*," 1920) by Nima Yushij announced the emergence of whole new vistas in the art. Nearly 500 lines long, this poem exploded on to the Iranian cultural scene like thunder and revealed a phenomenally rich language in harmony with the anxieties of modernity. Two years later, Nima published his *Afsaneh* ("*The Myth*," 1922) and *Ay Shab* ("*O Night!*," 1922), consolidating his status as the founder of a new movement in Persian poetry. By 1937, when Nima published *Ququus* ("*The Sphinx*"), he had carefully cultivated an entirely new form in Persian poetic diction. The language of *The Sphinx* is at once poetic and political, iconoclastic and revolutionary. Nima was in full control not only of the rich Persian poetic legacy but also of European romanticism, realism, and symbolism.

By 1939, Parviz Natel Khanlari, a prominent member of the literati, had translated Rilke's letters into Persian and written an introduction to them. The result was a major poetic manifesto which was to influence generations of poets. Khanlari's own poem *Oqab* (*"The Eagle,"* 1942) was a valiant attempt to modern-ize the language and diction of Persian poetry, although it never achieved anything like the significance of Nima's work. By 1943, Khanlari had emerged as a major theorist and advocate of the modernist movement in poetry. His journal *Sokhan* (*"Logos"*) became a forum for young poets. Although Khanlari's erudition was quintessential in the poetic learning of his generation, his political conservatism and identification with the Pahlavi regime prevented him from becoming anything more than a typical learned scholar. Nima, however, was the voice of a generation of hope and aspiration.

By far the most popular poetry of Kiarostami's early childhood, which *ipso facto* defined the culture of his upbringing, was a watered-down versification of constitutionalist nationalism that, under the dictatorial reign of Reza Shah, had lost much of its courage and imagination. But in the poetry of Farrokhi Yazdi and Abolqasem Lahuti, constitutionalist nationalism embraced Soviet socialism, a fact that led to incarceration, torture, and death for poets like Farrokhi Yazdi. The kind of nationalism that Reza Shah tolerated and indeed encouraged was a racist chauvinism directed principally against what it categorically and indig-nantly called "the Arabs," while "the Turks" also were not spared its biting sarcasm. A weak and weakened working class was evident in the almost total absence of poetic imagination organic to the proletariat. Meanwhile, the growing petty bourgeoisie, in tandem with its jaundiced comprador counter-part, was entertained by a brand of "romanticism" which celebrated solitude and individualism in pursuit of private romance.

The situation changed radically in the post-Reza Shah period. Kiarostami grew up during this period of revolutionary change in the Iranian political and poetic culture. Radical ideas, social realism, and anti-colonial sentiments flooded the creative imagination. Nima continued to dominate the most revolutionary poetry. His work combined a radical departure from classical prosody and the most progressive ideas. He became a cultural institution in himself. Nimaic poetics germinated a mode of subjectivity in which the very constitution of Iranian modernity could be re-focused beyond its colonially received mandates. Deeply rooted in the material realities of its time, Nima's poetry transformed those actualities into the aesthetic possibilities of emancipation. "In their relation to empirical reality," Adorno observed, "artworks recall the theologumenon that in the redeemed world everything would be as it is and yet wholly other."[2] Nima's poetry became that "redeemed world," in which Iranians could hope for a mode of being at once rooted in their historical realities and yet "wholly other."

THE 1950s

The first thirteen years of Kiarostami's life was a period of relative freedom in Iran. Political parties were flourishing: socialist, nationalist, Islamic. It would not be until 1953 that this period of relative democratic effervescence would come to an abrupt end through the CIA-sponsored coup in which Mohammad Mossadiq's democratically elected government was toppled, the Shah was returned to power, all major political parties were banned, and the institutions of a brutally repressive regime took root.

There was nothing in the Iranian cinema of the 1950s to anticipate the phenomenal developments that were to take place during the next decade. A few commercial filmmakers established film studios and hired actors from the theater to act in utterly inane movies. But the culture of the cinema was nevertheless taking firm root in the country. In all major cities there were now a number of movie houses. Cinema had emerged as the leading form of popular entertainment. There were still no television sets. Of course, radio was paramount among all social strata, from urban intellectuals to peasants in the field. But cinema occasioned a fascination beyond anything experienced before. Its sister art, theater, was far more limited in reaching a mass audience. Traditional forms of popular entertainment, such as *Naqqali* (public storytelling), *Ro-hozi* (popular theater), *Shamayel-gardani* (illustrated public storytelling), *Ta'ziyeh* (passion play), etc., were still current in Tehran and other parts of the country.

But the rapidly growing Iranian petty bourgeoisie found this new form of entertainment particularly attractive.

In the 1950s, Kiarostami was a teenager and the cinema available to him was imported from India, Hollywood, and occasionally Europe, or produced locally. The indefatigable Esma'il Kushan still dominated Iranian cinema and continued to explore the possibilities of a commercially viable industry. His *Contrite* (1950), in which he explores the themes of an active transformation of Iranian society from a rural to an urban environment, became a trendsetter for much of the later Iranian melodrama and was a commercially successful film.[3] A major development in the melodramatic films of Kushan was his casting of women in leading roles. Two distinguished Iranian vocalists, Qamarolmoluk Vaziri and Delkash, acted in one of Kushan's films, *Mother* (1952), guaranteeing its success. Vaziri and later Delkash were pioneering women who revolutionized Iranian music by singing publicly, despite the cultural inhibitions of their time. This was a period of gradual technical and aesthetic improvement and adjustment in Iranian cinema. Actors and actresses, many of them from religious and ethnic minorities, particularly Armenian, began to be drawn to cinema. Famous writers like Hejazi started writing scripts for films. Popular vocalists like Vaziri or Ruhbakhsh acted. The first 16 mm film, *The White Glove* by Parviz Khatibi, was made in 1951. More powerful projectors were purchased to show Khatibi's film.[4] Equally important in this period was the critical awareness of cinema as a medium in which, as one contemporary critic put it, "the eyes give a person much more pleasure than the ears."[5] The target of these technical improvements, however, remained mainly an audience of petty bourgeoisie with limited tastes and expectations. A characteristic scene of song and dance, the most famous performer of which was for years Mahvash, became the crucial staple of all Iranian films of the 1950s. The audience was so mesmerized by these scenes that even foreign films, American or European, were interrupted halfway through to cut in a song and dance routine by Mahvash.[6]

A crucial development of the 1950s was serious improvement in professional acting. Jamshid Sheybani established an acting studio in which speech, acting, theories of aesthetics, the history of theater and the cinema, make-up, and music were taught.[7] Films produced in the latter part of the 1950s reflect this greater attention to acting. But unfortunately, the most popular films still had as their leading actors rather talentless mannequins. Shapur Yasami's *Amir Arsalan* (1955) was a phenomenally successful film of this period. But nothing came even close to the success of Musheq Soruri and Samuel Khachikian's *Banquet in Hell* (1957), which featured Arham Sadr, a veteran comedian from Isfahan, as the lead character. Arguably, these two films were principally responsible for popularizing cinema as the dominant form of entertainment in Iran. This popularization soon took a nasty turn with Majid Mohseni's *Lat-e Javanmard* ("The Valiant Vagabond," 1958), which glorified a lumpen as the central character. Naser Malak Moti'i emerged in the 1950s and continued well into later decades as the most famous *Lat* in Iranian cinema. The *Lat*, a lumpen character feigning a degenerate version of chivalry, became a major figure in popular cinema. Amidst this vast sea of mediocrity, one occasionally notices a gentle wave such as Farrokh Ghaffari's *Downtown* (1958), which gave promise of a crucial change in the next decade.

None of these developments in Iranian cinema could compare in significance with the far more important events in the poetry of the period. The "children" of Nima were now coming of age. Nima's own early romanticism had branched out in the poetry of Fereydun Tavalloli and had resulted in the work of Nader Naderpour. But the politically far more important social realism of the more mature Nima now continued not only in his own poetry but also in that of Mehdi Akhavan Sales and Ahmad Shamlu. Although her poetry of the period had very little in it that anticipates her revolutionary blossoming in the 1960s, Forough Farrokhzad was also among the prominent voices of the time. Forough's poetic voice became a major force in the formation of the Iranian individual subjectivity. In the words of the distinguished Iranian literary historian and critic, Mohammad Reza Shafi'i Kadkani:

> Gradually, the universality of the beloved in lyrical poems, which was one of the endemic diseases of our classical poetry, diminishes. In this period, the features of the beloved become more evident and more specific. Poets abandoned the amorphous image of the Beloved and turned to more tangible matters about love and the relations between two human beings. When you read the poems of this period, whether it is a woman who speaks about her beloved (Forough), or a man who speaks of his beloved (Shamlu), you notice that this beloved is no longer that imaginary and abstract Beloved of the classical period. The relations between a lover and a beloved

are very real and concern the routine life of the bourgeoisie. The feudal Beloved abandons the realm of Persian poetry, and that condition of universality and non-individuality that defined the Beloved of the lyrical poetry of the previous period disappears. The lyrical poetry of this period reflects the realities of the age.[8]

THE 1960s

As Kiarostami emerges from his teenage years and begins his adult life in the 1960s, Iranian cinema still has not much to offer him or any other member of his generation. An average of twenty-five films are being produced every year, but each one as bad as another in their hackneyed images and ideas. Samuel Khachikian establishes himself as the master of the Iranian thriller with conventionalism written and pictured all over his screen. The thriller and the melodrama are the two principal genres of filmmaking in this decade. The Iranian middle class is increasing in size and the general population getting younger because of the decline in the infant mortality rate. There is a massive influx of migrants from the remote rural areas into major metropolitan centers. The most successful among these migrant workers join the petty bourgeoisie, whereas a sizable number end up in shanty-towns on the outskirts of the capital. The increasing size of the petty bourgeoisie provides a constant source of income for Iranian melodramatic cinema.

Society at large was on the brink of great upheaval. The death of Ayatollah Boroujerdi in 1961 created a major power vacuum in the Shiite clerical establishment. In a conference convened immediately after his death, the leading clerical and lay authorities began to address the issue of who would lead the Shiites in an increasingly complicated and hostile environment. The Pahlavi regime's official recognition of the state of Israel in 1960, which the clerical authorities opposed, was one clear indication that the state and the ayatollahs were at odds. The Shah had initiated major land reform in 1962, putting the clerics on the defensive. The placing of Iran on the American side in the world order had particularly agitated the clerical establishment. Even among the secular intellectuals of the left, this identification with the US and Western Europe was seriously challenged. The publication of Jalal al-e Ahmad's *Westoxication* in 1962 is perhaps the best indication of this dissatisfaction. Notwithstanding such discontent, and his cues coming from the Kennedy administration, the Shah launched his "White Revolution" in 1963. The religious establishment was caught off guard. Converging under the leadership of Ayatollah Khomeini, it countermobilized against the regime. The revolt of June 1963 was widespread and rather extensive, but it failed to destabilize the country. Khomeini was forced into exile and the insurrection subsided.

The Iranian intellectual scene was agitated; a renewed, albeit muffled, expectation was in the air. The Iranian cinema finally started to respond to these changes. The first sign of a radical departure from the nightmare of 1950s commercial cinema was Farrokh Ghaffari's *Shab-e Guzi* ("*The Night of the Hunchback*," 1964). A contemporary critic, Hazhir Daryush, jubilantly proclaimed the serious commencement of Iranian cinema with the making of this film, based on a story from *The Thousand and One Nights.*[9] This and two other major films, Forough Farrokhzad's *Khaneh Siyah Ast* ("*The House Is Black*," 1962) and Ebrahim Golestan's *Khesht va Ayeneh* ("*The Brick and the Mirror*," 1965) proved that indeed a whole new cinematic tradition was in the making.

But in the same year, by far the most famous and popular film in the history of Iranian cinema, *Ganj-e Qarun* ("*The Treasure of Qarun*," 1965), illustrated the continued taste of the Iranian mass audience for the melodramatic celebration of lumpenism, a plague that has never lost its influence and continues to perpetuate the worst traits of Iranian patriarchy. The commercial success of *The Treasure of Qarun* was such that the year after its production the number of Iranian films per annum increased from thirty-nine to fifty-two, the majority of those following the formula of this film, and thus giving rise to a whole genre of Iranian cinema called "*à la The Treasure of Qarun.*"[10]

The catastrophic consequences of these films was more than compensated for by much more significant developments in literature that matched the best of the 1960s cinema. Nima Yushij died in 1960, but his poetic offspring—Ahmad Shamlu, Mehdi Akhavan Sales, Forough Farrokhzad, and Sohrab Sepehri, chief among them—were defining the moral and intellectual atmosphere of the time. The publication of Farrokhzad's *Another Birth* in 1964 marked the most significant event in the history of modern literary creativity in the language. Before her tragic and untimely death in 1967, Farrokhzad would radically change the poetic disposition of her culture beyond anything before achieved. In the realm of fiction, no less significant events were taking place. The publication of Ali Mohammad Afghani's *Ahu Khanom's Husband* in 1961 was universally celebrated as a milestone in Persian literature. Sadeq Chubak's *Patient Stone* was published in 1966. Houshang Golshiri's *Prince Ehtejab* came out in 1969, as did Simin Daneshvar's *Savushun*. In film, fiction, and poetry, Iranian achievements in the 1960s would leave nothing for Kiarostami to regret.

A new wave of serious filmmakers was rising. Soon after the successes of Ghaffari, Farrokhzad, and Golestan, Davud Mollapour directed *Shohar-e Ahu Khanom* ("Ahu Khanom's Husband," 1968).[11] Based on the original novel by Ali Mohammad Afghani, *Ahu Khanom's Husband* steered clear of all the nauseating clichés of Iranian popular cinema, seeking a realistic portrayal of urban life. It was received with great critical acclaim and demonstrated that Iranian cinema could gradually escape entrapment in catering to the basest instincts of a mass audience. The year after that, Daryush Mehrju'i's masterpiece, *Gav* ("The Cow," 1969), based on a story by Gholamhossein Sa'edi, the leading Iranian playwright, became the defining moment of the Iranian cinema. With Ezzatolah Entezami's unforgettable performance as a man so obsessed with his cow that he goes mad upon its death, dawned a new age in Iranian cinema. Mehrju'i achieved for Iranian cinema what no one before him had been able to do: give it character and direction, articulate its potential, and bring it to global attention. Mas'ud Kimiya'i's *Qeysar* ("Qeysar," 1969) pales in comparison to *The Cow*, though it, too, attracted considerable praise. But *Qeysar*, despite its technical and directorial brilliance, did nothing for Iranian cinema except to glorify further the rampant lumpenism of the 1950s and 1960s. Central to *Qeysar* was still the lumpen machismo of the *film jaheli* genre in which the "honor" of the patriarch is vested in the chastity of his female relations.

The coming to fruition of the best in Iranian cinema in the 1960s coincided with the most glorious moments of modernist poetry: Forough Farrokhzad, Sohrab Sepehri, Ahmad Shamlu, and Mehdi Akhavan Sales defined the specific achievements of this poetry. Forough Farrokhzad emerged as the most eloquent voice of her generation, speaking not only of suppressed femininity but a whole spectrum of forbidden thoughts. Sohrab Sepehri cut through the thick politicization of his age to grasp a primal moment of wonder in the world. Shamlu's poetry celebrated a revolutionary pride in the very fact of being human. Akhavan Sales expressed the rising chorus of a whole nation's suppressed anger and search for dignity. No other period in the history of Iranian modernity is so rich with the metaphoric tremors of emancipation. Volatility became the theme of the age. The world was unstable, people were rootless, reality was amorphous, relations were changing, and ideals were mutable. But in the midst of all this fluidity of atmosphere, a certain consistency was in the air, a congruity between what the prophetic poets proclaimed and what their readers dreamed. In the poetry of Forough Farrokhzad and Sohrab Sepehri, in particular, there was a transmutation of the historicized person that Nima had made possible into an impatient realization of the self-transparency of one's presence in the world. The whole metaphysics of representation, from classical poetry down to its vestiges in the Nimaic revolution, Sepehri and Farrokhzad took gracefully to task by radically rejecting the aesthetic objectification of being. Their poetry is an active insurgency against that objectification in reaching for the immediate experience of the world *before* its mediated modulations. Theirs was an instrumental intrusion into the immediacy and facticity of that form of being wherein the world is de-worlded, life is de-experienced, reality becomes no longer self-evident, and the self-transparency of life is no longer inaccessible.

THE 1970s

In the 1970s, the film division of the Institute for the Intellectual Development of Children and Young Adults (*Kanun-e Parvaresh-e Fekri Kudakan va Noja-vanan*), or *Kanun* for short, became the focal point of a major movement in Iranian cinema. Abbas Kiarostami and an entire generation of young filmmakers were its pioneers. The establishment of *Kanun* was part of a general pattern of cultural development that the Pahlavi regime had initiated to engage the Iranian youth in politically harmless entertainment. But, as usual, *Kanun* turned out to be a Trojan horse for the government. From the poetry of Ahmad Shamlu to the fiction of Samad Behrangi, some of the most subversive works of literature were sponsored and distributed widely by *Kanun*.

The Shah, however, had much bigger fish to fry rather than to worry about the symbolically subversive counterculture under his nose. The position of Iran in OPEC had been strengthened in the early 1970s and revenue from oil reached unprecedented figures. The Siyahkal uprising in northern Iran and a host of similar guerrilla movements were brutally suppressed. Ayatollah Khomeini was in exile in Iraq and effectively cut off from his supporters inside the country. The monarch was in complete control. The Iranian economy was more than ever predicated on the export of oil and the import of just about everything else: wheat from the United States, potatoes from Pakistan, rice from Thailand, onions from India, oranges from South Africa, cheese from Denmark, chicken from the Netherlands, eggs from Israel, sheep from Turkey, and frozen meat from Australia. This catastrophic economic counterdevelopment meant astronomical wealth for the royal family and its cohorts, a massive increase in the size of the Iranian petty bourgeoisie, the spontaneous enrichment of the comprador bourgeoisie, the total devastation of the national economic infrastructure, the retardation of the growth of the working class, the totalitarian erasure of civil society, the cessation of all institutionalized and grass-roots political activities, the radicalization of religious and secular insurrectionary movements, and, ultimately, the generation of a politically muted group of isolated intellectuals. By early 1975, the Shah's megalomaniac proclivity had resulted in his finally abandoning all pretense to democracy and establishing the *Rastakhiz* ("Resurrection") Party as the only legal political organization in the state. The monarch ordered everyone either to join the party or leave *his* country.

Against the background of these brutal realities, Abbas Kiarostami was meticulously engaged in an entirely different domain. He was busy trying to teach us how to see the world differently. Like his kindred spirit Sohrab Sepehri, Kiarostami sought a re-reading of reality from a tabula rasa that would make the world once again meaningful and trustworthy. Kiarostami's cinema has always explored from a slight angle otherwise hidden from ordinary sight. In *Nan va Kucheh* ("*Bread and the Alley*," 1970), we see the earliest formation of Kiarostami's cinematic sensibilities. Having just bought a fresh loaf of bread, a young boy is heading home when a stray dog approaches him. First a moment of great fear, anxiety, and perplexity sets in. He then tries to follow a grown-up, who leads him astray and takes him off in unfamiliar and aimless directions. Then comes the intuitive solution of simply giving the dog a piece of the bread and going home.

The film's execution is typical of Kiarostami in its precision and clarity. The camera work is extremely smooth and perceptive (though occasionally flawed in its point of view) with both the young boy and the stray dog. Any "moral" to the story is so tacit as to be almost unnoticeable. If there are any "lessons" to be learned, they are almost immediately subverted when we see the young boy safely reaching his home, and the stray dog sitting comfortably at his door plotting its move against the next boy who approaches with a handful of groceries. The baffling predicament of the first boy is now compounded in the second, who has no obviously handy solution such as a piece of bread to help him negotiate his way past the menacing dog.

In studying the world of children with de-cultured eyes and a penchant for irony, Kiarostami detects momentous occasions wherein binary oppositions collapse; when, for instance, punishment can become pleasure. In *Zang-e Tafrih* (*Recess*, 1972) he narrates the story of a young boy who, having broken a window with his ball, is punished by being forced to stand in the hallway while his friends are still in class. On his way home he first witnesses a soccer match and then wanders off to the outskirts of the city. This adventurous day in the otherwise boring routine of school life quietly insinuates rebellious possibilities. From the playful smashing of the window, to the exhilarating athleticism of the soccer game, and finally to the uncharted outskirts of a restrictive urbanity, the narrative is colored by the initial transgression that occasioned this "recess." In *Recess*, we thus witness some of the earliest experimentation with the disquieting limits that Kiarostami's deceptively simple camera can reach. It will not be until the Rostam-abad Trilogy, and perhaps most significantly in *Zendegi va digar Hich* ("*Life and then Nothing*," 1992), that this particular feature of Kiarostami's cinema is fully charged and developed.

With *Tajrobeh* ("*The Experience*," 1973), Kiarostami began his remarkably muted but unbearably moving treatment of love in young adults. A young errand-boy working and sleeping in a photography shop falls in love with a young girl living in a middle-class neighborhood. In hopeful anticipation he goes to her home to offer his services as a servant. He leaves with some prospect of working there, but his hopes are dashed that evening when he receives a definitively negative response. With this film of not more than sixty minutes, Kiarostami managed to subvert the genre of poor-boy-meets-rich-girl that plagued mainstream commercial cinema *ad nauseam* in the 1960s and 1970s. To be sure there is not the slightest sense of rancor or parody about *The Experience*. Rancor, in fact, has never been a feature of Kiarostami's cinema. An effusive love radiates from his camera and embraces everything in its sight.

In the simplicity of his narrative and the courage to dwell deliberately on the innocuous, Kiarostami is remarkably similar to his contemporary, Sohrab Shahid Sales. Shahid Sales, who died in 1998 in self-imposed exile in Chicago, appeared suddenly in Iranian cinema. His *Yek Ettefaq-e Sadeh* ("*One Simple Incident*," 1973) is considered by many a turning point in Iranian cinema. In "*One Simple Incident*," Shahid Sales taught his camera patience and serenity in order to observe the life of a poor boy from northern Iran, evoking the composure and forbearance of a saintly disposition. Soon it became clear that there was something far more important at stake in Shahid Sales' opting for a simple narrative. The deceptive simplicity of his work began patiently to probe the nature of reality beyond its metaphysically mediated signification. In *Tabi'at-e Bi-Jan* ("*Still Life*," 1975), Shahid Sales observes the unbearable monotony of the life of a railroad worker whose sole function is to signal the passage of a train at the same time every day of the year. Here, what we see is not even the perceptible things themselves but things *before* their metaphysically mediated perceptibility—*before* they are perceived, understood, analyzed, judged. The sheer physicality of being, prior to any attribution of meaning and significance, is what begins to surface in his cinema. Shahid Sales soon left Iran for Germany, where he made *Dar Ghorbat* ("*In Exile*," 1975). He remained in Europe and then in the United States until his early death in 1998. He left an indelible mark on the narrative technique of Iranian cinema.

Kiarostami took this deliberation on the nature and aspect of reality much further. In *Mosafer* ("*The Traveler*," 1972), his sense of irony assumes one of its harshest and most self-effacing turns. A young boy from the provincial town of Malayer, Qasem is mad about soccer. When he learns that the national team is to play at the capital, he determines to see the game at any cost. Robbing his parents, swindling unsuspecting schoolboys by pretending to take their picture with an old, broken camera, and finally cheating his fellow fans by selling their soccer gear, he raises enough money to go to Tehran to watch the match. The overnight trip wears him out, but he does manage to get to the stadium in time,

In *The Traveler* Kiarostami explores with masterly understated irony the world of young children with a "misplaced sense of achievement"

only to fall fast asleep just before the game starts. In narrating the life of a young boy, Kiarostami is at his best. The film ends with a bizarre and inexplicable sense of resolution. There is a matter-of-factness about Kiarostami's form of irony, a kind of conspicuous carnivalesque in his weaving reality and romance together. We feel neither sympathy for nor indifference to Qasem. Instead, for the first time, we see him in the web of a fantastic reading of the world which is at once beautiful and inevitable. As a filmmaker, Kiarostami's principal contribution has been this ability to show inevitability and beauty simultaneously. We begin to see through his camera the distinction between reality as sheer physicality and reality as it is perceived via the legitimate and the legitimizing epistemics of a culture. How exactly it is possible for Kiarostami's camera to detach itself from the reality it thus de-sediments has probably something to do with his uncanny ability to use metaphor, mutate metonymy, upturn synecdoche, and imply irony, all in visual modification of the narrative. Irony is chief among the many such innocuous "optics," as we may call them, that are the instruments of de-sedimentation without constituting a metaphysics, or even an aesthetics, let alone a culture, of their own. It is his camera's ethereal ability to remain on the verge of abandoning a culture without entering another that ultimately defines his vision. This is the principal mechanism of aesthetic signification in Kiarostami's cinema, whereby art generates its own, materially anchored, reality. Kiarostami's cinema is thus a perfect testimony to Adorno's assertion that "if artworks are answers to their own questions, they themselves thereby truly become questions."[12] We are Kiarostami's audience by virtue of our inability to evade such queries. In that inability, then, resides our subjectivity beyond a colonially constituted modernity.

Kiarostami has not always been successful in keeping clear of the potential pitfalls that threaten his carefully balanced distance between reality and its undoing. In *Do Rah-e Hal bara-ye yek Mas'aleh* ("*Two Solutions for One Problem,*" 1975), one of his weakest short films, we see him falling victim to one of the most dangerous threats to his cinema: moral sentimentalism. By and large, Kiarostami has controlled this threat and kept it at bay with remarkable ingenuity—perhaps intuitive, perhaps cultivated, one can never tell, and that is a powerful aspect of his cinema. But in *Two Solutions for One Problem* we see what a slippery road Kiarostami has traveled. Two classmates face the dilemma of one of them having inadvertently torn the other's notebook. With the first solution, the "victim" would have his revenge but he prefers the second, his cooperation with the "perpetrator," which resolves the problem and preserves their friendship. Oddly enough, in retrospect, one develops a greater admiration for Kiarostami's cinema when one notices such occasional setbacks. For it is in films like *Two Solutions for One Problem* that one sees the relentless pursuit of a cinematic language in which Kiarostami emerges triumphant. Despite its structural failure and its aesthetic collapse into moral sentimentalism, *Two Solutions for One Problem* still bears the marks of the same type of experimentation in uncharted realms of sensibilities. What Kiarostami questions in this film—the nature of revenge as a human trait, one of the most enduring features of human hostility—he approaches through the perspective of children. Kiarostami has always sought to experiment with alternative modes of progression from identical moments of crisis. In a sense he is trying to recapture moments in cultural infancy in which tension and aggression have resulted in a particular course of action, while other modes of response have been left perilously unattended.

Taking issue with Hegel's idealist dialectic, Adorno, in his *Theory of Aesthetics*, accuses Hegel of having confused "the representational or discursive treatment of thematic material with the otherness that is constitutive of art."[13] The "otherness" of art is invariably evident in its dialectical relationship with reality, a relation that ultimately forces reality to reconstitute itself. Consider the following example from the work of Kiarostami: as part of renegotiating reality in alternative possibilities, Kiarostami has often looked at the boundaries between human and animal lives. A particularly brilliant illustration is his short film, *Manam Mitunam* ("*So Can I*," 1975), which is crafted with impeccable precision and brevity. Here, in less than four minutes, we see him crossing the transformative boundaries of three interrelated spaces. Two little boys are watching a cartoon. One of them interrupts every scene in which an animal performs an action by saying, "I can do it too," and then imitates that action. When two birds are shown flying, both boys are dumbfounded. The exemplary world of art (the television, the cartoon, the very magic of "cinema") and the internal logic of nature (the animals depicted in the cartoon) affectionately embrace the "real" world of the two children, prompting them to emotive and demonstrative responses. The two conflating realms of nature (animal) and nurture (art) have continually attracted Kiarostami, an inclination that again inspires artistic creation in the Rostam-abad trilogy, though, in the case of *Life and then Nothing* (1992), with the added twist of the devastating power of nature in an earthquake. In the latter case, it is the earthquake and television antennas that, as powerful symbols of nature and art, embrace reality as it is. The two realms of nature and nurture, or animality and its sublimation in art, are thus the two strategic toeholds that embrace and thus radically compromise our received conceptions of reality, forcing reality, in effect, to yield to art.

The kind of innocuous optics with which Kiarostami had been engaged extended visually what Sohrab Sepehri had already achieved poetically. Within both Kiarostami's cinematics and Sepehri's poetics, hitherto uncharted horizons of sensibility were discerned, so that a whole project of material resignification of the world was made possible or even self-evident. Consider "Plain of Color," a poem Sepehri composed in 1966:

The sky bluer than ever.
The water bluer even than ever.
I am in the courtyard.
Ra'na is by the pond.

Ra'na is washing the clothes.
The leaves are falling down.
Just this morning my mother was saying
That it is a sad season.
I said: "Life is like an apple.
We must bite into it skin and all."

The neighbor's wife is weaving a bride's veil
By her window,
While singing.
I am reading the Vedas,
And occasionally sketch something,
A stone, a bird, a patch of cloud perhaps.

The sunshine is dot-less.
The sparrows have come.
The nasturtium has just blossomed.
I seed a pomegranate and think to myself:
"Wouldn't it be wonderful if people's hearts
Were transparent like these seeds?"

The juice of the pomegranate gushes into my eyes.
I cry.
My mother laughs.
Ra'na too.[14]

Here we have a narratively explicit appropriation of time and being-in-time as a mode of countermetaphysically accessing the pre-interpretative moment of the world. This becomes exactly the mode of operation in Kiarostami's cinematics. Consider his *Rang-ha* (*"Colors,"* 1976), in which he extends the limits of his experimentation with the nature of reality by reaching for the particular parameters of its sense perceptions. *Colors* is an experiment with non-narrative cinema. Here, under the innocent guise of teaching children the names and designation of colors—red, green, yellow, blue, etc.—the particular properties of objects are given a renewed sense of significance. Again, the operation of the thematic unfolding of colors is rendered legitimate by the presumed targeting of young children. But at the same time, and with the innocent and yet vigorous energy thus generated, the proportions and properties of those real objects begin to assume unfamiliar closeness to our eyes. Defamiliarizing the familiar thus becomes the effective strategy of resignifying the world.

In *Lebasi bara-ye Arusi* (*"Suit for a Wedding,"* 1976), Kiarostami begins to succumb to the temptation to compare the world of children to that of adults, a comparison potentially very damaging to his cinema, due precisely to the same trap of moral sentimentality into which he fell in *Two Solutions for One Problem*. What usually saves Kiarostami's cinema whenever he lapses into sentimentalism is his cultivated intuition to let his camera be guided by the jagged logic of the child's world. In *Suit for a Wedding*, a young boy is taken to a tailor by his mother to have a new suit made for his sister's wedding. While the tailor and the mother negotiate the terms of their transaction, the young apprentice of the master tailor and the boy have their own little business to attend to: how to get the boy to try on the suit the night before it is due without getting the young apprentice fired.

Whatever the technical errors of *Suit for a Wedding*, it marks a transition in Kiarostami's view of the world of adults. For Kiarostami adults are finished realities, children realities in the making. In *Gozaresh* (*"The Report,"* 1977), Kiarostami experimented for the first time with the world of adults, while maintaining his fascination with the nature of reality. In *The Report*, Mohammad Firuzkuhi, a bureaucrat in the ministry of finance, is entangled in a corruption charge. At home, his situation is not much brighter. His landlord is evicting him and his family because he has not paid the rent for some time. He has all kinds of petty fights with his wife. In one of these quarrels, he beats her badly and leaves the house with his infant child. On his return home, he finds that she has attempted to commit suicide. He manages to get her to the hospital in time. Early the next morning, having been assured that his wife will live, he leaves the hospital.

In the same year that Kiarostami made *The Report*, Parviz Sayyad made *Bonbast* (*"Dead End,"* 1977). A brief comparison between *The Report* and *Dead End* makes the deliberate nature of Kiarostami's camera more pronounced. In *Dead End*, Sayyad portrays quite successfully the brutally sad irony of a secret police officer, pursuing a political activist. who is mistaken for a suitor by the sister of that activist. The fierce loneliness of the young girl, the numbing solitude of her life in a desolate house with her mother, the symbolic location of a *Dead End*, and, finally, the sad turning of a potential love affair into one of violence are all portrayed with a melodious numbness by Sayyad. But the narrative never lifts itself beyond its still sadness into a negotiating position with reality. Given the prior givenness of the real, no theoretical understanding of it can remain outside, or, as Adorno puts it, "Art negates the categorical determinations stamped on the empirical world and yet harbors what is empirically existing in its own substance."[15] What Kiarostami's camera manages to do is to make us conscious at once of the fact that the being-there of the real is pre-theoretically "there," and that, even more troublingly, we *are* that being-there. Thus, the being-there of the real is the furthest away from us by merely being always already theoretical, i.e., culturally militated. What Kiarostami manages to do, however, is to constitute the pre-theoretical givenness of the real in relation to "the world." But this "world" is no longer theoretically implicated by and in the culture. Thus, it can function as a horizon, pre-metaphysical grid, against which reality can at once be felt, sensed, and grasped, and in a way that is impossible through the always pre-established culture of understanding that reality. I will demonstrate later that in *Ta'm-e Gilas* (*"Taste of Cherry,"* 1997) Kiarostami reaches the pinnacle of this resubjection of his audience to a negotiating position vis-à-vis reality. In *Taste of Cherry*, he does that via a turning to reality through a being-toward-death.

Finding alternative resolutions of moments of crisis with their received solutions carved on their faces is one recurring theme in Kiarostami's cinema. In *Rah-e Hal* (*"The Solution,"* 1978), we see a young man trying to hitchhike back to his car with a tire he has just had repaired. When nobody gives him a lift, he simply starts walking after his rolling tire, which leads him to beautiful countryside with scenes and experiences he would not otherwise have had. He reaches his car with a fresh and unforgettable awareness of his surroundings. The particular aspect of these sorts of Kiarostamiesque diversions from the ordinary is that they emerge naturally from the situation itself, without the slightest sense of being concocted. This is where Kiarostami's choice of young boys (the conspicuous absence of young girls in his films until just recently is a serious problem) in most of his films helps him to explore an almost natural condition of curiosity, accidentality, and serendipity, and an almost snowball accumulation of events leading from one to another. The experiences that result, such as the boy's adventures in *The Solution*, thus appear to be almost unintended consequences of natural curiosity and accidents. What these apparently innocuous "accidents" do is quietly shatter the routinized matter-of-factness of the real. The being-there of the real is, as we can now begin to see through Kiarostami's camera, in and of itself the nearest to its ipseity, while its theoretical understanding is furthest from it, and yet not alien to it. By this counterintuitive, countercultural move, Kiarostami constitutes a horizon for sensing that reality *without* committing a violent metaphysical act to compromise its sensuality. Kiarostami's aesthetic countermetaphysics is thus constitutionally thing- and act-oriented, and not idea-oriented. Of Godard, Gilles Deleuze once said, "as someone who works a great deal, he must be a very solitary figure. But it's not just any solitude, it's an extraordinarily animated solitude. Full, not of dreams, fantasies, and projects, but of acts, things, people even. A multiple, creative solitude."[16] Kiarostami's cinema, from its very inception, is an aesthetics of the real, a countermetaphysics of the factual. It is there to filter the world and thus strip it of all its cultures, narrativities, authorities, and ideologies.

THE YEAR OF THE REVOLUTION

The period between 1977 and 1979 was one of shattering events in modern Iranian history. Anti-Pahlavi sentiments across a range of social classes ultimately coagulated under the leadership of Ayatollah Khomeini, a Shiite cleric with a lifelong history of antigovernmental activities. On 1 February 1979, Ayatollah Khomeini ended his fourteen years of exile and returned to Iran in triumph. The Shah had already left. His prime minister, Shahpour Bakhtiar, was in no position to halt the revolutionary march to overthrow the Pahlavi regime. On 30 and 31 March, Khomeini ordered a national referendum, in which the overwhelming majority of Iranians were reported to have officially chosen to have an "Islamic Republic." On 4 November, student activists occupied the American Embassy and took the American diplomatic corps hostage, a crisis that lasted 444 days. By the time the hostages were released on 19 January 1981, the constitution had been drafted and ratified by the representatives of the clerical establishment. As of 15 November 1979, Abbas Kiarostami, like thousands of other Iranian intellectuals and artists, and millions of other Iranians, was living in an Islamic Republic.

As Iran became wrapped up in a colossal revolutionary zeal, Kiarostami was concerned with an entirely different issue. In *Qaziyeh Shekl-e Avval, Qaziyeh Shekl-e Dovvom* (*"The First Version, the Second Version,"* 1979), he examined how children and adults deal with the issues of secrecy, commitment, and honor. Seven young boys are expelled by their teacher because one of them has disrupted the decorum and order of the classroom. The six innocent boys refuse to squeal on their friend, and accept the consequences of their camaraderie. Kiarostami shows a video of this incident to a group of adults and asks for their opinion. One of the boys tells on his friend after a week of expulsion from class. The same group of adults is asked to reflect on this incident. A variation on the nature of the Platonic "noble lie," this film sustains its narrative energy by examining the nobility that youthful conceptions of honor create. The adults cannot but pontificate and admonish on the basis of categorical imperatives, while an inarticulate sense of propriety holds the seven boys together. The "difference," always a subtextual Kiarostami-esque fixation, is the moral transformation of innocent nobility into aggregated prudence. This is by far one of the most subversive interventions into the ahistorical modulation of morality across time and space. A different kind of "morality," a "countermorality," emerges here that is entirely contingent on the reality of the event itself and not on abstract ethical imperatives. This dwelling on the pre-theoretical moment is what remains constant in Kiarostami's cinema. In that pre-theoretical moment, reality exudes its own manner and mode of propriety. Through such quiet and subdued erosions of the violence of the metaphysics,

Kiarostami has gradually established a counterculture within which things can at once mean and signify without the otherwise inevitable commitment of the innocuously real to the blatantly conjectural.

THE 1980s

The mood of the land in the wake of the Islamic revolution can be inferred from the voice of Ali Musavi Garmarudi, a leading poet, in "The Time Is Short," a poem he composed in autumn 1978:

> The time is short.
> We have to get going.
> We have to say hello
> To all the plants,
> One by one.
>
> We have to stay awake
> By all the fountains
> Of the world,
> And clean our faces
> In the mirror of their purity.
>
> We have to get up.
> We have to pray
> By the height of the waves in the sea.
>
> We have to learn humility,
> And spend every night
> In the modest handbag
> Of a snail.
>
> We have to slide into
> The bosom of the seashell,
> And endure our solitude
> In the beam of the pearl's light.

We have to,
Along with the caravan leaders,
Drink the night
Of the desert
All at once.

We have to kiss
Millions of callous-covered hands
At the brick-making factories
With the humility of the clay.

The time is short.
We have to get going.
We have to crush
Thousands of leeches
Upon the Silk Road.
We have to cleanse the rice paddies
Of all the leeches.

We have to,
Every once in a while,
Return
And put in order
The poles of the fences around the garden,
And collect the fallen fresh walnuts.

We have to plant.
We have to resume planting the asparagus,
And we have to throw away the magical marbles.

We have to learn
How to fly
From the migrant birds,
From the robins.
We have to learn.

We have to
Take away the ornamental feather
Of the crane
From the helmet of all the world conquerors
And with it rewrite
A good book.

We have to chop many heads
Off and spit the mucus of hatred
Onto its latrine.

We have to have an operation
With a cry
On the narrow throat of the early dawn.

We have to send the early dawn to Africa,
And we have to force into exile
The white.

The time is short.
We have to get going.[17]

The time is violent. It is a time of high promise. Souls are agitated. Men are in arms. Women are afraid. Brutality is running amok. A whole nation has opened its wounds. Revenge is the order of the day. The custodians of the sacred hold a saber in one hand and the holy book in the other. Men speak on behalf of God.

How in the midst of all this madness could people like Kiarostami think about a toothache?

In *Dandan-dard* ("*Toothache*," 1980), Kiarostami experimented with an ironic reading of pain. While the grandfather and father of young Mohammad Reza have long since passed the age of having toothaches and now enjoy the benefits of dentures, the boy suffers from a bout of toothache which results in his being excused from school and sent to the hospital, where he is given expert advice by a dental hygienist. The convenience of the father and grandfather's dentures renders the young boy's toothache quite paradoxical. Wouldn't he be more comfortable with a pair of small dentures? The narrative also rests on a typically Kiarostamiesque pondering on the relationship of constructed reality (dentures) to reality (teeth). Here the artistically re-created make-believe (dentures) is privileged over the naturally created reality (teeth). *Toothache* was made for *Kanun* and has all the appearance of a documentary to be shown around the country to teach children the benefits of oral hygiene. There are charts, cartoons of little devils working their nasty business on teeth, and the rather supercilious seriousness of the chief dentist at the hospital explaining the benefits of oral hygiene while the poor boy suffers under his gesticulating arms.

The rest of the country might have a revolution to worry about. In Kiarostami's world, however, the convenience of a set of fantastically clean-looking dentures is contemplated and contrasted with the sufferings of natural teeth. But why?

There is a story of a medieval calligrapher who lived in the city of Shiraz. One day a devastating earthquake reduced the city to ruins. After the tremors were passed and the extent of the destruction was clear, the neighbors of the calligrapher went to find out what had happened to him. They went to his house, which was in ruins. They began arduously to sift through the rubble in the hope of finding him. When the whole house had been searched brick by brick, the neighbors descended to the basement to look for any signs of life. Deep in a corner of the basement, under the debris, they saw the man bending over a piece of paper with his reed pen and ink in hand. "Are you all right?" they asked. "I have just perfected the letter *N*," was the reply. "No one has ever written a more perfect *N* than this."

The kind of redrafting of reality in which Kiarostami has been engaged, his persistent attempt to show us how to look differently, sketches out a mode of being that survives all the pains and promises of a revolution. What did the revolution promise? What did it achieve? Where is the place of Iran in the predicaments of modernity, neocolonialism, and the sharp response of "Islam" to all of these? Kiarostami's has been an entirely different kind of agenda, an agenda of liberation from the received mandates of the culture of death and negation, metaphysics and mysticism, concealment and doubt. His cinema is the vision of life on earth, certainty in the real, a celebration of the transitory, the festive embracing of being-toward-now. Let us now turn to the rest of his story.

One of the most subversive short films by Kiarostami is *Beh Tartib ya Bedun-e Tartib* ("*With or Without Order*," 1981). In this film, under the calm appearance of a simple exercise, the depth of the authoritarian motifs of obedience is revealed. In a series of short sketches performed by pairs of actors, Kiarostami demonstrates the peculiarities of "order." The film crew, however, finds trying to organize order quite difficult. Disorder defies the imagination and the skill of any "ordinary" person's will to organize. Disorder, in effect, defies ordering, organizing, managing, staging. The question this brilliant short film profoundly poses is how the received patterns of obedience can be subverted, if at all. Or, even more seriously, how can art be subversive? To be subversive, art must not collapse into despair: we are always on the edge of a suspicion that Kiarostami's sense of paradox and irony may lead him to pessimism and hopelessness. From his later films it is quite evident that he is too life-affirming and delighting in the senses to give in to despondency. But there are moments in his work where irony does border on a sense of quiet despair. In *Hamsarayan* ("*The Chorus*," 1982), he depicts an old man who is hard of hearing. On his way home, the street noise becomes unbearable for him, so he turns off his hearing aid. He arrives home in blissful silence. Next his granddaughter comes home from school, in vain ringing the doorbell in anticipation of her grandfather opening the door. Finally, her schoolmates sing in chorus to alert the old man. Here the hearing aid as a symbol is quite reminiscent of the dentures in *Toothache*: a concocted reality substituting for the real thing. But the same device that can help the old man hear his granddaughter come home or the song she and her friends sing is a source of aggravation and anxiety in the middle of a busy street. Just as art is a kind of construct, *concocted* reality is the experimental means of getting to know the *nature* of reality. What we ordinarily call "the nature" of reality is the thematized object of our observation, objects that have been *cultured* to be understood. Art denatures and dethematizes reality so that precisely its culturation and thematization become self-evident. Once thus dethematized and denatured, reality can reveal the metaphysical foundation of its appearance as significant, a feature of reality ordinarily concealed from our eyes by virtue of our being part of the same thematized reality.

In his strategy of denaturing "reality," Kiarostami can make the thematized reality as much anxiety-provoking as comic. *Hamshahri* ("*Fellow Citizen*," 1983), a satirical reading of Tehran traffic, is a peripatetic reflection on the nature of human relationships once people imagine themselves concealed in moving boxes. The brilliance of this, as always, paradocumentary meditation on the nature, function, and ever-changing effervescence of social interactions is that it can very easily be read as a subversive examination of how human societies operate on the verge of total collapse into anarchy. The presence of a moving box obstructing people's full public view of each other can so easily lead to anarchy and confusion that one wonders how the formation of the social contract was ever possible. Unlike E. M. Cioran, however, who was constantly in a perplexed fear of the impossibility of social agreement, Kiarostami can laugh at its sheer presence. Particularly when it comes to "social reality," we can see the complete erasure of the distinction between "nature" and "art" that, at least since Aristotle, we have categorically accepted. "For things come into being either by art," Aristotle maintained in his *Metaphysics*, "or by nature or by luck or by spontaneity." "Luck" and "spontaneity" ultimately collapse into nature and art, because Aristotle further maintained that "art is a principle of movement in something other than the thing moved [whereas] nature is a principle in the thing itself . . . and other causes are privations of these two."[18] By an aesthetic dethematization of "the real," Kiarostami has persistently demonstrated the precisely metaphysical presupposition at the root of "nature." "Nature" thus emerges as perhaps the most successfully thematized reality presumed beyond any inquisitive inroad.

Made some four years after the Islamic Revolution, *Fellow Citizen* can very easily be taken as a political allegory. For any other filmmaker, such a temptation would be irresistible. But the nature of Kiarostami's cinema defies simplistic allegorization. The bizarre confluence of concealed sentiments and social actions in a traffic jam does appear remarkably similar to the social psychology of the revolutionary crowds that began to gather under Khomeini's banner. But Kiarostami's gentle, comic camera never allows such political implications to get out of hand and become realities sui generis. Any resemblance of this traffic jam to the social psychology of revolutionary crowds ultimately leads to more satirical commentary on the very nature of humans as social creatures. The temptation to read Kiarostami politically is equally strong in his *Avvali-ha* ("*First-Graders*," 1985). Its release coincided with a period of gut-wrenching soul-searching by secular intellectuals who, having thought that the revolution was theirs, were now utterly disgusted by its theocratic turn and were blaming everything and

everyone from the heavens and stars to the CIA, the KGB, Mossad, and the
British intelligence service for their political predicament. In *First-Graders*, we
see a group of young students who for one reason or another are sent to the
school principal for disrupting their class. They initially deny any responsibility
for the mischief, but the principal's persistent questioning finally forces them to
admit their guilt. These scenes of confusion, disruption, denial, interrogation,
and confession are periodically interrupted by orderly scenes of morning exer-
cises in the school. The camera's sympathy is neither with the confusion of disruption nor with the maintenance of order. Instead, Kiarostami seems to be
particularly concerned with the nature of denial and the process of confession.

By the mid 1980s, the Iranian political scene is preoccupied with much
harsher realities. The Iran–Iraq war rages, with catastrophic consequences for
both nations. In Iran, the reign of theocracy is in full swing. Under the cover of
the American hostage crisis and the Iran–Iraq war, the ideologues of the Islamic
Revolution ratify a constitution in which the organs of civil society are entirely
incorporated into the state apparatus. Civil liberties are systematically and constitutionally eradicated. Thugs and hoodlums are officially employed by the
Islamic Republic to attack innocent people and impose a medieval code of
conduct. A succession of terrorist acts by the Mojahedin-e Khalq organization
shakes the foundations of the Islamic Republic. In retaliation, the Islamic
Republic brutally crushes not only the Mojahedin but every other kind of political opposition to their rule of terror. Hundreds of thousands of the Iranian
middle class immigrate to other countries. Those who remain are subjected to
the daily violence of a revolutionary, war-torn, brutally militant regime. Revolutionary leaders are either discredited and forced to flee for their lives, like President Bani-Sadr, or else assassinated, like President Raja'i, Prime Minister
Bahonar, and Chief Justice Beheshti. An average of 100 executions per day is
reported during these barbarous years.

"What is poetry for," Hölderlin is said to have asked, "in a time of despair?"
Kiarostami's cinema has always been the furthest from the political, and yet it
remains "political" in the most subversive sense of the term. Whether intention-
ally or not, his cinema is actively engaged in teasing out the hidden assumptions
underlying the constitution of the Iranian subject. By aiming at the heart of the
very conception of "reality," Kiarostami effectively confuses the subject who

claims to know it. As an effective strategy of resubjection, the confusion of
reality with the object of knowledge problematizes both the subject and the
object and opens their constitution up for renegotiation. This is by far the most
revolutionary implication of Kiarostami's cosmovision. His vision is simple and
simply countercultural. But it is not countercultural in the sense of proposing an
alternative culture: Kiarostami always stops short of any culture and thus celebrates the pre-cultural alterity of reality. "Only by conceiving of works of art in
their negative relationship to everything that is not art," as Christoph Menke
puts it in his *The Sovereignty of Art*, "can the autonomy of such works, the internal logic of their representation and of the way they are experienced, be ade-
quately understood."[19] In Kiarostami's case, an alert awareness of the fictive
transparency of the real is constitutional to his way of making the world yield to
alternative modes of signification.

By the late 1980s, Kiarostami was ready to make one of his masterpieces, the
first in what later became the Rostam-abad trilogy, *Khaneh-ye Dust Kojast* ("*Where
Is the Friend's House?*" 1987). The story cannot be any simpler: a young schoolboy,
Nematzadeh, is admonished by his teacher for not having written his homework
in the appropriate notebook. One more such offense, the teacher threatens, and he
will be expelled from school. As fate would have it, Nematzadeh forgets his notebook that day, and his friend and classmate Ahmad, puts it in his bag by mistake
and takes it home. As he sits down at home to do his homework, while being constantly interrupted to do various chores for his mother, Ahmad realizes that he has
Nematzadeh's notebook in his bag. What follows is Ahmad's relentless quest to
find his friend's house and return his notebook. The challenges the young Ahmad
meets on his way and the story's beautifully surprising end mark the maturity of
Kiarostami's craft.

Paramount in the character of Ahmad, the protagonist, is his solitude and
stubbornness.[20] As Kiarostami's alter ego, Ahmad is *different* in the strongest
sense of the term. Ahmad differs from just about anybody, from his teacher and
his petty-dictatorial mandates and rules, from his mother and her numbing
insistence for him to do his work, from his grandfather and his idiotic conceptions of etiquette and propriety. But, ultimately, Ahmad is distant from the
house in which his friend dwells and which refuses to surface on the face of the
earth. Ahmad is the child of a different future, of an altered destiny, of a revised

Kiarostami's *Where Is the Friend's House?* visually translates one of Sohrab Sepehri's greatest poems in unanticipated terms: how far will a young boy go to protect his friend from certain punishment?

vision of reality, of a redefined reason for being. Ahmad is the Adam of an Eden yet to be created, and even if it is never created Ahmad is already there. The mode of Kiarostami's resubjection never collapses into yet another metaphysics. All figures of authority—teachers, mothers, grandfathers, neighbors—are not so much defied as ignored. So Ahmad's manner of differing from others is never confrontational, violent, or based on principles. In Kiarostami's Eden, there is not so much "truth" as reality, not so much "morality" as manner. Ahmad's character is inherently noble not so much because he does the "right thing" as because he *just* has to return his friend's book. The return of the book remains always in the vicinity of that *just* an act. It never claims to rise to the metaphysical haughtiness of an act of "kindness." Kiarostami is the master not so much of destroying the metaphysics of morality as of ignoring it, rendering it irrelevant.

THE 1990s

By the early 1990s, the Islamic revolution was more than a decade old, and Kiarostami turned his attention to the nature of routinized violence via a brilliant and, as always, paradocumentary study of "homework." *Mashq-e Shab* (*"Homework,"* 1990) is a collection of interviews with schoolchildren in which they reflect on the difficulty, redundancy, and futility of homework. Whether one uses the word *mashq* (literally, "exercise") or *taklif* (literally, "duty") for "homework," there is a sense of violence in Kiarostami's grasp of the nature and function of education. What emerges from *Homework* is a frightful, yet perfectly innocent, indictment of the routinized violence imbedded in all systematized "education." The so-called process of "socialization" emerges here as a paradigm of the command-and-obedience nexus that becomes constitutional to man as a social animal. The power of Kiarostami's examination is that he scarcely touches on the all-important issue of the political uses of "education." While the Pahlavi government had an imperial reading of Iranian history piped into its educational apparatus, the Islamic Republic prompted the most radical Islamization of that same history. But what Kiarostami targets, as always, is something much more serious than such variations on the theme of indoctrination. What he does, through the perfectly pitched dialogues of the children themselves, is to uncover narratively the metaphysics of violence as normatively transubstantiated into matters of ethics, morality, responsibility, and literacy. The children's innocent references to television cartoons thus assume a splendidly subversive intonation, pointing to "film" as a countermetaphysics of alternative modes of being. *Homework* thus emerges as one of the most cogent deconstructions of dictatorship at the elementary level—that of children being "educated" in a culture in which "punishment" is perfectly understood and instantly associated with being beaten with a belt by a father, while "encouragement" has absolutely no meaning or significance whatsoever. By far the most disturbing sequence of the film is its last interview with a seven-year-old boy named Majid who is petrified at the sight of Kiarostami and his camera crew. With a paradoxical twist, Kiarostami's own rather scary face, with dark glasses, staring at these innocent children sitting in front of a monstrous apparition formed by the camera and the camera crew, becomes part of this apparatus of fear that he is obviously trying to undo. Majid is inconsolable except in the presence of his young friend Mola'i. At the end, Kiarostami manages to liberate himself and the audience from this abyss into which he has cast everybody by having Majid recite a beautiful hymn in which God is thanked for the beauty of the world and for giving us eyes to see it. The camera freezes on the faces of Majid and Mola'i while the same song is sung by a chorus. The geography of fear mapped on these innocent faces is the most enduring image of *Homework*, rendered even more fearful when seen against the background of routinized indoctrination, the "Islamic ethics" drilled into them every morning as they form obedient rows to go to their classes. As the virtues of the Shiite saints are being recited to them, the children evince a restless, jubilant, and fidgety resistance, which at one point becomes so pronounced that the Islamic censor forces Kiarostami to cut off the sound, at which point the subversive power becomes even more evident.

In the same year, Kiarostami took advantage of the true story of an imposter to achieve one of his most successful analyses of the nature of reality, before the completion of the Rostam-abad trilogy in 1994. *Nama-ye Nazdik* ("*Close-Up*," 1990) is the fictive recreation of the real story of a man named Ali Sabzian who so admired Mohsen Makhmalbaf, one of Iran's leading filmmakers, that he pretended to be him. Ali Sabzian even convinced an unsuspecting family that he was Makhmalbaf and that he was going to make a film in which they and their house would be prominently featured. The family, an elderly couple and their children, fell for the impostor "Makhmalbaf" and agreed to act for him. Sabzian was finally recognized for the impostor that he was and taken to court by the family for his deception and on suspicion that he was planning to rob their house. Kiarostami heard this story and immediately seized upon it. He found Sabzian and the family he had fooled and persuaded them to reenact their encounter. In the meantime, Kiarostami repeatedly asked Sabzian to explain his actions. The result was a sustained examination of the nature of reality in the face of its simulation.[21]

In *Close-Up*, Kiarostami contemplates the interaction of fact and fantasy in the story of Sabzian/Makhmalbaf. One could begin with either fact or fantasy. It would not make any difference, and therein lies the power of the film. Makhmalbaf is a filmmaker, a real man who creates fictional worlds. Sabzian fictitiously enters the real world of Makhmalbaf by pretending to be him. Or we can say that Sabzian physically enters the fictitious world of Makhmalbaf. He becomes so successful in his fantasy that he convinces a perfectly respectable family to cooperate with him, thinking that he is Makhmalbaf. Sabzian's fiction finally unravels and he is taken to a real court where he receives a real jail term. But this all happens before Kiarostami enters the scene. Kiarostami now subjects everything to a double erasure by asking the real people involved in the event to "reenact" for him what happened. But by doubly negating the real, Kiarostami's erasure confirms a reality: Sabzian now actually does act and direct for Kiarostami, the family does feature in a movie, and Kiarostami ends up making a film. The spectator is thus put in the bizarrest of situations, a succession of fact and fantasy, in which one knows one is watching a fiction (Kiarostami's *Close-Up*) that is based on fact (Sabzian's real story) that is based on fiction (Sabzian pretending to be Makhmalbaf) that is based on fact (Makhmalbaf as a leading Iranian filmmaker) that is based on fiction (Makhmalbaf making fictional stories in film) that is based on fact (the reality Makhmalbaf transforms into fiction).

The translucent nature of fact-as-fantasy thus becomes the diaphanous lens through which Kiarostami begins to show us ways of looking we never knew existed. In his next two films, *Zendegi va digar Hich* ("*Life and then Nothing*" [or "*And Life Goes On*"], 1992) and *Zir-e Derakhtan-e Zeytun* ("*Through the Olive Trees*," 1994), Kiarostami brings this particular angle in his work to perfection. And there are traces of this fascination with the nature of reality in many of his earlier films. But *Close-Up* is the first consistent instance of this distinctive feature of Kiarostami's cinema. By thus aesthetically subverting the metaphysics of "the real," Kiarostami has opened the way to radical dismantling of the structural violence of "meaning," upon which is predicated such metaphysical surrogates as "history," "tradition," "identity," and "piety." A pellucid reading of reality-as-fantasy begins to replace the opaque metaphysics of objectivity at the roots of all violent claims to truth. The fictive transparency of the real that thus emerges begins to eat into the legitimacy of any and every absolutist claim to truth, reality, veracity, having-been-there, having-seen-it.

The fictive lucidity of the real is the strategic attendance upon the reality otherwise concealed behind the metaphysics of presence, the culture of the significant, the ideology of the victorious, the politics of truth. Here, Kiarostami takes his aesthetic cues from the first poet of this transparency, Sohrab Sepehri:

By the sunset,
In the midst of the tired presence of things,
An expectant gaze
Looked at the hollowness of time.

Upon the table,
The noisy presence of a few fresh fruits
Was flowing towards a vague intuition of death.

And upon the carpet of idleness, the wind
Had graced the soft border of life
With the aroma of the little garden.

And just like a fan unfurled, the mind
Had held the bright surface of the flower
And cooled itself with it.

The traveler
Descended from the bus:
"What a beautiful sky!"
And the continuity of the street
Carried his loneliness away.[22]

In the poetry of Sepehri, reality becomes translucent. It is stripped of all its accumulated layers of metaphysics. Thus cleared of its historically accumulated burdens of "meaning," reality reveals itself as the object of mere observation. But this time around, the very act of observation is the result of a set of fresh eyes, eyes cleansed of all the dust of metaphysics, culture, ideology, politics.

In 1990, three years after Kiarostami had made *Where Is the Friend's House?*, a devastating earthquake struck northern Iran. Among the areas affected was the village of Koker in the Rostam-abad region, where Kiarostami had filmed *Where Is the Friend's House?* in 1987. As the entire country and the international community mobilized to help the victims of the earthquake, Kiarostami assembled his camera crew and technical support and traveled to the site of the tragedy to see what had happened to the people who had acted in his film. *Zendegi va digar Hich* (or *Zendegi Edameh Darad*) (*Life and then Nothing* [or *And Life Goes On*], 1992) was the result of this trip.

In a post-screening appearance on 26 April 1996 in New York, Richard Peña, the Programming Director of the New York Film Festival, and Abbas Kiarostami offered two complementary explanations of why the first title of this film, *Life and then Nothing*, was subsequently changed to *And Life Goes On*. When the film was premièred at the Cannes Film Festival in 1992, there was another film with the same title. In order to avoid confusion, Kiarostami changed the title of his film to *And Life Goes On*. He also added that the first title, *Life and then Nothing*, was probably offensive to those deeply involved in religion, who might feel that he was denying the existence of the afterlife. For this reason also he decided to change the title. As should become evident in any close reading of *Life and then Nothing*, Kiarostami has no metaphysical concern whatsoever, one way or another. The pun on *Life and then Nothing* leans much more heavily on "*Life*" than on "*and then Nothing.*" The "and then nothingness" of the pun collapses everything other than life, not just the metaphysics of it, into "life." I also think that perhaps in the back of Kiarostami's mind, when giving this title to his film, was the Persian translation of the Italian journalist Oriana Fallaci's Vietnam memoir, *Zendegi, Jang, va digar Hich* ("*Life, War, and then Nothing*").

What Kiarostami achieves in this film is so daring, so brutally and beautifully naked, nude, revelatory, and rambunctious that it brought him as much praise and admiration as it did violent condemnation and rebuke. What *Life and then Nothing* demonstrates, with characteristic simplicity, elegance, and matter-of-factness, is the boisterous, unruly nature of life, the fact that living is good, that death is just there, and that life in its bizarre accidentality has a logic and rhetoric, a twisted irony, entirely its own. Life is riotous and rowdy; no morality, history, culture, habit, manner, or propriety can hold it together, define it, narrate it. So disorderly and unruly is life, and yet so joyous and jubilant, that no earthquake, no calamity, no revolution, no *coup d'état*, no exile, no heartaches

Kiarostami's *And Life Goes On* is a magnificent homage to life in the midst of a misery untouched by theology or theocracy—a visual poem in praise of grace and beauty in the most unlikely circumstances

of dreams turning into nightmares, no emblems of hope becoming insignia of despair, can alter its enduring enchantment. Kiarostami showed children delighted by discussions of the soccer World Cup, young couples preparing for their wedding night, old men putting up television antennas, and all of these in the midst of the most brutal destruction of life and landscape. His camera, caring and caressing, intrudes with the gentlest presence, always knowing where to stop, when to look, how to gaze, why to turn. Iranian critics committed to "Islamic ideology," "revolution," "social responsibility," "moral standards," and, above all, to the metaphysics of fear and mourning were up in arms against Kiarostami after the release of this film. His entire *oeuvre* was ridiculed. He was accused of not knowing the fundamentals of filmmaking. Detailed readings of his films focused on his technical errors. "Foreigners" were accused of all kinds of plots, designs, and hidden agendas to give Kiarostami prizes in international festivals. But he also had supporters, admirers, and critically positive viewers of his films. What was certain after *Life and then Nothing* was that Kiarostami had touched something primordial, a raw nerve in Iranian politics, something visceral, subterranean, gut-wrenching, forbidden in Iranian culture. What was also evident was that in postrevolutionary Iran, cinema was effectively replacing poetry, plays, short stories, and novels as the most significant cultural medium. Whereas from the 1950s through the 1970s it was the poetry of Nima Yushij, Akhavan Sales, Ahmad Shamlu, Forough Farrokhzad, and Sohrab Sepehri; the plays of Gholamhossein Sa'edi, Akbar Radi, and Bahram Beiza'i; and the short stories and novels of Sadeq Hedayat, Ebrahim Golestan, Sadeq Chubak, Simin Daneshvar, Houshang Golshiri, and Mahmoud Dolatabadi that defined the terms of aesthetic engagement with matters of society and polity, in the 1980s and the 1990s, Kiarostami's films figured markedly in a movement that included Daryush Mehrju'i, Amir Naderi, Bahman Farmanara, Mohsen Makhmalbaf, Rakhshan Bani-Etemad, Samira Makhmalbaf, and by far the most visually learned of all of them, Bahram Beiza'i. Through Kiarostami's films, and because of the global audience he began to attract, the aesthetic apparatus of a remarkably rich literary culture cast its long critical gaze on Iran and its problems of cultural modernity.

And Life Goes On thus turns into a quest of its own, while articulating another version of *Where Is the Friend's House?*—a kind of unlearning of a whole culture of signification, an entire hierarchy of order. In Iranian mythology, civilization originates with King Kiyumars (Gayomartan or Gayomard, in the *Avesta*), who is considered to be the "first man." Kiyumars is the initiator of law and order, the state, and monarchy. He introduces order, commands the first army, leads the first community, establishes borders, demands obedience. Kiyumars' son Siyamak is killed by demons, the *divs*, and his grandson Hushang (the *Avestan* Haoshanha) continues his grandfather's civilizing mission. He develops agriculture and invents the crafts. It is finally left to Hushang's son Tahmuras (Takhma Urupi of the *Avesta*) to confront the *divs*. Among the deeds of Tahmuras is the capture of Ahriman (or Angra Mainyu) and riding on his back around the world. It is finally from the *divs* that Tahmuras, and with him humanity, learned the art of writing.

The captives bound and stricken begged their lives.
"Destroy us not," they said, "and we will teach thee
A new and fruitful art."[23]

The art of writing, the ultimate end of civilization, so that the glories of culture could be recorded, was thus given to primordial man by his fiercest enemy; it was born out of hostility and anger, come into being from fear and dread, taught by the demons. This ambivalence is at the heart of culture, according to the Persian myth of creation. Kiarostami's visual renarration of all manner of being always has a vividly antimythological bent, a matter-of-factness that denies the intrusion of any thematic metaphysics, or aesthetics even, into the non-sensicality of the sheer force of being. Kiarostami is not even the last metaphysician. He is an antimetaphysician, but only by completely abandoning the metaphysical project, not by opposing it. Abandoning metaphysics, and with it also aesthetics, culture, ideology, and politics, Kiarostami does not erect an alternative canopy. His is the open air of the absolutism of reality, to use Hans Blumenberg's term, and yet there is no fright on the face of that absolutism. All that is thrives in celebration. Here, Blumenberg's assertion that "[c]ultures that have not yet achieved mastery of their reality continue to dream the dream and would snatch its realization away from those who think they have already awakened from it,"[24] needs to be radically reconsidered. Because of Kiarostami's reconfiguration of reality in such an awakening way that always stops at the border of dreaming a dream, we can now imagine a mode of being beyond false and falsifying fantasies.

Among the rubble of the earthquake in Koker, Kiarostami noted a budding love between two of the young residents whom he had filmed in *Life and then Nothing*. It was a play on the on-screen/off-screen variations on that love story which became the content of *Zir-e Derakhtan-e Zeytun* ("Through the Olive Trees," 1994), the third of the Rostam-abad trilogy.

What *Through the Olive Trees* did was to confirm and bring to a dramatic climax Kiarostami's perennial fascination with the nature of reality, with the fictive transparency of the real. Through the innocent act of role-playing by two non-professional "actors," the mere reality of fiction makes an impossible love possible. Kiarostami's gentle and unobtrusive gaze is fixed on the borderline of

In *Through the Olive Trees*, Tahereh Ladania's prolonged silences and Kiarostami's long takes map out uncharted territories in human emotion

that (im)possibility where fact and fiction, reality and fantasy, wish and fulfillment, negotiate the terms of their respective enchantments. Through this gaze Kiarostami has succeeded in teaching us the infinite possibilities concealed beneath the received impossibilities of cultures as violent metaphysics.

Finally, in *Ta'm-e Gilas* ("*Taste of Cherry*," 1997), Kiarostami carried his fascination with the nature and disposition of reality to an examination of being-unto-death, an antimetaphysical examination of suicide. In an interview with Kiarostami in New York, when he was making *Taste of Cherry*, he was asked why he had turned to the subject of suicide. He replied that he had become interested in the matter when he read the aphorism of E. M. Cioran: "[h]ad it not been for the possibility of suicide, I would have killed myself a long time ago." The difference between Kiarostami's *Taste of Cherry* and Cioran's *The Trouble with Being Born*, his frighteningly gloomy reflection on the absurdity of life, lies precisely in Kiarostami's ability to turn that absurdity into a tolerable, one might even say celebratory, reflection. Cioran's brilliance rests on his morbid disposition: "Nothing is a better proof of how far humanity has regressed than the impossibility of finding a single nation, a single tribe, among whom birth still provokes mourning and lamentation."[25] Kiarostami, however, does not dwell on actual lamentation. He can manage to bring a character into a suicidal man's car who will sing the most beautifully accented song in praise of life, as evident and palpable in the taste of two pairs of cherries. He can have his camera dwell on the motionless face of the same suicidal man so long, deliberately, and persistently that the screen oozes with the whole might and majesty of life. "I endure myself," Cioran replied to the man who asked him, "What do you do from morning to night?"[26] This is not what Kiarostami would answer. "I make films," he would probably say. There is a manifest plainness about Kiarostami's reading of life, a kind of tangentiality to all philosophies and all metaphysics, that cannot suffer the consequences of too much self-reflection as a prelude to volumes of self-pity.

Even at the most disquieting moments of despair, Kiarostami, like Sohrab Sepehri, his poetic counterpart, sees beauty in the benign brutality of being:

The sun was setting.
The sound of the intelligence of all
Vegetation could be heard.

The traveler had arrived
And had sat upon a comfortable chair
By the lawn:

"I am sad.
I am terribly sad.
On my way here all I could
Think of was but one thing.
The color of the pastures
Was so dazzling

And the lines of the road
Were lost in the sadness of the prairies.
What strange valleys
And the horse, do you remember,
Was white
And just like a clean word
Was pasturing on the green silence of the meadow.
And then the colorful strangeness of the village by the road,
And then, the tunnels.

"I am sad.
I am terribly sad,
And nothing
Not even these aromatic minutes
That are dying on the branches of the orange tree,
Nor the sincerity of the word
Exchanged between the silence
Of the two leaves of this wallflower,
No, nothing can relieve me
From the attack of the emptiness of my surroundings.
And I believe
That this harmonious melody
Will be heard for ever."[27]

Inheriting this lyrical gift to see beauty and life in the midst of the unbearable inevitability of being, Kiarostami is the first visual poet of his nation.

THREE

THE SIGHT OF
THE INVISIBLE WORLD:
THE CINEMA OF BAHRAM BEIZA'I

One of the most brilliant Iranian filmmakers, dramatists, and scholars of the performing arts, Bahram Beiza'i (born 26 December 1938 in Tehran), is universally recognized as the leading framer of a radically revised aesthetic vision of his culture. A creative visionary of uncommon clarity, Beiza'i has redefined the Iranian performing arts to meet the challenges of a modernity he openly embraces with an uncompromisingly secular gaze. At the service of that revolutionary gaze is Beiza'i's stunning record of artistic and scholarly achievements in three distinct but interrelated areas—film, theater, and scholarship in the performing arts. During one of Beiza'i's visits to the United States, in the course of which he screened a number of his films banned in Iran, I met him on 13 March 1995 for a conversation on Iranian culture and the inner workings of myth in its historical development. I excerpt portions of that interview here, and then trace the dynamics of mythological imagination in some of Beiza'i's major films.

Hamid Dabashi I'm very interested in your views on our pre-cinematic visual and performing arts, and the influence they might have on our contemporary cinema. In your judgment, what impact, if any, have the visual and performing arts had on the texture of our culture? I am particularly concerned about the fact that Persian painting was in effect concealed in books and thus available only to very few people. So in what way can we speak of the presence of visual and performing traditions in our culture?

Bahram Beiza'i

Bahram Beiza'i   So far as our visual art is concerned, what was accessible to the public was of course first and foremost what people could see on the doors and walls of mosques and similar public buildings. These are the so-called abstract designs, which are in fact stylized calligraphy of Qur'anic verses, and the visual designs in carpets, rugs, and kilims. In addition to these, communal rituals are also modes of "performance" that depict certain images—images of certain beliefs.

HD   By "ritual," you mean religious rituals?

BB   No. Not at all. In fact, I don't believe that any ritual in Iran was originally religious. I believe that all religious rituals are deeply rooted in ancient non-religious rituals. Even in such rituals as the collective cooking of soup (*ash*) in certain villages, for example, in which every household contributes one of the ingredients, and all of them make the soup and eat it together, we observe communal participation in a creative act.

HD   As in *samanu-pazun*, for example?

BB   That's right. Consider also that the same soup is even used for fortune-telling: they would let it cool for a while, and then interpret the lines that would form on the surface of the soup. They would read those lines as, for example, the sign of its being "accepted" by whatever patron saint it was intended for. But the whole event signified that, by bringing together all these rituals and activities as the soup is made, something had been created. Thus, it was a kind of distribution of fertility, a collective act of creation. Such rituals may not have a direct connection to the specific question of "visual art" that you are concerned with. But nevertheless, one needs to pay attention to them. More specifically, though, for the longest time the visual arts as such were forbidden in Iran. They were objected to on theological grounds, that painting was a kind of participation with God in creation, which was of course forbidden.

HD   Well, I hope we come back to this question of forbidden painting because it appears to me that these prohibitions were invitations to transgress. But that's a different issue. I do remember the form of ritual you are referring to from my own childhood, what was called *samanu-pazun*: women in the neighborhood made a stew of wheat germ, *samanu*, for the New Year.

BB   Correct. But my point is that for a long time, it was difficult for Iranians to display formally the relationship between their actions and their thoughts. Thus, rather than openly indicate that one was working in accordance with one's own imagination when engaged in an act of representation, one would instead proclaim that one was merely assisting in the execution of divine will and thus was a minor participant in creation. As evidence of this assertion, paintings were not openly displayed, but rather were hidden in the pages of books and served solely in an illustrative capacity. Moreover, such paintings were typically kept within the confines of the rich households that acted as patrons to the artists. Consequently, the isolation of these works, which were never displayed in public, resulted in a widespread ignorance of their very existence. Even today, these lavish manuscripts are not usually available to the general public, because the majority are printed abroad, meaning that these texts were stolen from Iran, sold abroad, printed, compiled, and then sold back.

HD   You mean the so-called "Persian miniatures"?

BB   Exactly. In fact, the collection of miniatures on which I am currently working has been printed abroad. For example, our information about miniatures, which, I might add, is in itself a misnomer, is quite recent and derived from paintings we have received from abroad. Also, those that actually have been printed within Iran are usually of a substandard quality; their details and intricacies are extremely difficult to decipher and appreciate. I should reiterate that these illustrations are inaccessible to most people—and that makes it exceedingly difficult to determine the history of *pardeh-dari*, for instance.

HD   In what way?

BB   Whether it originated in the coffeehouses or village squares. Unfortunately, we lack any record with respect to the real history of these arts, and I feel that we even lack the means to commence such a project. Some time ago, I worked on the history of Iranian theater and drama with the assistance of Mehrdad Bahar, the distinguished scholar of Iranian mythology. While I was engaged in this project, I located evidence of *pardeh-khani* within the rites of Manichaeism. When we read phrases such as "look, here is a sinful woman," or "look at that." This may suggest that the subjects of the book were viewing panel paintings.

HD   So this may very well be because of Mani's putative interest in painting?

BB   Yes. I like to think that this type of *pardeh-khani* persisted throughout the Sassanian period and then disappeared temporarily until it again resurfaced in remote villages and began to be used in the service of Islamic propaganda. If my estimation is accurate, this type of artistic expression observed in the past 100–150 years prevailed long ago as well.

HD   So again my question is, are you tracing the origin of these ritual performances to any specifically religious ceremony?

BB   Well, the story is not yet complete. When this type of artwork was customarily displayed, it was not done so freely, nor all at once. It was revealed in small installments for two reasons: first, because it was forbidden in Iran for images of saints to be depicted—and for this reason alone they would slowly uncover one portion of the painting while simultaneously concealing another facet of it, so that the images would not be left vulnerable to devils and evil spirits. In addition, these paintings would only illustrate the deeds of their subjects in an adulatory fashion, and this has traditionally been continued in the images of such religious figures as the prophet Mohammad, Ali, and so on. Another example of image construction within the theater is the art of the marionette and shadow-puppeteering. The Chinese art of shadow-puppeteering is particularly perfected and complete, especially in Southeast Asia. Moreover, I am aware that in Indonesia one of the celebrated religious heroes frequently depicted in drama is Hamzeh. Our version of this art form was not quite as complicated as theirs, though it still retained some significance and, within the books of poetry which I have consulted for the purpose of playwriting, a great deal can be discovered concerning this topic. By virtue of the fact that the marionettes in puppet shows are not life-size, the problem of not being able to represent certain subjects proves irrelevant to this dramatic form. Also, this art form was practiced in many places, and thus was not tied to any specific area. Yet another art form highly comparable to that of puppeteering is the dramatic technique of the magic lantern show (*fanus-e khial*), no longer practiced today. In the Safavid era, certain poems were composed that describe the details of this kind of performing art. In the magic lantern, images were projected onto walls and glass surfaces. There is also a strong possibility of finding these images in the *Shah-nameh*, the stories of Nezami, and even in mystical tales in which there are no human subjects, unlike those of the *Shah-nameh* which specifically deal with human conditions.

HD   Would you consider this array of visual art as perhaps the antecedent of Iranian cinema?

BB   No. We must hesitate to jump to such conclusions concerning its origins. The first filmmaker in Iran, as you know, was an Armenian by the name of Avanes Oganians, although his being an Armenian does not imply that he was a stranger to Iranian culture. He was indeed an Iranian. As you know, the Armenian culture and religion have been heavily influenced by Iranian culture, and by Mithraism in particular. There are many Iranian names and terminologies within their religious practices. Armenians had Iranian names, Iranians had Armenian names, and that was not a source of aggravation for anyone. Avanes, however, relied on cinematography, which was an exclusively European invention, to synthesize images, and thus promoted the use of such foreign inventions in the production of his first cinematic work. Like everyone else in his generation, he had a "photographic memory," as it were, for photography had been around for about half a century by then. The invention of photography had made it possible for people to look at mechanical reproductions of themselves. He also knew of the invention of cinema, which was very recent at the time. The significance of the invention was that one could actually see oneself moving on the screen. There does not have to be a specific historical precedent within the country for everything we do in Iran.

HD   True. But my point was the specific visual "accent" we give to cinema in our culture, which must inevitably have its roots in our visual and performing art—as is perhaps best evident in your own cinema—the uses of *Ta'ziyeh* motifs and *Arusak-bazi* in particular. The *medium* was of course invented elsewhere. But I wonder whether we use it slightly differently in the light of our visual and performing arts that predate cinema.

BB   Yes, in that respect you are right. And many people still do not know why it is necessary to be rooted in a historical genealogy of one sort or another, as in the cases you just mentioned. In fact, when we look at some of the greatest films ever made, we note that the filmmaker has a literary, or visual, or theatrical history which is instrumental in his cinema. In Japanese cinema, in particular, you see the strong presence of Japanese theater. It seems that in many instances, if one were to show a person walking in the street or any other daily activity, one need not have historical documentation to validate that act. Yet in other circumstances we need a more contemporary and philosophical expression of the history and culture of the past.

HD   What does it mean to have a "contemporary and philosophical" expression of our past?

BB   If you wish to show a person just walking down a street, you do not need to have a historical or cultural antecedent for that ordinary act. But if you wish to show a more complicated relationship between individuals, you need to have a more comprehensive control over your visual, literary, and theatrical culture.

HD   Then how would you assess our present cinematic culture? Do you think that we are rooted in our visual, literary, and performing arts, that we have succeeded in cultivating our own specific angle on cinematic vision?

BB   I believe that many of our filmmakers lack the slightest understanding of such antecedents. Many of them think and say that they have learned their cinema in the streets and from "the people," and other statements to that effect. Of course this is not peculiar to Iranian filmmakers. Many American filmmakers also lack a historical knowledge of their own visual and performing arts. Many filmmakers think that one can learn how to make a film by looking at other people's films, or by watching television, or similar methods. In general I believe that, with few exceptions, there is a remarkable ignorance of the literary, visual, and philosophical background among our filmmakers. I also do not believe that a knowledge of this sort would hurt our film critics either, or that they would be accused of being backwards if they knew about these things.

HD   I wonder about the relationship between creativity and scholarly or archival documentation of a particular mode of performing arts. Is it correct to say that your cinema is, in addition to everything else, an archival reservoir of our visual and performing arts, and thus has that kind of presence and influence in its immediate surroundings?

BB   I have never intended to do anything like that. But when I am working on a film, occasionally I notice, or other people notice, that the roots of what I am doing are deep in one tradition or another. I am very happy that these things are noted. The more we know about these traditions the richer our cinema will be. Unfortunately, a major difficulty is securing accurate information about these kinds of arts. There is, as you know, a substantial body of scholarship produced outside Iran, about which we know very little inside the country. There is of course an equally impressive body of literature produced in Iran. But I do not find it to be very useful. It is an extremely difficult task to sit down and read all of these and examine them carefully, especially for those of us who are not academically trained. But we have no choice. We have to sit down and systematically examine these sources, and then try to find answers to our questions in them. It is extremely difficult.

HD   But don't you think that you are combining the task of a scholar and the creativity of an artist together here?

BB   Of course I am. But the fact is that Iranian history is an extraordinarily complicated history, with quite a number of crucial questions about it that no one has given an answer to. If a person immerses himself in these questions, he may indeed get lost in them, except that he himself may occasionally find his way in one direction or another, and thus create his own answers. At any rate, I have asked these questions and have tried to find answers to them.

HD   What exactly are these questions?

BB   Questions I have had as an intellectual, as a thinking subject. Who am I? Where do I stand? Or, even more fundamentally, since our chatacters are fundamentally determined by our culture, who are we? Where do we stand as a nation? Why are we afflicted with our present predicament? What are the solutions to our problem?

HD   If you think that these questions disappear if you leave Iran, you are wrong. They don't.

BB   I have always felt a psychological need to ask these questions, and as a result they have found their way into my cinema. I did not ask these questions in order to make films. I have always sought to find an answer to my inner, more intellectually expansive questions. They have expressed themselves, as a result, in my cinema and theater quite naturally. Many of the younger generation are also seeking an answer to their own questions in my work. If the answer they find is useful, I would consider myself quite lucky.

HD   Still this fascination of yours with "history" is quite intriguing to me. Why "history"? You seem to have quite serious existential questions of identity, of subjectivity: "Who am I?" "Where do I stand?" you know, questions of that sort. But why do we need to go back to "history" to find answers to these questions? What would a knowledge of the Qajars or the Safavids provide in response to these kinds of questions? Don't you think that the defining moment of an artist is his creativity, his moral uprising against the so-called "traditions," his defiance of "history"?

BB   Perhaps. But let me be more specific. Perhaps the greatest shortcoming that we have in our country is the absence of a history of the people. The history of the literature and the history of the official people are written by official people. But I want to know how the rest lived. Of course by "people" I do not mean anyone affiliated with a specific political party. It's a very personal kind of a conception that I have. And in fact you may have noted that in my own work I have been "writing" a kind of a history of these people, a kind of history that has not been told in official "history." I have read, just like you and everybody else, the official history that they gave us at school, for example. I realized that even when I saw a popular drama, a *Ru-howzi* comedy, or a *Kheimah-shab-bazi* play, they were all related to the ordinary people, the populace. They were not the work of the literati or of prominent artists. Nobody ever hears of these artists. In effect I wanted to know where these people came from, what their origins were. I was thus gradually drawn to our literary sources, to our mythology, anthropology, and certain ritual performances that were later co-opted into religious rites, things of that sort. I started something with no immediate intention of going in one direction or another and yet gradually it turned into a kind of genealogical search. I did not begin with a well-thought-out plan of action. I just noticed that most of our people are attracted to this kind of performing art. Right now, if you were to stage a *Ta'ziyeh* performance somewhere in Tehran, or a *Ru-howzi* comedy, ordinary people would soon discover their own problems and predicaments in it and start crying or laughing accordingly. These would certainly not be the stories of their imams and saints. These would be the stories of their own predicaments and problems, and they would seek their own salvation in them as well. There is a constitutional difference between this kind of ready-made theater and the more complicated, intellectual, and engaged theater that is intended to convey very complex psychological issues. As a result, when I want to discover the power of this theater, its origin, etc., it is more on performance that I tend to concentrate. I need to be in touch with ordinary people.

HD   What would that contact mean for the nature and function of your art? I mean how can an artform like cinema, which, as you just said, is a quintessentially modern art, be useful in a society that in many of its social and political institutions is still pre-modern? Don't you see an incompatibility here, especially so far as our visual culture is concerned?

BB   There is no problem in that regard. Remember that cinema is a multidimensional art. Consider documentary filmmaking, for example. One could produce very compelling pictorial evidence of this pre-modern society, that could be extraordinarily significant. It is not necessary for filmmakers to have learned or mastered all those visual and performing cultures we just spoke about. They can simply document aspects of reality as they see them. Later, others who know the culture better may discover hidden layers there. Or it may be completely the other way around. That is to say, a filmmaker may make a film about this society without adding anything to it; in other words, the filmmaker may know nothing about the past culture of the society and may simply be using it for superficial commercial purposes. I do not approve of such people because they are only in the business of making films. I approve of those people who at the very least document this society for us so that we can begin to see it in ways we did not before.

HD   When you look at your own work over the last three decades, do you think you have succeeded in teaching us a new way of seeing things, at both a popular and a critical level? Are we now more visually "literate," so to speak? That's what I mean by the incompatibility of the two worlds, of the possibility of learning how to look. The direction of an actively ocularcentric trait in our cultural disposition is what I have in mind.

BB   First of all, I have no claim to teach anyone anything. I must say here that my work began and has continued against extraordinary opposition, because many people who write criticism of the Iranian cinema do it because they don't have anything better to do. They have been writing about Iranian cinema without knowing about anything integral to it. As a result, they repeat opinions of one sort or another. It is really a perfectly easy thing to do, to write film criticism. And yet they suddenly saw the emergence of a kind of cinema that they could no longer understand with their customary simplicity. Unfortunately, this is what happened to my cinema. I was confronted with the worst kind of religious, moral, and ethical accusations. The reason was very simple. They had not a clue what I was doing. Now, in retrospect, I see that the younger generation finds answers to their particular problems in my cinema, except when they think that my cinema is very symbolic. But I have never intended to make very profound kinds of films. I was simply experimenting, and things that I did show had a certain kind of inevitability about them. I could not not show them. You see what I mean?

HD   Yes, I do.

BB   Just like the poetry of Hafez. When you read it for the first time, you get something out of it, and you like it. But later on others come and interpret it, and in reading them you may notice other significant points. My primary concern with a film is that people will actually enjoy watching it. I have never intended to impose a second or third layer of meaning on my films. But it seems this has nothing to do with my intent. It somehow happens in and of itself. When these second and third meanings are discovered they really excite me.

HD   But you cannot deny that while you are making a film you have certain philosophical and cultural concerns?

BB   Of course. This happens quite naturally. When I think through a problem, my thoughts are obviously reflected in the film.

HD   But this points to a larger issue. This notion of your films being supposedly complicated or appearing to be complex in fact feeds on what appears to be our innate disposition to expect additional "layers" of meaning in everything. Especially when a poet like Hafez or now a filmmaker like you develops a certain reputation for being complicated, suddenly an avalanche of "hidden meanings" buries the work. I wonder why? What do you think are the reasons or causes for this overwhelmingly metaphoric language or expectation of a metaphoric language?

BB   The origin of it might be in our language, or in the culture of our region. Perhaps it can be traced back to social and geographical causes. Things of that sort. And it is not limited to Iran. I believe it is something peculiar to the range of cultures in our part of the world, which have a proclivity to complication, as opposed to the ancient Greeks, who had a culture of revelation. It is a culture of unveiling, a culture of nudity. Just look at their statues. It is an art of revelation, an art of glorifying beauty, and an art of praising daily realities. Iranian art, on the contrary, is an art of concealment. Everything about us is hiding, concealing, and protecting.

HD   What you say is a bit too essentialist for me. But do go on.

BB   Even members of the aristocracy and the nobility, men and women, always covered their faces. By such kinds of concealment, certain unfathomable dimensions were added to their character. They became mythologized in a way. Nobody dared to talk about them any more. As you know, the ancient Iranian kings used to cover their faces with a mask. The function of this mask was not just to give certain luster to their presence, something which must have been related to Mithraism because they were thought of as the representatives of Mithra on earth, but the more important point is that their human frailty was invisible. You could not penetrate their character, because nobody could actually see their facial features and expressions. The same was true of women, particularly the women of the nobility. This was so that nobody could imagine or fancy them. That's why, I believe, that today we have this unfortunate problem of mandatory veiling in our country. But it is not limited to Iran. Even in China, or among the Native Americans, or in Africa, you have the same phenomenon.

When the Native Americans wanted to go to war, they painted their faces, so that they would appear more frightful and horrific, and their enemy would not see their fear.

HD   I am not quite sure about this link you make between the practice of the nobility and contemporary veiling in Iran. The practice of royal magic, as it were, to generate fear and uncertainty among subjects is rather different in nature and disposition from the contemporary conditions of the mass veiling of women, which is a specifically urban phenomenon. But as for the things you say about painting the face, we do have similar cases in the famous story of Babak Khorramdin's covering his face with blood when executed by the Abbassid caliph, or Rostam in the *Shah-nameh* wearing a leopard skin. But, still, what you say sounds a bit too generalizing to me.

BB   Of course there are exceptions. But my point is that this metaphoric language that you refer to has to do with the fact that Iranian art is far more concerned with covering and concealing things than revealing them. That's why, except for Naser Khosrow's travelogue, we have no realistic account of world travel. All travel accounts are of the hinterland, or of the travel of birds, a kind of metaphoric trip. All the metaphors are directed at these kinds of things, toward the so-called City of Love, and its two guards, which are supposed to be our two eyes, or its fortress into which no one can enter.

HD   But there are many examples of earthly concerns as well. Look at Ibn Battutah's *Travelogue*, or all those geography books, such as those of Hamdollah Mawstowfi or Ibn Hauqal, which indicate actual knowledge of geographical regions that must have involved traveling.

BB   My point is that the act of thinking is in and of itself a peculiar thing that can make things even more complicated than they actually are. In our own time, we have been engaged in constructing new social metaphors. During the course of the recent revolution, there were rumors that Khomeini knew nine foreign languages, that he played the piano like Beethoven, and that his picture was seen on the face of the moon, things of that nature. And the same thing was true of a number of certain political heroes of our time, about whom legendary stories were being told—about how they evaded the police, for example. They gradually emerged as mythological figures. You know that the same kind of psychology must have been at work in many other legends and myths, complicating and mystifying them into stories about the other world, about Heaven and Hell, about the story of Karbala, and so on, ad infinitum.

HD   How do you read this proclivity to mythmaking? Is it to escape reality, or is it a mechanism of dealing with it?

BB   Probably it's a kind of necessity. But the key question here is in what particular direction is it used. We have an innate need to transcend reality. Many of the rituals and ceremonies in Iran are intended to help us do that, to transcend, to get beyond ourselves.

HD   How do you mean?

BB   What I mean is that a metaphor does not do anything except try to get beyond daily, routine reality, and give higher and more noble human features to heroes, in order to ascribe them more sublime human characteristics. When this reaches a particular level, well, it turns into a myth. This could be a good myth or a bad myth. Gradually, all our fears are accumulated in one particularly nasty myth. We suddenly begin to attribute to our enemies characteristics of mythological proportion.

HD   This Manichaeism is still with us, isn't it?

BB   Well, there are always metaphoric ways of explaining the world. There are people in this world who represent what is good in it. And there are people who represent what is evil. They are ultimately a kind of explanation for the world. And yet they are a kind of explanation that make things even more complicated than they actually are. Thus, you can actually consider cinema a kind of modern mythmaking. Every filmmaker, every philosopher, or every religious person does two things at the same time. One is to erase the previous art by fighting against it with criticism or negation, or by virtue of the alternative visions he proposes, and by virtue of this fight he is engaged in the making of a new myth.

HD   Take Na'i in *Bashu*, for example. Is she the new mythological construct of a woman with which you wish to erase the image of woman we have today in Iran?

BB   Well, everybody struggles against his or her culture. The way it works is that a culture proceeds on its course. In those societies that harbor a certain traditional image, any new kind of image is censored. They try to erase it. Censorship in fact means precisely upholding this stable and proper traditional image which they demand and exact from you, and as a result they oppose any kind of change, provocation, suggestion. They won't tolerate it.

HD   This is a far more crucial conception of censorship than merely political censorship.

BB   Yes. I have said this repeatedly. Censorship is not just political.

HD   When you were talking about cinema as a kind of mythmaking, I was thinking of dreams and the obvious correspondence between the mental images we have of alternatives to experienced realities and their creative expression in art or in dreams.

BB   This is something quite universal, not limited to one culture or another. As you know, there has been a lot of new discussion about the relation between manifestations of a person's culture and his or her dreams. People have been collecting and comparing their dreams. Some of the things they have found are rather startling. There seems to be a common repertoire for people who live under similar conditions in sharing a common set of dreams in correspondence with their culture. There are many common themes that are repeated in their rituals, their customs, their paintings, their art, and their dreams. Some of these are sexual themes that have been repressed. Some are related to common instinctual motifs. There are also themes that have been culturally constituted, for example, the sign of the cross, which could be a sign of an embrace, of salvation, of death, of everlastingness, or many other similar kinds of signs. But the question is that when you are making a film, either consciously or subconsciously you use these signs in one way or another. For example, in a Hitchcock film there is a courtroom scene in which the camera zooms in on a man who is playing with a cross in his hand while whispering something under his breath, as a sign that he does not have much faith in the proceedings. He is reaching for something metaphysical, extraordinary, clinging to a hope of salvation. So you see, it is a universal phenomenon, a collective kind of sentiment, expressed in many cultures. But the point is how it is expressed, in what context, for what purpose.

HD This cross that you mention reminds me of a scene in *Bashu* which is very crucial in reading it, and that is when you draw the shadowy figure of the father from that of the scarecrow under whose shade Bashu is sitting.

BB This image is very much related to your earlier point about a redefinition of the role of women, a redefinition which is, or rather should be, endemic in our culture. But this is also a redefinition of men as well. As a matter of principle, in fact, any redefinition of women is, *ipso facto*, a redefinition of men too. Because these two cannot be defined independently of each other.   .

DAYBREAK

My reference to Bahram Beiza'i's Bashu: Gharibeh-ye Kuchak *("Bashu: the Little Stranger," 1986) in the course of our interview was based on my long-standing interest in the place of myth in his cinema. The strongest defining force in Beiza'i's films is his uncanny ability to generate that authorial moment when a culture is in communion with its mythical subconscious. In what follows I will trace the contours of Beiza'i's visual access to that subconscious.*

In one of the earliest scenes in *Bashu*, the protagonist lifts up the thick cover he has held over his head in the back of the truck that has carried him in a nocturnal journey from war-torn southern Iran into the northern regions. He has had a hellish night, in complete darkness and deadly solitude, and takes with him even ghastlier memories of the war in his homeland and the death and disappearance of his entire family. From death, destruction, and frightful isolation under a thick cloth, and through a nighttime journey during which he has been as good as dead, he now throws off his protective cover, and rises as if resurrected right in the middle of a paradise. The truck has stopped, and the driver is having breakfast. Bashu has no idea where he is. But there is a green serenity in the surroundings, a quiet splendor, a reassurance in the air. The nightmare is over. Day has broken.

There is something mythic about this early morning scene in *Bashu* which is quintessential in all of Beiza'i's films. Whether his settings are legendary or historical, contemporary or ancient, urban or rural, Beiza'i always reaches for the *mythos* in order to stimulate and release the *nomos*. In my conversation with Beiza'i, I engaged him specifically in a discussion of myth so he could articulate what I believe is central to his cinema. No one in the history of Iranian performing arts comes anywhere near Beiza'i in his command of the Persian mythological culture and his ability to force it into creative convulsion. Thus predisposed, he reads the metaphysical underpinnings of Iranian society mythically, and reduces them to their constituent *mythos*, from which their *nomos* and *logos* are articulated. From this critical angle, his camera works in an entirely different way than that of his contemporary Abbas Kiarostami. Kiarostami focuses on the factual evidence of the world with such a persistent gaze that every ounce of metaphysical energy is sapped out of it. He strips reality naked and places it right in front of our eyes, rests his case, and declares: "Here you are! Look at it!" Beiza'i works in exactly the opposite direction. He challenges the metaphysical elements by plunging deep into them, colliding head on, and there in the realm of *mythos*, he engages its angelic and demonic forces, fights and wrestles with them in the hope that the echoes of his mythic battles will be reflected onto our contemporary realities. In entering the realm of the *mythos*, Beiza'i goes one village upstream to seek the parabolic source of our present ills, and there and then cleanse the water and clear the air before it reaches us mortals below where we live and breathe. Beiza'i's cinema, as a result, becomes the mirror of an invisible world, the mythic challenge of the real, where all our enduring assumptions about the world can disappear into thin air, just before they make sure we remain law-abiding citizens of their republic of fear.

By the time that Beiza'i made *Gharibeh va Meh* ("*The Stranger and the Fog*," 1974), he was completely at home with his richly suggestive and pregnant mythological language, a language that despite its allegorical implications has a profoundly earthly quality. The emerging affection between Ra'na, the coastal woman of permanence, and Ayat, the maritime man of migration, in *The Stranger and the Fog* is rooted in the twilight zone of land and sea, life and death, reality and myth. The village of Ra'na, the young widow, is ethereal; it is somewhere in the north of Iran or perhaps nowhere at all. On the edge of a maritime abyss, it is as foggy as real, as imaginary as material. On that borderland of life and death, Ayat has to fight against the demons that have chased him from the sea into the security of the village, to fight with the same ferocity with which Ra'na has to battle the ghosts of her dead husband's ancestors, which haunt the villagers with the same intensity as does the fear of an invading army of sea monsters. The crucial aspect of this dual, circular, warfare is that Ra'na and Ayat fight together, on two simultaneous fronts, land and sea. Ayat is haunted by his fatal attraction to the sea, Ra'na by the phantom gaze of a dead husband. The invading sea monsters, apparitions of Ayat's own fears of the unknown and the insinuating, are no more scary than the invisible ghosts that haunt the village in the form of "traditions," "customs," "habits," and "manners." In the end, Ayat, Ra'na, and the entire village fight as much against the invading sea monsters as against the monstrous apparitions, a whole genealogy of fear, that they have themselves invented.

The protagonist of *The Stranger and the Fog* is neither Ayat nor Ra'na. It is the fog. In this furiously foggy subjugation of the real, the real can yield alternative visions of itself. The cloudy atmosphere of *The Stranger and the Fog* represents all the received cognitive categories through which a culture views itself. It is then that the symbolic structuring of the universe of imagination called *culture* is actively mutated through this hazy vision of the real. As a visual projection of the subconscious, Beiza'i uses the fog to melt away the presumed rigidity of the evident. The result is a spectacular alteration of the obvious. After viewing the atmospheric mistiness of *The Stranger and the Fog*, we can no longer view reality with the same submissive matter-of-factness, thinking there is nothing we can do about it. With the vaporous effusions of the visible, the authority of sight itself is reconstituted, negotiated anew, implicated in a whole new hermeneutics of subjectivity.

In Beiza'i, we see not through the dead or dying myth but through the resuscitated reinventions of them. Georges Bataille is correct in holding that through a dying myth we can see the world as even more profoundly mythical. But that is only if we have first benefited from the fruits—and not merely suffered the dire consequences—of its illusions. In the colonial outposts of the Enlightenment, we have an entirely different attitude towards our myths. We need, like Beiza'i, to reinvent them in a way that affirms for us our place in the world, one that does not deny us our particular historical inflection. Because our needs are of a different sort—the need to be born into the modernity of the world—we cannot have any conception of a "joyful suffering." We have had too much "joyful suffering" in our neck of the woods. We called it "Sufism."

REMYTHOLOGIZING THE REAL

By the time he made *Cherikeh-ye Tara* ("*The Ballad of Tara*," 1978), Beiza'i had thoroughly mastered the active remythologization of Iranian culture, in order to negotiate a new angle on reality. Without a full command over the inner work-ings of the layers of Iranian mythological memory, it is impossible to do what Beiza'i has achieved, at once resuscitating *and* manipulating, forcing them to yield to alternative modes of meaning. The reason that Beiza'i has become prover-bial among his Iranian critics for the "incomprehensibility" of his cinema is pre-cisely the deep-rootedness of these mythological referents in the mind of his Iranian audience. Beiza'i has tried to defamiliarize these myths in order to move his audience into a renewed pact with them.

With a gaze fixed on contemporary realities, particularly the condition of Iranian women, Beiza'i forces the most ancient traditions to justify their claim to sacred certitude, to unquestioned authenticity. Beiza'i chose the archaic word *Cherikeh* for his title, not in a vain search for authenticity but in order to shock the familiar with the unknown, the comfortable with the mysterious, the overtly remembered with the actively forgotten. These are all effective strategies of alien-ating the world from its way of cozening itself into the habitual. Any number of other words—*ostureh*, *hekayat*, *afsaneh*, *qesseh*—would have equally conveyed the sense of a ballad. What *Cherikeh* does is to force a lazy audience to pause and ponder, to dwell on the unknown, to distance itself from the habitual, even to dis-trust the received definitions and locations of our place in the language we call home. "The main function of myth," in the judicious words of Åke Hultkrantz, the distinguished myth scholar who conducted extensive fieldwork among the Wind River Shoshoni Indians, "is to sanction the establishment and condition of the world and its institutions, thereby safeguarding the existence of people and society. In many cases, the very recitation of the myth is so filled with power that it influences—or is thought to influence—the course of actual events."[1] But myths as such tend not just to make the world possible, but to make it possible with the heavy price of the tyrannical subjugation of one reason or gender to another. Beiza'i's cinema allows visual access to that mythical universe, in order to renegotiate newer, more just and equitable myths for the world.

In *The Ballad of Tara*, which, next to *The Stranger and the Fog*, is Beiza'i's most mythologically narrated film, he opts for a cinematic rendition of the creation myth. Here, he draws on any number of ancient Iranian mythological narratives in order to generate and render operative his own, by virtue of the quantitatively reducible variations on the theme of a given myth.[2] In this narrative, Tara is a woman: earthly, seasonal, in tune with the land, assiduous in her attendance on the real. She is part of nature, constitutional to and a constituent of its celebration of life: a mother of two children, ready for any season, with no sign of self-consciousness about her. The description of Susan Taslimi as Tara by Shahla Lahiji is quite accurate:

> The impeccable acting of Susan Taslimi as Tara is the indication of a perfect choice and of the remarkable capability of the actor in the cultivation and performance of her role. This capability is evident not only in her acting but also in her physiognomy. Susan Taslimi—in her wheat-like complexion, elongated nose, set-back but penetrating, open, and intimidating eyes, which at times have that affectionate look, bony and sculpted cheeks, the wrinkle of power at the side of her mouth, the thin line of thought on her long forehead, her tall stature, and then that authority in her demeanor and speech—is the very epiphany of Mother-Earth: That very mythological vision of woman that can very well belong to yesterday, today, or tomorrow, and all the time remain thoroughly woman.[3]

Tara as earth, nature, and fertility appears at a moment when she has lost two of her men: a husband and a father. Meanwhile she is being courted by four others: the brother of her husband and probably his murderer, whose love for her is sickly (his name is Ashub, meaning "chaos"); Qelich, who like her is earthly and who digs for water in the depths of the earth; the Historical Man, who comes to get the sword she possesses but falls in love with her; and a half-crazed boy. She is placed squarely between two male groups of dead and living attendants, and whatever Tara inherits from her paternal ancestry she distributes to everybody in the village, much to their delight. She even has to bear the responsibility of a sword which no man will take because of fear of its being haunted. She is given back the sword but she does not quite know what to do with it. She tries to cut wood, chop vegetables, or use it as a doorstop. She throws it into the sea, much to the anger of the Historical Man, but to her surprise the sea returns it. She discovers the use of the sword when a wild dog attacks her and her children and she kills it, much to her astonishment. Among awe, delight, surprise, and anger, Tara defines the world, locates herself, and articulates the reality of the earthly life that she lives. She is the original point of departure for whatever exists, for whatever should and does matter.

The women of *The Ballad of Tara*, like those of all other films of Beiza'i, hold a place of dignity through their work. Tara is a farmer. Her children, her domestic animals, her farm, and the routine that holds them together are at the center of a universe over which she presides. In the pre-moment of history, only work matters. Tara tries to put the sword to work. But it is a useless, work-less, instrument. History having not yet begun, there is no use for the sword. When Tara and the Historical Man meet, he can only speak of death, destruction, and honor, while she tries to see whether he has any skills she can put to use. The Historical Man wants her sword to defend his honor, but while here in the pre-moment of history he falls in love with Tara and cannot leave until he is sure that Qelich loves her and will actually take care of her children in his absence. Then the Historical Man goes back to history, having found cause to enter it again. Beiza'i in effect holds history hostage to mythological renegotiation in the pre-moment of its beginning. For the Historical Man, as he enters this pre-moment, honor precedes life, whereas Tara places life, in which dwells her love for the Historical Man, before any Historical constitution of manly "honor." She has no use for such cultural abstractions, particularly when defined by useless men. Tara is *noble* in the pre-cultural materiality of the term. He speaks of honor in History, she of love in a life that is too real to collapse into any temporality. Central to this distinction is the function of the sword: she first tries to use it practically, or sell it, to harvest grain with it, or throw it away. Yet the people of the village have no use for it. The sword, however, belongs to the lost honor of a tribe. When she kills the dog she learns its use and is petrified by it. She gives it to the Historical Man so he will leave, but by then she is told that he will not go back because he has fallen in love with her: history is taken hostage in its own pre-moment.

Far more important than defining myth as a "sacred tale" or "traditional tale,"[4] it is crucial to see the act of mythmaking as a form of communal signification. In the absence of such collectively binding myths that make life meaningful and trustworthy, the world atrophies into confusion and chaos. Beiza'i's cinema in general, and his *The Ballad of Tara* in particular, is a successful negotiation with the enduring parameters of the Persian mythologizing imagination. One of Beiza'i's crucial achievements in *The Ballad of Tara* is to subvert time and narrative in a way that enables his story to find and demonstrate its own internal "logic." Consider the narrative elements of this ballad: the Historical Man has left history and entered its pre-moment in order to retrieve his sword, and yet is held there by a love affair. The grandfather is dead and yet he speaks from beyond the grave as the solitary sound of an authority that defies death and time. Equally paramount in this pre-moment of history is a sword that always mysteriously reappears, against all reason, despite all resistance, in tune with a narrative logic that only a myth—or perhaps more accurately in Beiza'i's case, a "countermyth"—can generate and sustain. The dialogue in *The Ballad of Tara* varies in accent and intonation, indicating no particular time or location. The costumes are not all from Tavalish, the region where the film was made, but are the symbolic regalia of a pre-moment in the world. The sights and sounds here do more than just express ideas; they define the terms, as they constitute the parameters, of a different world, the world of the story, the realm of the unreal, to which the real must yield. The stylized gestures are pantomime invitations to view the unseen, the place of the pre-moment of being-in-the-world. In *The Ballad of Tara*, Beiza'i enters the realm of the myth in order to force his audience to leave the routinized world, alerted to a wholly different consciousness of reality.

To achieve that reconstitution of the real cinematically, visuality becomes the central mechanism of Beiza'i's narrative, which must begin to teach its primarily audile audience how to see. Foregrounding the visual possibility of color and shape as the constituent forces of the narrative results in their active stylization, which in turn leads into a theoretical articulation of the visual. Ornamenting movement comes next, aided by an almost self-conscious formalization of the camera movement and angles. All of these lead to the constitution of a visual world, legitimately operative on its own terms, aesthetically irreducible, giving palpable reality to film as the visual substitution of the real, from which we can reconstitute the real by contesting it. No other filmmaker has this kind of command over scenes so richly rooted in Iranian visual memories, or can pull this off without collapsing into the museumization of the culture. To grasp Beiza'i's remarkable ability, all one has to do is to see Shahram Asadi's *Ruz-e Vaqe'eh* ("*The Fateful Day*," 1995), which is based on one of Beiza'i's scripts and yet visually collapses into an awful museum piece of tourist attraction. Beiza'i is no museum curator. He is the puppeteer of our forgotten memories.

By renarrating the myth, Beiza'i in effect creates the visual site of a ritual, a sign of his lifelong dedication to and fascination with *Ta'ziyeh*. Bringing the "ritual" to climactic closure is the last sequence of *The Ballad of Tara* in which Tara picks up the sword and attacks the Historical Man as he retreats into the sea. In a stunningly shot and acted scene, Tara strikes futile blows against wave after wave. Beiza'i drowns his camera for the longest time in the sheer futility of Tara's actions, choreographing the effects of the ritual to the last detail. Yet Beiza'i opts to end on a different note: when the Historical Man has gone, Tara tells Qelich they will marry at the next harvest.

MYTHOLOGIES

In a short attack on Mankiewicz's film *Julius Caesar*, Roland Barthes deplores the fabricated spontaneity of trying to pass off the fake as real. Reading the implications of sweat as a sign of physical exertion, Barthes formulates a short cut into what he calls "an ethic of signs."[5]

> Signs ought to present themselves only in two extreme forms: either openly intellectual and so remote that they are reduced to algebra, as in Chinese theatre . . . or deeply rooted, invented, so to speak, on each occasion, revealing an internal, a hidden facet, and indicative of a moment in time, no longer of a concept (as in the art of Stanislavsky, for instance). But the intermediate sign . . . reveals a degraded spectacle, which is equally afraid of simple reality and of total artifice. For although it is a good thing if a spectacle is created to make the world more explicit, it is both reprehensible and deceitful to confuse the sign with what is signified. And it is a duplicity which is peculiar to bourgeois art: Between the intellectual and the visceral sign is hypocritically inserted a hybrid, at once elliptical and pretentious, which is pompously christened "nature."[6]

The ethics of signs that Barthes proposes here opens a whole new window on the workings of the mythic. Beiza'i's cinema is somewhere between Chinese theater and that of Stanislavsky, as Barthes describes them here. His cinema is at once archetypal, or what Barthes calls "openly intellectual and algebraic," and rooted in the moment. Beiza'i makes a cinematic virtue out of mythically impregnating the present. "Simple reality" and "total artifice" collapse in Beiza'i's cinema on the site of a "ritualistic" constitution of the real. Barthes is disgusted with the duplicity of the pretension to "naturalness" in *Julius Caesar*. But in his anger he issues a manifesto in his ethics of the sign which is theoretically limited. He is correct that between "the intellectual and the visceral," Hollywood has "hypocritically inserted a hybrid, at once elliptical and pretentious." But he loses sight of the possibility of collapsing "the intellectual and the visceral," as Beiza'i does systematically in almost all his films, on the site of a mythic-ritual reconstitution of the real. Barthes did not see this possibility because the context of bourgeois art in which he launched his critique was, in the late 1950s, as it indeed still is in much European theorization of the aesthetic, oblivious to the functioning of the aesthetic in the colonial outposts of the Enlightenment, where no autonomous national bourgeoisie could have existed, and, as the result of an entirely contingent social formation of creative consciousness, art was predicated on a different kind of critical disposition. In this particular case, the cross-fusion of "the intellectual and the visceral," far from feigning "nature," cultivates an extraordinarily revolutionary angle on the real.

To see that possibility in practice, we can do no better than to turn to *Bashu: the Little Stranger* (1986), in which Beiza'i brings Tara into history. Na'i is a demythologized Tara in the heart of history. By pulling Tara from the premoment of history into history, Beiza'i mythologizes the *now* of the moment, or, in Barthes' terms, faces "the intellectual and the visceral." With the *now* of the moment mythologized, the *then* of the myth is historicized. This confluence of time and narrative is crucial to our reading of Beiza'i's cinema. It is wrong to separate Beiza'i's cinema into the historical and the mythological.[7] He is a filmmaker with no sign of visual schizophrenia. By historicizing mythology and mythologizing history, Beiza'i visually crosses the received borders of both and takes us into a third territory, at once historical and yet radically alerted to its self-inflicted wounds of mythologizing urges. The site of the confluence between the *mythos* and the *logos* in Beiza'i is his fascination with "ritual." "Ritual" for Beiza'i is the performative microcosm of a universe in which collide both the

Far from his home in southern Iran, Bashu is reborn through the love of his new mother, Na'i. In *Bashu: the Little Stranger* Beiza'i reaches down into the deepest mythological layers of Persian culture to narrate an immaculate conception

logos of history and the *mythos* of its being comprehensible, meaningful, trust-worthy, significant.

In *The Absence of the Myth*, Georges Bataille seeks to capture the moment of the un-myth as itself mythical: "Night is also a sun, and the absence of myth is also a myth: the coldest, the purest, the only *true* myth."[8] "The world" itself being mythical, and "the myth" worldly, as someone almost condemned to realism, Beiza'i cannot but underline that cross-fusion. What is thus evident in Beiza'i is the fictive transparency of the real, the therapeutics of mythmaking in the face of the fear of reality. *Bashu* is the critical evidence that the binary opposition between "history" and "myth" does not hold for Beiza'i. For in his cinematic cosmovision he has brought together the two and posited a third world in which we become radically conscious of the *mythos* in the operative energy of *logos*.

Despite the critical intelligence in her feminist reading of Beiza'i, Lahiji falls squarely into the trap of a patriarchal definition of "motherhood," without pausing to ask whether or not that power-basing definition is remotely "instinctual." There is nothing "instinctual" about a *definition* of "motherhood" which is historically constituted. In haste to celebrate Na'i as the ideal typical "mother,"[9] Lahiji entirely forgets to consider that on more than one occasion Na'i's attitude to Bashu is inexcusably racist. In their first encounter, Na'i makes a nasty reference to his dark complexion (he is from the south of the country), and asks, "Are you an animal or a human being?" She is at first very protective of her own biological children and treats Bashu as a dangerous animal in her rice paddy. The leitmotif of racism persists in *Bashu*, resulting in one of the most definitive scenes, in which Na'i ritually gives birth to Bashu, but not before buying a new bar of soap to wash his dark skin in an attempt to make him white. Having failed to do so, she says, "No use, he will never become white." None of these racist comments, however, have the slightest effect on the earthly dignity of Na'i's character. In the absolute brilliance and self-confidence of his characterization of Na'i, Beiza'i knows only too well that she must share the racism of her village, the universe of her physical location and material imagination, before transcending them. Na'i is no "mother" in a patriarchally constituted sense. Na'i is earth incarnate. To her, Bashu, her own two children, the animals she cares for, the sprouting rice in the paddy are one and the same.

RITUAL BIRTH

To understand Na'i better, and what Beiza'i does in his characterization of her, we need to see her in the context of mythological motifs and against the two opposing myth-types of the world parents.[10] In the most familiar world parents myth-type (A625 in Thompson's motif-index), a sky father and an earth mother are parents of the universe. This myth-type is found in a vast geographical expanse that ranges from ancient Greece to India, eastern Indonesia, Tahiti, Africa, and North and South America. The less widely known world parents myth-type (A625.1 in Thompson's motif-index) is exactly the reverse: the mother as sky and the father as earth.[11] Na'i is of course immediately identifiable as a mother-earth figure (A625). However, Beiza'i does not just give a text analogue to the motif-index and leave it there. He is an artist, not a folklorist.

Throughout *Bashu*, Na'i's husband is absent, and when he does appear in the very last sequence of the film, the most visible phallic symbol, his right hand, has been cut off, presumably in a war or work-related accident. We are never told. Bashu as a result is "born" to Na'i symbolically; she *ritually* gives birth to him. Visually, this *ritual birth* has a number of representations. One is Na'i's washing of Bashu in a river during which, in Beiza'i's extremely accurate mise-en-scène, his head is precisely beneath Na'i's womb. With his body completely in the water, his head exposed and in Na'i's hands, Bashu is ritually born to mother earth. In another sequence, Na'i fishes Bashu out of a small brook with a net that she casts towards him. Bashu does not know how to swim and has just fallen off a branch on which he was frolicking. While all the men are standing by completely paralyzed, Na'i casts her fishing net towards the drowning Bashu. In the pool-like brook, Bashu appears to suffocate, as if in Na'i's womb, or, more specifically, aspirate the plasmatic meconium of the fetus. The grayish-green color of the water is particularly reminiscent of meconium, the dark greenish mass that accumulates in the bowel of the fetus and is discharged shortly after birth. Na'i pulls Bashu out with a movement that is remarkably similar to birthing. She saves and thus "gives life to him," as he would have died otherwise, unaided by the impotent men standing about, and then holds him to her bosom exactly as if he were newborn from her own womb. There are many other instances of ritual birth, such as Na'i's hallucinatory, surreal dance to Bashu's magically therapeutic drumbeats, that resembles the twisting and turning of the body during the final stages of labor. It is just after this scene that we see Na'i washing the clothes she wore while she was sick, as women do after giving birth, and dictating a letter to Bashu to be sent to her absent husband. "My son Bashu writes this letter," Na'i says proudly. "Like all other children, he is the offspring of the earth and the sun." Bashu has been conceived immaculately. The only remote "contact" with the husband comes in the form of this letter *after* the ritual birth of Bashu to Na'i.

This ritual birth in the conspicuous absence of Na'i's husband leads us to the precise site of remythologization in which Beiza'i has narrated his version of world parenting. To see the central place of Na'i as mother earth in this cosmic vision, and the revolutionary reimagination of the world through a reinvention of the world parent myth, we ought to look at the original myth itself before Beiza'i's reconstitution of it.

The splendid work of Professor K. Numazawa of Nanzan University of Nagoya, Japan, on the related motif of the creation myth (Thompson index-motif A625.2), "The Raising of the Sky,"[12] although written by a Japanese scholar in German, published in Paris in 1946, and predicated on Japanese mythology, corroborates Beiza'i's film in a surprising way. It is precisely this unexpected similarity that shows the insight that *Bashu* offers into a range of universal myths. Numazawa's observation of the "Raising of the Sky" motif of the creation myth supports the theory of a link between agricultural communities and mythmaking. The significance of agricultural communities—also the setting of *Bashu*—is in their approximation to the earliest forms of human society. Myths that have to do with the origin of the universe, in which a mother earth and a father sky play the central roles, take us directly to the formative communal context of patriarchal and matriarchal patterns of socialization. The myth of world parenting usually begins at the pre-moment of the world, a moment central to both *The Ballad of Tara* and *Bashu*. How did the world appear at this pre-moment? "There is, common to nearly all the myths I have spoken of," Numazawa observes,

> the idea that darkness filled the universe before the separation of the sky and earth, and that light appeared for the first time in the universe when the sky and earth had been separated. And with the coming of the light, everything on earth which had been hidden in the darkness appeared for the first time.[13]

Recall that until the very last sequence of the film, we do not see Na'i with her husband. He is present by virtue of Na'i's speaking of him. Her neighbors, some of whom are her husband's relatives, remind her of him, and of course her two children are presumably the result of their marriage. The husband arrives *after* the ritual birth of Bashu to Na'i. So the narrative moment of *Bashu* is the untime of the world; that is, father sky has left, but his marks are on mother earth, and thus the world is evident. And yet, there are many nights and days, i.e., the death and resurrection of the world, without a visit from father sky. According to Numazawa,

> This is precisely what we see every morning at the break of dawn. The breaking of dawn starts with the union of the sky and earth in the darkness of the night. This union is the union of father sky and mother earth, and all things that appear with the rising of the sun are born of these two.[14]

But we never see Na'i sleeping with any man. There is no sign of father sky. The repeated emphasis of Beiza'i's camera on Na'i's sleeping patterns, in the course of which she has to keep an eye on the rice paddy, leaves no room for speculation. She sleeps alone, in the dark. Beiza'i's intuitive grasp of this myth, at once critically intelligent and creatively subversive, leads him to have Na'i ritually give birth to a son *in the absence of her husband.* As Numazawa comments,

> The myths in which father sky leaves mother earth in the morning show clearly traces of the custom of visit marriage (*Besuchsehe*). When morning comes, the man, like Uranos, must leave the woman. Therefore the myths have merely transferred what happens every morning to the first morning of the beginning of the universe—in other words, to the morning of the creation of all things.[15]

The Japanese practice of "the visit marriage," or its patriarchal counterpart in the Shiite *"mut'ah,"* or "temporary marriage," is far closer, as Numazawa suggests, to the original matriarchal custom whereby the husband is at hand only to cause the conception of the child and then goes away. In Beiza'i's case, what is important is the virtual elimination of the father. By Bashu's ritual birth to Na'i even the "temporary marriage" is rendered superfluous. But Na'i and Bashu become parent and child not simply through a cinematically staged ritual but far more effectively by "working" together. "Work" is constitutional to the emerging parental relationship between Na'i and her son. At first Bashu does not work, and the neighbors ridicule Na'i for giving shelter to a useless boy. Then she makes him work, and her neighbors criticize her for turning the boy into a slave. From this bit of social satire emerges Na'i and Bashu's relationship, which is developed through work. This theme climaxes when, after her illness, Na'i rises when it is still dark and finds Bashu already at work in the rice paddy.

The return of the absent father threatens the archetypal dyad of Bashu and Na'i

A smile of satisfaction appears, barely visible, on her face. If we now keep in mind Beiza'i's glorious long shots of rice paddies in a film made on the Caspian coast in 1986, we find startling corroboration of his story of Na'i and Bashu from a Japanese scholar half-way around the globe in 1946:

> A principal feature in so many myths, particularly those whose motif is the banishment of heaven, is agriculture, specifically agriculture whose chief product is rice. The central figure in these myths is a woman, and the principal animals are cows and pigs. In the social system one may see the prevalence of visit marriage (*Besuchsehe*), the

earliest form of marriage in the matriarchal cultural sphere that developed out of the status that women had acquired economically in the course of social development. From such facts one may conclude that the myths we have been discussing are products of the matriarchal cultural sphere.[16]

The location of the film in an agricultural community, the pivotal importance of a rice paddy, the centrality of a woman to the story, domestic animals, the economic autonomy of Na'i—all these are the surprising evidence of a conscious basing of *Bashu* on a universal myth that anchors its narration on the centrality of the idea of mother earth before launching the cosmic vision of a radical reconstitution of the myth, liberating Na'i and the entire people that she represents from mental, moral, mythological, cultural, historical, and political bondage. Beiza'i is unrivaled in his ambitious thrust towards a radical reconstitution of Iranian culture.

Alan Dundes has offered an Oedipal explanation of the myth type that Numazawa has examined, the myth in which a male offspring of world parents strive to separate them by pushing the sky father off the earth mother.[17] This is quite suggestive in the case of *Bashu*, particularly in light of the final sequence when the father returns with his right hand, an obvious phallic symbol, cut off. The first time we see the father is when Beiza'i masterfully draws his figure from a scarecrow that Bashu has made. The father stands in front of the sun, creating a momentary darkness, and asks Bashu who made the scarecrow. Sitting, Bashu has a conversation with the father, not knowing who he is, while in his shadow as an extension of the scarecrow. After this conversation, during which Bashu gives a cup of water to the father, Bashu hears from his friends that Na'i's husband has returned. On his way to Na'i, for some inexplicable reason nervous and even frightened, he picks up a stick and runs towards the rice paddy where they live. When Bashu gets there, Na'i is already engaged in a quarrel with her husband, objecting to his demand that Bashu be sent away. Bashu comes in hurriedly, stands between Na'i and the father, and instinctively raises the stick to attack him and protect his mother. The angle of Beiza'i's camera here is astonishing. From the father's right side, we see the stump of his right hand, Bashu's raised stick, and Na'i safely behind her son. Beiza'i has by then rendered the scarecrow figure of the father symbolically castrated, obviously redundant, and socially irrelevant. That is the beginning of a whole new definition of the family, of father-mother-and-son, and the relation of power which holds them together.

URBAN LEGENDS

In the colonial frontiers, myths die hard. Perhaps because we keep reinventing them, sometimes for the right reasons. What Beiza'i has achieved in his long creative career is precisely to prevent the collapse into a universe without myth. In our case, the old myths continue to haunt us. We are always at the mercy of falling into the abyss of the nothingness of things. Beiza'i's cinema has always worked towards a new revelation of the universe in which we, as Iranians, as colonials, as those written out of the history of their own modernity, can be reborn.

Under the calm, even prosaic, surface of *Shayad Vaqti Digar* (*"Perhaps Some Other Time,"* 1988), Beiza'i has a far more ambitious agenda, even more formidable, I venture to say, than anything achieved in *The Stranger and the Fog*, *The Ballad of Tara* and *Bashu* put together. *Perhaps Some Other Time* is predicated on a suspicion: Modabber suspects his wife Kian of having an illicit love affair, while she is trying to conceal a succession of inexplicable nightmarish memories, perhaps even the symptoms of schizophrenic paranoia. While pregnant, and striving to conceal her psychological predicament, Kian finds out that she is not the natural child of her parents and that they had adopted her. Meanwhile Modabber, who is going mad with suspicion, finally locates Ranjbar, the antique dealer whom he suspects of having an affair with his wife. Kian is desperate to conceal her condition from her husband. Modabber is frantic to prove his wife's fidelity. They give each other the wrong signals, add to each other's confusion, and lead each other to false conclusions. Modabber then finds out that Ranjbar is married to a woman who looks remarkably similar to Kian, and in fact turns out to be her lost twin sister. Kian discovers that her recurring nightmares all stem from her early childhood memories, when her mother, desperate and destitute, had abandoned her on a street corner, where she had been picked up by a caring couple.

Through the very simple narrative of *Perhaps Some Other Time*, Beiza'i examines the function of "evidence," and the mechanism of gathering it in the establishment of truth and falsehood. The role of women in this work is of an entirely

In *Perhaps Some Other Time*, Beiza'i starts off from two premises—one masculine, the other feminine—to challenge the primacy of instrumental reason. A case of mistaken identity turns an urban setting into an archaeological excavation of hidden assumptions

different sort than in his previous films. Here, he is after something far more universal, far more significant, and achieves it in a much more ingenious way. Despite its contemporary setting, *Perhaps Some Other Time* is infinitely more mythical than either *The Ballad of Tara* and *The Stranger and the Fog*. Its urban setting is deceptive to those who are accustomed to seeing the working of myth in rural settings, archaic clothing, or antiquated dialogue.

The film begins with both Modabber and his wife Kian tormented by visual representations: Modabber by a video of his wife, Kian by nightmarish images the meaning of which she cannot fathom. But—and here is the key difference—

Modabber sees something that he is not watching, while Kian watches some-thing that she does not see. He sees a complete stranger to him, the lost twin sister of his wife, but he thinks he is looking at his wife. She watches in her dreams the real images of her infancy, but she does not have the complete data and interpretative frame to realize what it is she sees. Modabber begins to inter-pret the video images on the false exegetical premise of marital infidelity. Kian begins to accumulate data, piece by piece, from her dreams and from observing her husband's suspicious behavior, but does not have the epistemic parameters to interpret them. Hermeneutically, he is deductive; she inductive. Logically, he operates a priori; she a posteriori. He collects indubitable data only to end up proving himself wrong. She collects dubious data, only to prove herself right. Beiza'i thus makes a historic judgment on the masculine proclivity to abstrac-tion and metaphysics, and, conversely, on the feminine proclivity to material fact and always substitutional propositions.

The two character types, the mythical images that Beiza'i presents and exam-ines here, are those of the woman as "food-gatherer" and the man as "hunter." Kian gathers the data of her early childhood with the infinite patience of a pre-historic woman. Modabber hunts for absolutist abstractions, caring very little for the facts. Kian is after no absolutist abstraction. She just wants to accumu-late/gather enough data/food to make sense of/feed her perturbed imagina-tion/household. Modabber cares very little for the facts. He just wants to hunt/abstract for a final explanation/absolute certainty that will establish his wife's infidelity/the truth. Kian lives in and by reality. Modabber is a metaphysi-cian par excellence. As a result, *Perhaps Some Other Time* is Beiza'i's ingenious manifesto against a whole history of phallogocentricism.

The brilliance of one cinematic blow seeking to alter, or at least visibly and narratively challenge, the age-old authority of a phallogocentricism that for millennia has managed to conceal itself behind a metaphysical culture in which veiling is second nature requires not only a perfect command of but also a criti-cal intimacy with the mythological workings of the culture. That "changeability is one of the specific characteristics of myth"[18] is an academic insight achieved after a long and arduous examination of myths in their cross-cultural, and trans-historical settings by Professor T. P. van Barren, an Egyptologist at the Univer-sity of Groningen. He considered examples of behavior in mythological

Susan Taslimi's career changed forever the face of professional acting. The versatility of her performances (here, in *Perhaps Some Other Time*) was instrumental in the success of Beiza'i's cinematic career

narratives in settings as diverse as Tahiti, among the Anuak (a Nilotic tribe on the Upper Nile), among the Papuans of the Wantoat region in northeastern New Guinea, and Tikopia. But to initiate mythical changes that are as much rooted in the contemporaneity of our problems as they are launched towards an emancipation of our future necessitates a critical intelligence of an entirely different sort. Here, Beiza'i demonstrates an unusual combination of scholar and artist. His exceptionally detailed knowledge of both Iranian mythology and performing arts is completely at the disposal of his creative imagination, which is geared towards a radical, surgical break from the historical bondage to myths that has occasioned our slavery.

The mirror of an invisible world, the mythic bracing of the real, Beiza'i's cinema crystallizes all our enduring assumptions that have disappeared into the thin air, just before they frighten us into citizenship of a republic of fear, just at the moment when they can be held accountable for the promise that they give, the hope that they are.

FOUR

BAHMAN FARMANARA:
TWICE UPON A TIME

It is impossible to exaggerate the impact of Bahman Farmanara's Prince Ehtejab *(1974) when it premièred at the Tehran Film Festival. Adapted from one of the milestones of contemporary Persian fiction, Houshang Golshiri's* Prince Ehtejab *(1968), Farmanara's stunning visual adaptation brought to a new synergetic height the successful marriage of Iranian film and fiction, inaugurated a few years earlier by Daryush Mehrju'i's* The Cow *(1969), the groundbreaking adaptation of a story by Gholamhossein Sa'edi.*

Born in 1942 in Tehran, Farmanara received his college education first in London and then at the University of Southern California (USC). By the mid 1960s, he was back in Tehran promoting art films on national television. By the early 1970s, he had made his first short films. Prince Ehtejab *established him as one of the leading filmmakers of his generation. In the wake of the Islamic revolution in 1979, he made yet another screen adaptation of a story by Golshiri:* Tall Shadows of the Wind *(1978) has "the dubious distinction," as he puts it half-jokingly, "of having been banned by both the Shah and Khomeini's regime."*

After the Islamic revolution, Farmanara and his family left Iran and eventually settled in Canada. He had a leading position in a successful film distribution company when obligations to his family's textile company took him back to Iran in the mid 1980s. Almost immediately upon his return, he began submitting scripts to the Islamic censor for approval. None were approved until Smell of Camphor, Fragrance of Jasmine *(2000) marked his return to Iranian cinema after an absence of some twenty years.*

Returning to camera, both behind and in front of it, after an absence of some two decades, in *Smell of Camphor, Fragrance of Jasmine* Farmanara became the missing link between two generations of filmmakers

The following conversation took place in New York City on Thursday, 28 September 2000 when Farmanara attended the US première of Smell of Camphor, Fragrance of Jasmine *at the Thirty-eighth New York Film Festival.*

Hamid Dabashi   As I said to you yesterday after the screening of *Smell of Camphor, Fragrance of Jasmine*, it is a great pleasure to see you back in Iranian cinema with such grace and confidence that it is as if you had never left. You were sadly missed during this twenty-year absence. I must confess that I was a bit nervous when I sat down to see your film. Much has happened in Iranian cinema over the last two decades. Still, you have joined it without yielding in the slightest to any temptation to alter your vision or narrative, and yet you have something to teach the younger generation. I want to take you back to the point where you left the world of Iranian cinema. So let me start with the beginning. You were born in 1942—

STUDYING IN LOS ANGELES

Bahman Farmanara   Yes, I was born in 1942, and in 1958 when I was sixteen I went to England to study film. When I got there I found out that there was no film school, so I went to an acting school. When my father found out that I was studying acting instead of directing—well he was quite enlightened in allowing me to study directing, but not enlightened enough to let me study acting. So he immediately came to England and, within ten days, shipped me to the States. By sheer accident my mother's cousin was getting his degree in public administration at USC, so he sent me there.

HD   How long where you in England altogether?

BF   A year and a half. I then went to the film school at USC. I graduated in 1965.

HD   Is this the time that Mehrju'i was also in Los Angeles?

BF   Yes, you are right . . . Mehrju'i went to UCLA [University of California at Los Angeles] and studied philosophy. Haritash was also there.

HD   Did you know each other?

BF   I had met Haritash because he was at the same school as I was, but I did not know Mehrju'i. I met him when I went back to Iran.

HD   And after you got your degree you went back to Iran?

BF   I actually stayed for another year to study for my master's degree because I did not want to go back to Iran. I was too comfortable in California. Then my mother came and convinced me that I should go back, and so I returned in 1966.

HD   What about your siblings? Were any of them interested in the arts or cinema in particular?

BF   No, none of them. And that was the strange thing. I have two brothers and a sister, and they all worked in the family business—textiles. We used to go to the movies once a week. From the age of seven on, I was always the one who chose the film we were going to see as a family. So whether it was *East of Eden* or *Barefoot Contessa*, I chose the film because no one else cared. They just wanted to get out of the house because that was our evening out.

HD   What about Los Angeles—what sort of cinematic exposure did you have besides Hollywood?

BF   I liked European films. There were a couple of theaters there. One in particular, the Western Theater, on Western Avenue and Wilshire, showed films such as *Hiroshima, Mon Amour* and *L'Avventura*. Once a month, they would sell you a ticket for twenty-four hours. That's when I saw Andy Warhol's work. It was an experience that exposed me to movies other than the ones we saw from Hollywood. And then there was one theater that showed foreign films. I saw many Japanese films there, because, except for Kurosawa or Ozu, Asian films were not regularly distributed.

BACK TO IRAN

HD   In 1966 you returned to Iran. What did you do then? Did you go to work for the national television network?

BF   When I went back to Iran the first thing I had to do was my military service, because very soon after I arrived I decided I did not want to stay, and I could not easily leave the country again without first doing the required one and a half (this was the last year before it became two) years of military duty. Towards the end of my service, I got married. Then one thing led to another and I went into television. Iranian National Television at this time employed a bunch of young people, about my age, that Reza Qotbi had brought together. I knew Hazhir Daryush from the time that I was a student at USC in Los Angeles.

HD   Did Hazhir Daryush have an official position at the National Television?

BF   He was the head of a group that was introducing the arts—movies, music, painting, etc.—to viewers. But I knew him from before. When I was in England I used to write for the periodical *Setareh Cinema* [*Movie Star*] as a reporter. Hazhir Daryush was writing for them from Paris, and Kamran Shirdel was writing from Rome. So we knew each other by name. I went to the television offices and filled out an application, and about four days later they called me up. I started working in Hazhir's division. For two years—actually three years—I did a program about current movies—film criticism, that is.

THE EARLY FILMS

HD   What kind of films were you introducing in this program?

BF   Again, we were reviewing some Iranian films but also a lot of American ones. All the American companies had offices in Tehran, and it was around that time that behind-the-scene films were beginning to be produced and we would also show some of those. In the meantime I made two documentaries.

HD   One was about caviar, right?

BF   Yes, it was called *Noruz and Caviar*. Noruz was the name of the fisherman. They sent me off to make a film about caviar because they were going to use it as some sort of promotional piece in areas where caviar was little known. I visited the man who was working there, catching the most expensive food in the world. He was making about 1200 tumans per year [less than $200 at the official rate of exchange at the time] for going to the sea twice a day, because the net for catching the fish was vertical and had to be adjusted. So I made a film that was dead against such exploitation, and it was banned after one screening by the television authorities. This was in the late 1960s or early 1970s. Then I made another film—

HD   *Tehran: Old and New?*

BF   Exactly. This particular film was narrated from the point of view of a cab driver who starts way in the south of Tehran and takes passengers to different parts of the city, and so the viewers saw the disparity between the rich and poor parts of the city. This film was not distributed or shown on television simply because it revealed how much disparity existed between the different sections of the capital.

HD   Did you find any discrepancy between Qotbi's bringing together a group of young Iranian artists and intellectuals at National Television, and then finding what they produced rather objectionable?

BF   Well, you see everyone was discovering the power of television. I mean everybody knew about it, but it was the first time that we had a national network. Things were being broadcast locally all over the nation. Of course they were very protective of what they were showing. My own interests from the very beginning were the political and sociological problems we faced in the country. Somehow my films appeared as though I was criticizing the situation too harshly.

HD   1969, the year of your first film, is also the year of Mehrju'i's *The Cow* and Kimiya'i's *Caesar*. What was your place in this milieu?

BF   Well, I knew Mehrju'i when he was making *Diamond 33*. In fact I did the first television interview with him, because he had Nancy Kuwack as his star— and Fazeli. At the time John Neglusco was making a film called *The Heroes* for Moulin Rouge Studios in Iran with Stuart Whitman and Elke Sommer and a few other people. I was working with John Neglusco on that film. It was at the same time that I did this interview with Mehrju'i. But neither *Diamond 33* nor *The Heroes* was our kind of filmmaking. I remember the night we heard that Mehrju'i's *The Cow* had won an award at the Venice Film Festival. We were in the Marmar Bar, the regular hangout for the Tehran intellectuals, with Gholam-hossein Sa'edi, Mir Ala'i, Golshiri, and a few other friends, and I proposed a toast to the hope that from then on Cannes would be open to our films because they did not want to miss one like *The Cow*.

HD   Had you seen *The Cow* before its Venice première?

BF   Yes. That was actually the start of a movement in Iran that Kimiya'i's *Caesar* also contributed to. I knew Kimiya'i from the time he and I worked together on *The Heroes*. But my feeling then was that this was not the kind of film I wanted to make. In fact the first film that I ever wanted to make was an adaptation of Golshiri's *Prince Ehtejab*.

HD   Before we talk about *Prince Ehtejab* I want to talk about *Qamar Khanom's House*. What was your involvement with it?

BF   I had a friend who is now dead, Manouchehr Mahjoubi, who used to write for the satirical journal *Towfiq* and soon after the Islamic revolution he brought out another satirical journal called *Ahangar*. As they were making *Qamar Khanom's House*, I used to give them ideas for the structure of each episode. There were actually a few of us doing that, Hadi Khorsandi, Mahjoubi, San'ati, etc. Because I was Mahjoubi's friend, I used to be present when they were hashing out each episode. After the serial went off the air, they were trying to turn it into a feature. They were involved with a producer/cinematographer called Barbad Taheri. One day Mahjoubi called me and said that they had got themselves into some sort of financial trouble in their contract with Taheri. They had given him some promissory notes. Mahjoubi asked me if I would help them finish the film.

HD   So the film was based on the television series.

BF   Yes. I mean, the same characters. The only thing that attracted me to it was that, for me, *Qamar Khanom's House* symbolized Iran and the way it was ruled. You had the representation of every class of people. But I accepted the job for the wrong reasons, so it was a film that I routinely directed because I wanted to help them with their problems with the contract, and it was not successful, in so many ways . . .

HD   What year was it released? Do you remember?

BF   I think it was released in 1972, but this was after I had submitted the script for *Prince Ehtejab*. Soon after publication, the novel by Golshiri that the script was based on was banned, and we thought they would not allow us to make it into a film. So when this other film was offered to me, I went ahead and did it. But after I finished *Qamar Khanom's House*, we took Golshiri's and my name off the script, put my wife's name on it, and submitted it again. And this time it was accepted, and we went ahead and made the film.

HD   Now let me take you a few steps back. When did you read Golshiri's novel for the first time?

BF   Actually, because of his death recently, I was taking a look at the dates. It was 1348–49 in the Iranian calendar, which is 1969–70 in the Gregorian. It was one of those strange coincidences. Quite a number of my friends knew that I was looking for some story or novel to make into a film, and two of my friends, Mahjoubi and Jamshid Arjomand, and another person on the same day in different meetings, suggested this novel. And I took this as an omen, so I bought and read it. It was the 27th of Esfand (17 March), which is two days before the Iranian New Year. I didn't know Golshiri. I went to Isfahan. I knew he lived there . . . I found him through a mutual friend, Mohammad Hoquqi. We had a meeting, and by the time I returned to Tehran two days later, he had assigned me the movie rights of the book without receiving a penny.

HD   I see.

BF   And so, we went ahead and wrote a script together, and we thought that with *Prince Ehtejab* as the title, they wouldn't accept it, so we submitted it as *Agha* ("*Sir*"), not realizing that in the ministry they called their ministers and a few other important people *Agha*. So they turned it down.

HD   But why was it turned down, while the novel itself was published?

BF   Movies must always have their script approved . . . I still have what they wrote about it.

HD   By "they" you mean the Ministry of Culture. Who was the Minister of Culture at the time? Pahlbod?

BF   Yes, Pahlbod. The response was just two lines saying that permission is denied . . . for this script to be made into a film, and this body allowed no discussion of the matter. I always considered the people that sit on censorship boards to be idiots, because they think they know better than 60 million or 40 million or 37 million people, so discussions were rarely a point. But I knew that they were touchy about Golshiri's name, because Golshiri had just been imprisoned and kicked out of the Ministry of Education—he was a teacher in Isfahan, and they were very suspicious of his name because he was a leftist writer. That's why the second time, after *Qamar Khanom's House*, we submitted the script with my wife's name on it. She went to the Ministry of Culture, and received half a page of commendation for one of the best scripts that they had ever read.

HD   What is your wife's name?

BF   Farideh Labbakhi-Nezhad. And that script is still in the Museum of Cinema in Iran with my wife's name and the stamp of the award given *Prince Ehtejab* at the Iran Film Festival on it.

HD   That's wonderful.

BF   But that shows how arbitrarily, you know, these things are decided.

HD   I want now to talk a bit more about *Prince Ehtejab* because it's one of the milestones of Iranian cinema. Did you and Golshiri collaborate on the script?

BF   Yes.

HD   Were you at all nervous about this, you and your crew?

BF   Yes, it was difficult. *Prince Ehtejab*, like the books of Marquez, has so many things happening on one page, that we had to streamline it for the movie audience. I told him you write for one person, because when somebody reads a book, they're doing it by themselves. I have to think about a thousand people sitting in a theater at the same time, so I have to simplify things for them, in order for them to understand it. And he immediately understood that. So, for example, there were five generations before we get to Prince Ehtejab himself, and we brought them all together in the grandfather character. When Telfilm, which is a subsidiary of Iranian National Television, agreed to produce the film, they were also producing another film, the *Mina Cycle* by Mehrju'i. We had two actors that were going to play in both of our films . . .

HD   Who were they?

BF   Ezzatolah Entezami and Ali Nassirian.

HD   Yes.

BF   I went to Mehrju'i and asked, "Could you postpone your film, because if I don't make this film this year, it's going to be difficult for me to make it later on?" He now denies it, but he refused point blank: "I don't care whether you make your film or not." So I put aside Entezami and Nassirian, and chose Mashayekhi and Kasbian for the roles, as well as Shirandami and Khorvash and everybody else who was supposed to be in the film. Pezhman had never scored for a film, but I'd heard the music that he had written for the Children's Development Institute on the poetry of Nima that Ahmad Shamlu had recited . . . and that kind of music that sets the mood for a poem, that was what I wanted for my film.

HD   Why did you opt for black and white?

BF   Well, at the time, it was cheaper. The whole budget of the film was 700,000 tuman [about $100,000 at the time], and, also, we really didn't have the money to build a set, and when I went on location, most of these old houses had stained glass windows, and I wanted to control that in the film . . .

HD   It first premièred where? In Tehran?

BF   Well, it was shown at the Tehran Film Festival in 1973. That year, the jury consisted of Gilo Pontecorvo, Alain Robbe-Grillet, Shadi Abdolsalam, and a few others. That year Liliana Cavani's *Il Portiere di Notte* (*The Night Porter*) was also in competition. Apparently, it and our film had reached the finals, and Robbe-Grillet and Pontecorvo had written in defense of *Prince Ehtejab* that it was an antifascist movie and the other one was profascist.

HD   Then what happened?

BF   Well, there were three Iranian films in the festival. Beiza'i's *The Stranger and the Fog*, Kimiya'i's *The Deer*, and mine. My film won the Grand Prix for best film. In Kimiya'i's film, Behruz Vosuqi won the award for best actor.

HD   What about its international reception?

BF   It was shown at the 1973 festival in Tehran; then, in 1974, in Cannes, it was shown at the Director's Fortnight. And then, it was screened at the London Film Festival and a lot of other places, but I only went to Cannes. My feeling about a film I have made is that I give it up after the first screening because it no longer belongs to me.

HD   What was its fate inside Iran after the Tehran Film Festival?

BF   We had to cut about nine minutes in order to get it released, simply because the film was too provocative, both religiously and politically. But everybody was so eager to see it that it ran for nine weeks in a 2000-seat theater, the Cinema Capri, which is now called Cinema Bahman. It had a very successful run in Tehran, and they stopped showing it only because we reached *Noruz* [the Persian new year] and they wanted to show *Two Fellow-Travelers* with Behruz Vosuqi and Googoosh, for which they had a contract for the New Year. But it was shown again in another theater and had a good run.

HD   I can understand why the Shah's regime, a monarchy, would object to it, because the political aspect is evident both in the novel and in the film. But in 1973, the religious establishment was not yet in a position to make any kind of formal protest, although I do remember that the film has one very provocative nudity scene. Do you recall the reaction of the religious establishment to your film?

BF   Well, as you know, according to the rules and regulations of the censorship board, there were four taboos prior to the revolution: first, you could not criticize the constitution; second, you could not criticize the royal family; third, you could not criticize Islam; and fourth, you could not criticize the armed forces. Despite the religious undercurrent in the country, I did not get any negative reaction to the film prior to the Islamic revolution. However, I did get an earful about it after the revolution, when they also banned *Tall Shadows of the Wind*. But prior to the revolution, there were friends of mine who would say that if the royalists don't get you, then the religious authorities will. Indeed, the scene you refer to was very provocative. I don't think it will ever be done that same way again, with a parallel cut of a masturbation scene with religious rites.

AFTER *PRINCE EHTEJAB*

HD   What happened, then, between 1974, the year of *Prince Ehtejab*, and *Tall Shadows of the Wind* which was released in 1978?

BF   Well, when I was at the Cannes Film Festival, Dr. Bushehri, who was the husband of Princess Ashraf [the late Mohammad Reza Shah's twin sister], had a company called the Film Development Company of Iran. They had already made a film, not a good one. He offered to let me run the company, on condition that for two years, I did not direct myself but only produced films. This was a major opportunity to run an Iranian cinema company that actually had a lot of funds. They had an office in Paris and an office at Twentieth Century Fox, and they were already working with Orson Welles and a few other people, when I took over the company.

HD   Did you have any moments of doubt? You had just turned one of the greatest contemporary novels by one of the most progressive writers into a very successful film, and now here you were working for a company directly related to the royal family?

BF   Well, I always look at the risks and the possibilities—and as long as I chose the subjects of the films we were doing, and could defend them, I did not have any problem with where the money came from. And it gave me the opportunity to produce Abbas Kiarostami's first feature film, *The Report*. And I did a film by Beiza'i, *The Crow*. I also produced *The Divine One* by Haritash, and *Wind and Chest* by Mohammad Reza Aslani. They also had a contract for a film called *The Desert of Tartars*. We finished a film with Orson Welles, and we were also in the midst of shooting Orson Welles' last film, *The Other Side of When*. They gave us 75 million tumans for Iranian cinema, in fact. It was the largest amount of money ever allocated.

HD   My intention is not to pass any judgment. I am just trying to grasp the context of such an undertaking. Were you based in Paris or in Tehran?

BF   We were based in Tehran. One of my strongest passions was that I hated taking orders from any foreign interest in order to do a film, and one of my conditions was that the decisions should be made in Iran, and that the films should be done where they were supposed to be done.

HD   What prompted your quitting?

BF   Well, when they gave us 75 million tumans for Iranian cinema, Dr.

Bushehri and his cohorts decided to use this money to finance an American coproduction called *Caravans*. I hated the script.

HD   Who was it by?

BF   I forget now, but it was a bad script, and the director, at first, was supposed to be Sidney Polack, but Sidney Polack quit, and they hired a director who had made a *Dirty Harry* sequel. I was totally opposed to the project. And when I was ordered to do it, I said that it was not part of our agreement, and I quit. So I left the company for that reason, and just to show you how the country was run, I was called in by SAVAK a couple of times. I was beaten up.

HD   Because of having refused an order from—

BF   The order was from Princess Ashraf, and I had said that I'm not taking her orders, so I was actually punished for that. Bushehri used to spend ten days in Iran and then forty days outside Iran. One time when he came back, I told him what was happening, and then it stopped.

AT THE DAWN OF THE REVOLUTION

HD   When did you write the script for *The Night Never Ends*?

BF   I didn't. I had written the original story, seven pages long, called "Wanting." Zhila Sazegar wrote the script from that and Sayyad directed it, and the film became the all-time biggest moneymaker. If you consider that the tickets at three and four tumans at that time would now cost 800 tumans, it is the highest grosser in Iranian film history. That gave us some leeway to do other things, and I found some investors for *Tall Shadows of the Wind*, which was, again, based on a story by Golshiri, and in 1978 we shot the film.

HD   We are now in 1978, in the midst of the revolutionary upheaval.

BF   Well, some movements had begun.

HD   Exactly. Where did you shoot it?

BF   In a village called Hanjan, near Natanz.

HD   And again you worked with Golshiri on the script.

BF   Yes. Because the story is only four pages long, we worked on it for about two years until we got it to twenty-five pages, and I wrote the full script from that.

HD   When did you finish it?

BF   Well, we finished the film, and while we were editing, we did a trailer for it. We wanted to put it in theaters. Once we sent the trailer in to get a permit for it, they seized the film. It was banned on the basis of the trailer. We only got a duplicate negative made of the film. I still have the duplicate negative in a friend's house in Iran after twenty-odd years. But then, we were entering the period of time when most theaters were being closed or—

HD   Or burned down like the Rex Cinema in Abadan.

BF   Exactly. But the film was banned officially by the Shah's regime before the revolution really started. A year and a half after the revolution, the film got a release permit, and five stars on the ratings scale. We opened in three theaters. But one morning, after three days of screening, they called me from the theater—

HD   This was 1979 now?

BF   No, 1980. And they called from the theater to tell me that the Committee for the Prevention of Sin had banned the film. So I went to this committee—

HD   Now, the revolution had been successful and Khomeini was in power.

BF   Yes. I was put through a nine-hour interrogation. Nine hours. A young clergyman was doing the questioning; apparently, he had been briefed on films, or he liked films—I don't know. First, he accused us of burning fourteen scarecrows in one scene, as a figurative burning of the fourteen saints. I really was taken aback, because I knew we had made thirty scarecrows for that particular scene, but I thought that maybe there were fourteen in the shot that we used, although I could hardly remember. But I said, no, that's not true. They had a moviola set up in that office, and I asked them to look at the scene.

HD Right there in their interrogation room?

BF Yes. So I helped the guy put the film on the moviola for them to see. We began at the head of this one particular shot, and I started counting the scarecrows, and the total was sixteen; they hadn't counted the first two, because the camera was moving so fast. The interrogator, when he saw it was sixteen, accused me of adding two while he wasn't looking, and I said, "Come on, how could I do that?" He knew nothing about films. But one thing that really shook me was when he referred to *Prince Ehtejab* saying that all the films that I had made had been against religion. When I asked how he could say that, he said that I had parallel cut a religious ceremony with the masturbation of a whore. I knew that the phrase "parallel cutting" was not in this clergyman's vocabulary. I knew that . . .

HD He used exactly that phrase.

BF Yes, and so I knew that somebody from the cinema establishment was feeding him information, and that's when I really became worried, because as long as I had to deal with the clergy, I could cope, but if somebody from the film industry was involved and was helping point out these vulnerable sections, I was in trouble. And it was then and there that I decided to leave Iran, because I thought, OK, the film has been banned. I can't fight it anymore. The cultural struggle was becoming too complicated, and I couldn't waste my time. But I also had done something that put me in good financial standing. When I saw the beginning of the revolution and that things were moving very fast, I went to Paris, and brought four films for distribution in Iran, the films that were banned at the time in the country: *Z*, *State of Siege*, *The Battle of Algiers*, and a documentary about Chile.

HD This was in 1980.

BF Yes, 1980, and my wife and three kids left the next Sunday. And I left behind all the films that had not been distributed, like *Christ Stopped at Eboli*, and many other films that I owned, as well as two of my partners, in Iran. I have never really looked back.

HD How long did you stay in Paris, and what did you do?

BF Seven months. I went to the Canadian Embassy's library and started to look for something to do in Canada. My father was already living in Vancouver so I expected to get a Canadian visa. And that's when I made a proposal to begin a children's film festival in Vancouver.

HD   How long did you stay in Vancouver?

BF   Almost two years. Aside from setting up the film festival, I also started a film distribution company. I found two people that would put up $50,000 each. In 1981, I went to the Cannes Festival. I bought Andrej Wajda's *Man of Iron* for $100,000 for US and Canada four days prior to its winning the Grand Prix at the festival. The film was then in great demand, and those who wanted to buy it were told that somebody in Vancouver had already bought it. I sold the rights to Euro Classics for $175,000 about twenty-five days later. Because of that success, we found some investors in Toronto that put up $4.5 million dollars to start a bigger company, and this was the first Canadian company to have distribution offices in New York. So I started a company called Spectra Film in Toronto. Our office here in New York was on 34th Street between Fifth Avenue and Sixth Avenue, right in front of the Empire State Building. I used to spend three days in New York and four in Toronto. I distributed the films of people like François Truffaut, Alain Renee, Billy August, and many others.

HD   Is that company still around?

BF   No. I received a call from Iran telling me that my mother was very ill—

HD   When was that?

BF   In 1985. I went back to Iran, thinking that it would take about a week. I had asked my brothers in Iran to check whether or not I was on the list of those not allowed to leave the country, and they had said I wasn't. But the day I wanted to leave Iran, the authorities told me I couldn't, and the reason was *Tall Shadows of the Wind*. It was a coproduction of the Ministry of Culture, television, and myself, and they wanted to go over all this stuff, because I was also the producer of the film. It was all a misunderstanding, but clearing up this misunderstanding took about two and a half months. By the time I got back to Canada, the investors in Toronto had decided that I was not coming back, so they had made some changes in the company. When I came back I was depressed, and when I saw what they had done, I sued them. We settled out of court. It was at this time that Cineplex, the small chain that used to distribute our films, had just taken over Odeon. Since I was the only Canadian they knew with business experience in the US, they asked whether I would go to Los Angeles to found a distribution and production company. Thus, Joel Michaels and I set up Cineplex Odeon Films in Los Angeles, and we produced *The Glass Menagerie* with Paul Newman, *Talk Radio* with Oliver Stone, *Madame Sousatzka* with John Schlesinger, *The Last Temptation of Christ* with Martin Scorsese, *Mr. and Mrs. Bridge* by James Ivory, *The Grifters* by Stephen Frears, and *Prancer* by John Hancock.

HD   Did your family move to Los Angeles with you?

BF   Yes, in 1985. Then Garth made an attempt to take over the company.

HD   Did you have shares in the company?

BF   The options I was given because, as an officer, I was one of the four executive vice-presidents of the company. And Garth couldn't raise all the money. So when he had to go, those of us who were part of his team had to go as well. But they settled our contracts very generously, and I was able to start a company called Open City Entertainment. I was in the middle of producing a film called *Liolo* with Jean-Claude Luzan when my father called me. My younger brother, who was running the factory in Iran, had had a heart attack, and my father asked me if I would go and help.

HD   Your father was then living in Canada?

BF   He was actually then in LA also. And since this was the first time my father had asked anything of me, and because I was the one son that had never worked in the textile industry, I really couldn't refuse him. I left the film to my coproducers. I settled my accounts and went back to Iran, thinking that it would take me about a year or a year and a half before my brother recovered.

HD   Did you take your family with you?

BF   No. My two sons were just starting college. My daughter came with us, because she was working already, and my wife. But a couple of things happened. Not only did I get more involved in the company—

HD   Was the company Tehran-based?

BF   Tehran-based, and in a very bad shape financially. I became more and more involved. My brother returned to his job, but he was working only four to five hours a day. So I ended up becoming the CEO of the company, and in order to keep sane, because I had never thought that I could go into the textile business and be happy, after six or seven months of being in Iran, I submitted my first script to the Ministry of Culture to see whether they would allow me to work. But I had two strikes against me. First, I had been very famous and successful before the revolution. Second, since I had left the country after the revolution, I was considered to be against the revolution. And this section of the Ministry of Culture were dead against my working.

HD   Who were they?

BF   Well, various people, mostly revolutionary guards.

HD   But there were also some who were sympathetic, right?

BF   Some were sympathetic, but when I wanted to make films, they always suggested that I produce them instead. They said the best way for me to begin my return to cinema was as a producer. I adamantly refused to produce any more films. I wanted to go back to directing; that was the only thing that gave me joy. I think they also wanted to make an example of my defying them. Then they suggested that I sell Iranian films on the foreign market, and I said this is going back to what I was doing, selling Oliver Stone and John Schlesinger movies, and I refused to do that again. So this became a yearly battle. I would submit a script. After eight or nine months, they would summon me to a meeting, or sometimes not even have a meeting. They would just send me a message that the script was not approved, without giving a reason. But when there was a meeting, they would say that the committee has refused it. In fact, Beheshti, who was in charge of Farabi, liked my scripts, and so did the minister at the time, Larijani—who is now the head of television—but their employees rejected them. I realized what their game was. I think most of us who work in the arts in Iran have bouts of depression. I had my share, and thank God for Prozac. I think that the textile business kept me sane, because we had so many problems in the factories that I worked eight to nine hours a day on the job.

HD   In this period, after 1989, when you had just gone back to Iran, the Iranian cinema was gaining momentum. Kiarostami, Makhmalbaf, Bani-Etemad, Beiza'i, etc. Were you in touch with them?

BF   Oh, I was always in touch. Kiarostami had been my friend since *The Report*. Beiza'i and I had been friends, but we didn't meet as much as before. I used to play tennis with Mehrju'i. I also started teaching at the university.

HD   When did you do that?

BF   When I went back, starting, I think, in 1992, I taught for about four years at the Arts University, Cinema Section.

HD   They didn't object to your teaching?

BF   No.

THE RISE OF A NEW GENERATION OF FILMMAKERS

HD   How would you characterize your attitude to the new filmmakers who were now emerging in cinema at the time?

BF   I set up a tour of sixteen Iranian films that began at UCLA. My only condition was that I was to choose the films myself, because I was adamant that Beiza'i's films be part of the tour, as well as those of Amir Naderi, who had left Iran. So I knew most of the filmmakers, and they knew me, since I had been acting as a producer. I'm one of those people who have never been part of any clique. I've worked with everybody. I've always supported young people, and Makhmalbaf was the only exciting person coming out of that new generation. I remember when I met with Beheshti, I had by then seen Makhmalbaf's *Peddler*. Beheshti asked me what I thought of the film, and I said, "Well, this knife that you have sharpened for our throats has become double-edged." He didn't like that comment, but I have been proved right. Makhmalbaf's a very talented guy, and once he saw that what they had told him all these years about what goes on in the outside world was an absolute lie, he really started taking a second look at his career. Once this movement had really started, there were two things that were really important to consider in Iran. The first was that the Farabi Foundation, which was set up to support our films in international festivals, also greatly promoted their success inside Iran. All of a sudden, audiences realized that Iranian films were being admired everywhere, and this was quite good. Governmental support was very, very important. The second thing was that banning foreign films brought a new kind of audience to the Iranian cinema. Before the revolution, only American and French films had an audience, and people despised Iranian cinema, and thought it beneath them, because they were supposedly more upper class, better educated, and so on. But later on, they were forced to watch Iranian films, and thought it beneath them, because there was nothing else available, and the success of these films outside the country also surprised them. So now, Iranian cinema has an audience that it did not have before—before the revolution, Iranian films never moved beyond Shah Reza Avenue in downtown Tehran because all the cinemas in the upper part of the capital were in the hands of American companies. So, all this helped, and now we have a really new generation of filmmakers like Samira Makhmalbaf and Bahman Qobadi. If Iranian cinema is unique in structure, it is because it has three generations of filmmakers working successfully side by side.

HD   But before we get to the younger generation, you were enumerating causes of this renaissance in Iranian cinema. The banning of foreign films was a critical factor, as you said, but it is not true that Iranian films were shunned and looked down on by the middle or the upper middle class, because the most celebrated Iranian filmmakers were the staple of high culture among the Iranian bourgeoisie. We are of course talking about the younger members of this class. You do remember the great hoopla around the Tehran Film Festival. Our best filmmakers, beginning in the mid 1960s, were in fact the heroes of high culture.

BF   True. But we're talking about the general audience, and our films, even before the revolution, were not widely distributed. *Mina Cycle* was never released before the revolution—our films always played to a limited audience in Iran, even before the revolution.

HD   But wouldn't you say that still is the case with a film like *Taste of Cherry*, for example, which was not as successful as commercial movies that are made inside Iran?

BF   Yes. That is true, because with the sociological situation in Iran, which is highly charged and pressurized by economic factors, two things have happened to movies: They're looked upon as pure entertainment and nothing else by most audiences. And also, 65 percent of the country is below the age of twenty-five, so these people also want their own lives reflected on the screen, not those of my generation. I was surprised at the Tehran Film Festival when they paid a lot of attention to my last film, *Smell of Camphor, Fragrance of Jasmine*, but then again we have a new generation of university graduates, and so on. Every year, we have millions of high school graduates entering the job market.

HD   Last year, it was 3,000,000.

BF   Yes. So what is happening is that they are moving the industry in that direction. Famous producers only want things that relate to youth, but, at the same time, films like *Taste of Cherry* still made 30 million tumans in the box office, which is not a lot in Iranian terms at the present time, but it still means that a lot of people were curious to see the film. But it's not a film that is helped by word-of-mouth, simply because you either get it or you don't. And I always tell Kiarostami that you do everything to make the audience get up and leave, but your genius lies in the fact that they don't leave.

HD   I'm not trying to underplay the sociological and demographic changes that you mention. They're absolutely true, and they're certainly instrumental in what is happening in Iranian cinema. But I want to know whether, from your perspective, as somebody who was central to Iranian cinema before the revolution, you notice something aesthetically different, something schematically, thematically different about the newer films. In your judgment, is our cinematic culture changing? For example, the use of unprofessional actors, which has started very recently. It has been pivotal in Kiarostami. Our most significant filmmakers in the prerevolutionary period always opted for professional actors. But now, our leading directors—Kiarostami, Makhmalbaf, Panahi—don't use professional actors.

BF   Well, when a director like Kiarostami becomes world famous, it is the nature of cinema that other filmmakers try to follow the same road. In the case of Panahi and Qobadi and other people who used to be his assistants, it's very

The use of non-professional actors became the hallmark of the postrevolutionary cinema. Farmanara proved that he could still make magic with professional actors—here, in *Smell of Camphor, Fragrance of Jasmine*, Roya Nonahali

natural that they have taken that path. But Makhmalbaf also followed. So I think the success of Kiarostami really affected the kind of filmmaking that Samira Makhmalbaf is now also practicing and other young people as well, in not being afraid to use non-professional actors. And the films resemble semi-documentaries, but they are extremely well controlled.

HD   Yes, I understand that. But the fact is that if you look at the career of Kiarostami from *Bread and the Alley* to *The Wind Will Carry Us Away*, there's a consistency that runs through his films.

BF   He's the only one who hasn't changed.

HD   Exactly. Because of his fame and his significance, he has had a critical effect on contemporary filmmakers. That's perfectly understandable. Other than the obvious and perhaps inevitable influence of Kiarostami, do you sense some other elements becoming evident? Have the revolution, the war, and any number of similarly critical factors had effects on the nature of the Iranian cinema today that make it qualitatively different from the cinema of your generation? There's something precocious about this generation that has been born to a revolution and then grew up during a brutal war.

BF   Well, I think the censorship and codes have forced everybody to look at new ways of presenting their ideas. Oscar Wilde said that censors are necessary, because, otherwise, people would say what they think, and where would we be then? And when you compare ours with the Eastern European cinema before the the Berlin Wall fell, you see that there are a lot of exciting things coming out of that region, which also had a very strict censor. Here circumstances have forced us to take a new look at this cinema, and sex and violence have been taken out. You have to go back to the basic human stories that are very much elements of Italian neorealism. Now, we are using it in a different sense, though they used non-professional actors, as well.

HD   True.

BF   Iran remains a more restricted society than even Italy was. So in our cinema, especially because of its success outside Iran, and the money that it's possible to make from outside distribution, some directors are losing connection with the people inside while trying to reach those outside.

HD   What about your own most recent work?

BF   Well, the last script that I submitted to the Ministry was called *I Hate Kiarostami.*

HD   I heard about that. Is it your own script?

BF   Yes, it is my script, and the title is really to throw off the censor more than anything else, although there is a character in the film that has very strong opinions about what kinds of movies we should see, as he argues in a discussion. The whole action of the film takes places in an insane asylum, but this is not made clear until the end of the film.

HD   What stage is that script in now?

BF   We wanted to shoot it, and I thought that after Khatami won the election I could do it, but they rejected it because it was too political.

HD   But there is no longer a requirement for a script to be submitted to censors.

BF   I know. But still, the film is very, very political, simply because at the end of the film, you realize that the insane asylum, your prison, is the country.

SMELL OF CAMPHOR, FRAGRANCE OF JASMINE

HD   But before we talk about what hopefully will be your next project, let's go back to what led to the making of *Smell of Camphor, Fragrance of Jasmine*.

BF   Well, after this particular script was refused, I really went off the deep end. I had one of my most severe bouts of depression, and I thought they were never going to let me make films in Iran.

HD   After you returned to Iran in 1989, did you ever visit the United States?

BF   Sometimes, for ten days or so.

HD   But you had been actually living in Iran since 1989?

BF   Yes.

HD   After an absence of almost a decade?

BF   Yes. So because of that depression, I wrote the synopsis of the script for *Smell of Camphor, Fragrance of Jasmine*, which is about a director who is not allowed to direct. He's dying of heart disease, and he decides to make a film about his own funeral with a video camera, because that does not need the permission of the Minister of Culture. And, really, as a joke, I gave it to the Ministry. I submitted it one morning, and they called me the following morning. It was so fast it really

In *Smell of Camphor, Fragrance of Jasmine*, by arranging for his own funeral, Bahman Farjami's character becomes a "posthumous" self-portrait of Farmanara himself, casting a long critical look at Iranian culture

got my attention. They asked why I hadn't submitted this before. I said it was because I had just thought of it at the end of the meeting last week. They asked how I could write scripts that fast. I said, "Well, you know, at my age sometimes things come a bit faster than usual." So they asked me to write the full script. I still didn't believe that I was going to get a permit, but I wrote the first draft of the full script.

HD   This was now 1998.

BF   Yes. Since I was sure that they were not going to approve it, and *Prince Ehtejab* was being shown at the Brooklyn Museum, and I also had a real health problem—I used to pass out—I used the need for a medical checkup as a pretext to come to New York. I was away for a month, and while I was away my assistant called me and told me I had received the permit. I went back to Iran, and I had a really good look at the script because now we had to make a film. I think by the time we actually shot the film, the script that I used differed by about 40 percent from the one they had actually approved. But since two different bodies looked at the film, one at the finished film and one at the original script, there was no problem. It went through about eleven drafts before I was satisfied.

HD   Does it capture in any way your feelings at the time? Were you nervous about going back behind the camera, after almost two decades?

BF   Of course I was a bit nervous. I am always very nervous until I see the first couple of days of rushes, and then I'm sure that I have not lost my touch for capturing what I want on the screen.

HD   But that is a sort of anxiety that is actually quite positive. It's productive. My point is something slightly different. Twenty years have passed. You know that a seventeen-year-old kid, Samira Makhmalbaf, is off making her second film and winning awards all over the world. In a way there is a three-generation gap and there's something constitutionally different about the Iranian cinema. Meanwhile you represented the *crème-de-la-crème* of a generation of filmmakers that has been overshadowed by this new generation. They are precocious, winning prizes that your generation always coveted but never won. So my question is not about the natural anxieties of a filmmaker, but the particular circumstances in which you were going back behind the camera. That new generation, a new mode of filmmaking, the new political and cultural environment—were you at all conscious of these?

BF   Well, I've always felt very sure of myself and what I could accomplish. I never doubt. I mean, if there is doubt, I think you can't go on and do it. And I feel that my filmmaking is different from theirs in many ways.

HD   Very much so, and that is precisely my point.

BF   I see those films and I appreciate them. Abbas Kiarostami and I are friends, and we always discuss all the films he makes. But I never show him my scripts.

Simply because we have different outlooks, and he's become so famous that I sometimes feel that if he comments on my work he may influence my state of mind, and that's why I always show him my work only after I've shot the film, rather than before, though we talk several times a week. But I'm sure of the kind of cinema that I want to be part of. The new cinema of Iran and the way that the younger generation are making films—I don't think it's going to affect me, simply because I have a different agenda for the kind of film that I want to make.

HD   As *Smell of Camphor, Fragrance of Jasmine* shows, you have not been affected by this cinema. But you have introverted it. You have incorporated it into your own vision, and the vision of your own generation. This is something that some of the greatest filmmakers of your generation have not been willing or able to do. I say "introverted" it, which is a kind of concocted term, because *Smell of Camphor, Fragrance of Jasmine* shows a critical intimacy not just with what has happened in the Iranian cinema of the last two decades but also with Iranian society at large. Masters like Kiarostami and Beiza'i have been making one kind of cinema and have progressively developed their respective visions. Yet even a master filmmaker like Beiza'i seems to be entirely oblivious to, or appears not to care about, or probably even dismisses what has happened in postrevolutionary cinema, the exception of course being Kiarostami. The same with Mehrju'i. He, too, continues to make the same kinds of films, though with a major shift in his cinematic vision since the death of Sa'edi. But in your case, it seems to me that after twenty years of silence, or is it darkness, you come out with a film that is deeply grounded in your own cinema, deeply rooted in the cinematic culture of your own generation, and yet organically related to what has happened over the past twenty years. So this restores dignity to a cinema that nowadays is forgotten; yet, equally important, it is a very contemporary film.

BF   Yes, I understand. You see, structurally I tried to be different from what I was doing before, and that's actually what I like to do with each film. The next film, again, is going to be totally different, because that's the only way I can make films. They have to be different from one another, although now, looking back on a number of films I have made, I notice similarities in them. You spoke of some of them. I see other things as well, or things that other people point out. But what I had to do with this particular story was first break it down into a structure that allowed me to unburden myself, weave together a lot of things that have not been said for so many years, and say them in one film—I wanted to get rid of them. All the bitterness—

HD   A sort of exorcism.

BF   Yes, exactly. An exorcism, because I needed an exorcism from my soul, and because nobody in our cinema industry ever said, "Why aren't you letting this guy work?" The fact that we don't have the unity and the support that people in other countries have has made me very, very bitter. I was friends with all these guys; whenever they asked for my help, I gave it. I taught at the university. I read many scripts, correcting them and getting involved in other things that went into making the films of the younger generation, because they would bring their work, and ask my opinion. But I, myself, whenever I attempted to make a film, I ran into a brick wall. So all of this gave the impetus that started this project—you know, let me show them what I can do . . . that all the good things—

HD   Did you feel vindicated and triumphant when your film was acclaimed and won an award at the Fajr Film Festival?

BF   I'm always surprised by the reaction to my films. And, you know, I was walking a very, very thin line. I was playing the lead, which was not part of the plan—and I knew a lot of people were waiting for me to fall on my ass with this film—not only was it my personal story, but I was the star; I was in forty-two sequences out of forty-three.

HD   What prompted you to cast yourself?

BF   I had cast Aydin Aghdashlu, the famous painter, in the lead. We had done the test. It was great. And we went ahead on the basis of that and signed all the other contracts. Everything was done. We were one week from the shoot. Then he called me 11:30 at night and said that he was not going to do it.

HD   Why?

BF   I think he freaked out, because he's a famous painter, a writer. He had never acted in films, and he got cold feet. So I lost the lead actor one week before the shoot.

HD   Your camera crew was ready and—

BF   Everybody was ready. So we tested about twenty-eight or twenty-nine people that week.

HD   Meanwhile, in the back of your mind—

BF   Kiarostami from day one had said, "If you don't do the part yourself, nobody's going to believe it."

HD   And he was right.

BF   Well, I found out that he was right, but I had wanted a non-professional actor for the main part. I didn't want to have the role typecast by having a famous actor play the lead. So we tested writers, painters, and some actors who were not that well known, but we got to about forty-eight hours before the shoot and I had to have a session with Kalari, my DP, and our assistants to decide what to do. If I had started it a year before, I would have postponed production for seven or eight months until I found the person I wanted to play the lead, but the fact that I had not worked for twenty years and now had permission to do so, and since things were always rapidly changing I really had no other option. So we decided that I would play the lead.

HD   Did you find yourself making changes in your directorial habits because it was the first time you were on both sides of the camera?

BF   No, it just made for much longer days. I always have the film in my mind. I never put down actual direction until we get to that particular shot, on that day—but I always know what I want from a scene.

HD   How long did the shooting take?

BF   We shot for twenty-seven days in one month.

HD   And did you see the rushes regularly?

BF   Yes. Almost every other day.

HD   Did you edit it yourself?

BF   No, I work with Ganjavi on all my films. I edit when I'm directing, for the most part, because I don't shoot anything from eighteen different angles, and then decide on the moviola. I know what I want. I know the look that I want, so the editor that works with me has a more mechanical task than actually putting something together.

HD   Do you shoot narratively, A to Z?

BF   No. I mean we shoot according to the schedule that is given to me by the production manager, based on what's available.

HD   In Iran your film was greatly acclaimed and won many awards.

BF   It won best director, best script, best film, best original score, and best supporting actress.

HD   For that woman with the dead child.

BF   In the car, yes.

HD   A stunning performance. Were you surprised by its reception at the international festivals?

BF   Well, there were quite a few representatives from various festivals at Fajr.

HD   Marco Müller was there from Locarno, and Alberto Barbera from Venice. So was Mohammad Haghighat on behalf of Gilles Jacob.

BF   Yes. But I had decided that I was not going to send the film to the Cannes Festival anyway.

HD   Why did you decide that?

BF   Last year—the year before last—an Iranian film called *Stories from Kish* was submitted to Cannes, and Gilles Jacob said that if the Beiza'i episode was cut, he would show the film. The producer had no right to accept this condition, and Gilles Jacob had no right to demand such a cut, because when you accept a film, you accept it as a whole. A gallery owner can't tell an artist to paint apples instead of oranges if he wants his paintings to be exhibited.

HD   But you know that Gilles Jacob always cuts people's films, and many great directors, people that you and I know, love, and admire, listen to him and cut their films in order to be featured at Cannes.

BF   Well, many directors work with him on making cuts. You are right. But, in this case, the producer had no artistic rights to this film. I wrote to Gilles Jacob and told him that he had exceeded his authority as the head of the festival. I said, "You made an agreement with the producer, rather than the director, to cut the film. As long as you're the director of the festival, I will never give you a film of mine."

HD   Well, he's no longer the director.

BF   I know. But the film was chosen for the Director's Fortnight.

HD   I see.

BF   But I still did not submit it, because, in Iran, people see it all as part of the Cannes Festival.

HD   True. What about Venice? Did you submit your film to them?

BF   I did not submit it to Venice because the director of the festival was there. He saw the film, but he had also seen Panahi's *The Circle* in a private screening.

HD   I see.

BF   He never suggested that we submit it to Venice. We submitted the film only to the New York Film Festival.

HD   You sent it directly to Richard Peña?

BF   I sent it directly to Richard. Toronto had accepted the film, and Vancouver had accepted the film, and the only reason for delay in the announcement was that Toronto wanted to have the world première of the film, and they didn't want me to go to Montreal. I said that I had already given my word and that the film was in competition in Montreal. But we didn't get any offers. We didn't send the film.

HD   I dwell on this is because you have lived in Iran for the last decade. With all our celebration and delight in every Iranian filmmaker who is globally renowned, those of us who know the history of Iranian cinema over the past few decades are always wondering what Beiza'i, Mehrju'i, Naderi, and Farmanara are doing. When you decided you didn't want to make films or didn't have a film—well that's different. But when Beiza'i or Mehrju'i does make a film, and it isn't released abroad, it always seems like a cat whose whiskers have been cut on one side and walks sideways. You know. The world knows only half of the story. Iranian cinema walking sideways. There are of course many great Iranian filmmakers whose films are really very parochial and simply do not translate and thus do not get released abroad. For example, Ebrahim Hatami Kia's films such as *From Karkheh to Rhein* or *Glass Agency*. But this is not true of films by people like Mehrju'i, Bani-Etemad, or Beiza'i. I am deeply disturbed by the inordinate power that festival directors exercise in defining Iranian or any other national cinema through very selective representation. It is a sort of Kiarostamification of Iranian cinema. We all love and admire Kiarostami, but he is only one of our great filmmakers. The same is true of the relationship between cinema and our other arts. Yesterday, at the Q&A after Panahi's *Circle* had been screened somebody in the audience asked about the relation between Iranian cinema and Persian literature. At that moment, I was thinking that you were in the audience, and you are the one who has worked directly with a leading literary figure in modern Persian fiction. Recently we invited to New York five leading literary figures: Mahmoud Dolatabadi, Sepanlu, Mojabi, Mandanipour, and Lahiji, who represented the publishing industry. We put together an event for them at the Asia Society. Susan Sontag was on the stage sharing with them her admiration for Iranian cinema, but wondering why she knew nothing about Persian literature. The point is that there are organic links holding together any given culture, Iranian or otherwise. The relation between you and Houshang Golshiri, between Mehrju'i and Gholamhossein Sa'edi, between Kimiya'i and Sadeq Hedayat, and between Kiarostami and Sohrab Sepehri, just to name a few pairs of director and author, is quite crucial. My excitement about *Smell of Camphor, Fragrance of Jasmine* is that in it we have a glimpse of the totality of Iranian culture in its literary, poetic, visual, and performative aspects. That's why people are beginning to wonder, well, if the Iranian cinema is the tip of the iceberg, what and where is the iceberg?—which leads me to my next question, more

specifically about the film itself. Many people see it as a dark film, a contempla-
tion of death. But I don't see it that way. It's a heart-warming, life-affirming
film. Are you surprised by the readings that it has received?

BF   I have always felt that death is easy. Death is no trouble. It's life that is a
great deal of trouble because of all the conflicts we have to face. I have always
kept my sense of humor in looking at what happens to us. But the actual idea of
the film emerged out of a very frustrating and depressive period when I simply
was not allowed to work.

HD   Were you improvising as you shot, or were you following a script?

BF   Well, some things were improvised. My inclination is to have the script
exactly as I want it to be. This is the first time that I had to give myself some
leeway simply because I felt that I needed to put a lot more than you see on
screen in the script. I shot those parts and then eliminated them because I
thought I didn't need them. I started cutting in the middle of the scenes, rather
than having a beginning, middle, and end. So, in most of the scenes, we enter in
the middle, which is the heaviest part. And that's something that happened after
the shooting—and some things were totally eliminated because they were
slowing the pace. What I wanted to be able to say, really, as far as the structure is
concerned, was that I show what's happening and never dwell on anything too
much.

HD   The lead character, Bahman Farjami, is one of the most vivid portrayals of
an Iranian intellectual. Right before your film, in Daryush Mehrju'i's *The Pear
Tree* we have yet another depiction of an Iranian intellectual but in a very pessimistic and dismissive manner, as a sort of succession of failures: individual
failure, political failure, philosophical failure, etc. But the lead character of your
film is not a pessimist. He is not a broken character for the following reasons:
first of all, from his literacy and culture, we understand that the formation of his
character predates the 1979 revolution; he is far more deeply rooted. From his
taste for Ahmad Shamlu's poetry, we know that he identifies with contemporary
poetry. From his knowledge of Kafka and Poe, we know that he's cosmopolitan
in his literary taste. So the indications are that he is a secular intellectual from
before the revolution. But at the same time, we see on his table most of the

reformist newspapers of the Khatami period. So he also identifies with the reformists; in fact, you give a forum for a speech by Khatami. So, Bahman Farjami is an intellectual of the prerevolutionary period who also identifies with the reformist movement. This is in sharp contrast with much that has happened over the last quarter of a century to the Iranian secular intellectuals who initially identified with the 1979 revolution and were subsequently alienated from it. As a result, he is a positive portrayal of an Iranian intellectual, one who has hope, who is engaged and follows the news, and who has not abandoned politics. He is concerned about the fate of the Iranian writers and about the serial murder of the secular intellectuals. I wonder—and this is the link that concerns me, the link between the prerevolutionary intellectuals and what is happening after the revolution—I wonder whether, in your own creative construction of this character, you see him as the representative of the intellectuals of the prerevolutionary period who had their hopes and aspirations in the revolution and yet were disappointed. This was not really the revolution that they were hoping for, and yet your character begins to place hope in the reformist movement, yet not in a way that will denigrate the prerevolutionary intellectual culture, but in fact, restore dignity to it. How much were you conscious of this?

BF   I was conscious of it simply because Golshiri and I had a very close relationship; aside from a professional relationship, we were very close friends. He was an example of a truly revolutionary intellectual who was affected by the revolution and in fact wanted it. When the revolution happened, he fought against the repressive regime, but at the same time, devoted his full energy to create something positive from the change that happened in the postrevolutionary period. And if I have a model for this character, it was Golshiri who was always in the back of my mind. This is a man who grew through time. He did not get locked in the past but actually developed with the movement. Young writers such as Mandanipour, Kourosh Asadi, and Moniru Ravanipour would come to visit him and he would sit with them for hours listening to what they had written, because he wanted to give back what he had gained from the culture to the new generation. That's also the way I always felt in my own relationship with young filmmakers and writers. In my mind, Golshiri is really the model. I have created this character because I am a filmmaker and this is my story as well.

It's a personal story, but also illustrates that if you don't move with time, you are not true to anybody, including yourself. And some of our friends, both writers and filmmakers, got locked in that past, and out of opposition to things that are happening in Iran, they also locked themselves out of the new developments, which, like the younger generation, I find very exciting. So, that is the kind of thing that I like. I'm not a pessimist by nature. I work fourteen hours every day, and I always create a job for myself. The last sequence in *Smell of Camphor, Fragrance of Jasmine* quotes Kafka: "When you throw a stone in the water, you can't control the waves." I wanted him to throw the stone, regardless of how murky the water is, because, in effect, he is saying, "I'm alive. I'm back and I'm going to keep working." This is the way I've always related to my country, even during the ten years that I was living abroad, by keeping in contact with friends like Kiarostami, traveling back and forth, reading voraciously, and so on. I always try to keep in touch with what is happening. But during the last ten years living in Iran I realized, "OK, this hand has been dealt to us. What are we going to do?" Either we are going to roll with it and try to make something positive out of it, or we can bang our heads against a brick wall and not be positive.

HD   How far were you in the making of this movie when Golshiri died?

BF   He died after I finished the film. He saw the film the last time he was in my house—I always celebrate the last Friday of the year and have thirty or forty people over. After seeing it he said, "You know why I'm very happy with this film? First, because now they can't say that *Prince Ehtejab* was a fluke. Second, it wasn't based on any of my stories, you wrote it and now you can take full credit for it."

HD   So as fate would have it, your film became a homage to Golshiri?

BF   Yes. It did. And that's why I'm actually going back to one of his stories for my next film. It's called *The Dark Hand and the Light Hand*. I've based the script on a story of his called *The Dark Side of the Moon*. Well, he was an important part of my life, both as a close personal friend, and as a writer. I still feel a deep sorrow; I am still grieving for his death. So, yes, it became a homage to him. At the same time, it also predicted the death that has greatly affected me.

HD   It seems there is a parallel: you and Golshiri, Mehrju'i and Sa'edi. I hope that what happened to Mehrju'i after the tragic death of Sa'edi does not happen to you—I think the nature of Mehrju'i's cinema just changed.

BF   No. You see a new door has opened in my life. I now actually have more of a tendency to write my own scripts, and not base them on stories. But there are some contemporary novels I really like.

HD   Such as?

BF   *The Winter of '62* by Esmail Fasih, and his *Story of Javid*. I would never give up contemporary literature as a basis for my films. But not all my films are going to be based on other people's writing because I have some very, very personal things I want to explore—personal relationships, as in the scene with my mother. My mother has Alzheimer's disease, which is one of the greatest tragedies of my life. I want to explore things such as losing touch with your own past, losing touch with your own country, things like that.

HD   I want you to zoom out, as it were, into a long shot and place yourself within the broad picture. I believe that after the 1979 revolution, with Ahmad Shamlu's *Dead End*, modern Persian poetry entered a cul-de-sac, and that not even one major work of fiction has been written since the revolution, despite the fact that Mahmoud Dolatabadi is still alive, and Houshang Golshiri died only very recently. Golshiri never surpassed his *Prince Ehtejab*, nor did Dolatabadi ever surpass *Klidar*. Suddenly, there's this cinema, which is deeply rooted in our poetry and in our fiction, but has assumed, as in your own career, a direction of its own. There is an invisible poetry in this cinema that we know only locally and that is totally lost internationally. But that doesn't matter. I think the more Iranian cinema is misinterpreted, the better. How do you see the relationship between what has happened in our cinema today and Persian poetry and fiction?

BF   Well, I don't agree with all of what you suggest, simply because I think Shamlu still wrote poetry after the revolution. Golshiri's *The Enclosed Mirrors* is a really beautiful story. But what happened, really, is that cinema, because it's such a far-reaching art form, bridged the gap between the two. Books were being banned. Besides, the maximum print run of a book is five thousand copies, and usually it's two thousand. For a nation of sixty million, that's nothing. Cinema jumped ahead and brought poetry forward in a way that a couple of thousand copies of a book couldn't. And, in a way, it has started actually moving writers like Mandanipour and Kourosh Asadi ahead. They are closer now, this new generation of writers, to what movies are doing in Iran than Dolatabadi and other past writers simply because the latter had become so big that changing direction was not easy for them. Golshiri was the only one who was pushing the new generation forward, telling them they have to change the manner of their storytelling. He tried it in books such as *The Magi's Victory-Book* and other works. So cinema, in fact, tried to bridge the gap between prerevolutionary literature and that written after the revolution, which of course is minimal. It was not a total loss, but was minimal for a variety of reasons. I think we are now in the process of the two joining again together.

HD   I want to take you now into the global arena, because I see this slightly differently. I think what has happened is a visual mutation in our creative imagination. As you know, throughout our history, we have not been a visual people. We are a very verbal and audile people. What has happened in Iranian cinema over the past few decades has had a major catalytic effect on our creative imagination. But if we look at it globally, the first time that a form of Persian art became globalized was when Goethe adopted Hafez in his *West-Östliche Diwan*. That was the first occasion in modernity that one aspect of Iranian art, namely, Persian poetry, became international through its European reception during the Enlightenment. The second time was Fitzgerald's translation of Omar Khayyam. The cinema of the past few decades is the first form of Iranian art that has been massively globalized. We are not just talking about major film festivals in Europe and North America, but also about Asia and Africa, the Arab world, the Indian sub-continent, Latin America. All you have to do is go to Amazon.com and read the comments of people who have purchased a video of an Iranian film. I find them far more instructive than many film reviews I read here in the US, or in Europe, or even in Iran. The Iranian cinema has developed globally beyond anything we have ever known. Never in the history of Iranian art has anything like this happened. In your judgment, what is the effect of this global audience on our art? We have always been speaking to ourselves in the dark. We are now out in the open, in broad daylight. What is the effect of this global audience?

BF   Well, I think what has happened to us is that we have found, aside from our own countrymen, an audience that maybe does not understand us completely, but definitely has its own concept of what we are talking about. When you "globalize," as you characterize the way the Iranian cinema has expanded, two things happen. The first is that we can earn income from an art that we once imported. When changed into Iranian currency, it is always such a large amount of money that when I tell people *Smell of Camphor, Fragrance of Jasmine* was made for $70,000, they're amazed because they know that once we sell it, we're in the black—and that does not usually happen, especially with art films. At least, it doesn't happen anywhere else in the world. This forces us to look to the foreign market more than to the domestic.

HD   That's the economic factor.

BF   But it does affect the films because now we're being accused of making films aimed at the French audience's conception of Iran. I want to reverse this trend. I want to succeed commercially inside Iran as well, in a way that promotes a better kind of filmmaking. We have now gone back to commercial love stories, murders, and low comedy, which is very strange in Iran. This now constitutes 90 percent of our films. I really just want to speak to the people of Iran, to appeal to the youth of the population. For me, if the French and Americans and the British like my films also, that's the icing on the cake.

HD   Well, I'm not sure of that and let me tell you why. I have nothing against the acclaim of the Iranian cinema in Cannes, Venice, Berlin, New York, etc., at all. Quite the contrary, I rejoice in it. We have a great art and the world is entitled to delight in it. Not only do I not think that that celebration is at the expense of the Iranian audience inside Iran, but I think it has a critical, catalytic impact on the art. The usual conception of the French, the Americans, and the British that we have in Iran is false. It is a nineteenth-century colonial conception.

BF   Yes, I agree.

HD Here's an example to illustrate my point. Once I was walking with Mohsen [Makhmalbaf] in Paris, and an Algerian came up to him, embraced him, and said, "Thank you Mr. Makhmalbaf for this wonderful film, I loved it." There are North African migrants in France, South Asians in Britain, Turks in Germany, and all of them in New York. Massive demographic changes caused by labor migrations into the major metropolitan centers have changed their nature and disposition. Half of the people who were here in Alice Tully Hall today watching your film were Arabs, Iranians, Turks, Indians, Koreans, Japanese, etc., and yet they are all Americans. This conception that we are making films for the French and the British is simply wrong, ludicrous, and entirely derived from a Manichaean conception of the world, based on a colonial division that is no longer legitimate, just an outdated misconception. The globality of the reception of the Iranian cinema is not that now we are making films for Gilles Jacob to approve and the French to acclaim. No. You have to look at the demographic composition of France, Germany, Britain, and particularly the United States. We are no longer dealing with blue-blooded "foreigners," as we used to imagine them.

BF I understand that. But I look at it also from this point of view: when you have a country with a population of sixty million, forty million of whom are below the age of twenty-five, you also have an obligation to communicate with a very young population. I know that not a film, not a book, not a painting, nothing in its own right changes history, but there are many movements totally opposed to what we stand for in our films. We have those on the far right that think that the draconian laws of Islam, like those of the Taleban in Afghanistan, should be enforced in Iran, and to hell with films, television, the Internet, and all of that. But because Iran is not Afghanistan and has a cultural history, the same designs cannot be implemented in Iran that the Taleban have imposed in Afghanistan. But that doesn't mean that nobody's trying. They're trying very hard. The struggles between different power groups that you have right now are precisely because this has been attempted. So, as a filmmaker in this country, I feel that, OK, for my part, on my own behalf, as my contribution, I want to reach the young people. This does not mean that I'm ignoring the globalization of movies. I live outside Tehran. When I wake up in the morning, my computer is next to my bed.

I go on the Internet and read the *New York Times*, and *Variety*, probably before you in New York read them because I'm eight or nine hours ahead.

HD   The same way that in New York I read the Tehran newspapers, before people in Tehran are awake.

BF   Exactly. The whole equation is changing. Now, at the same time that we can be relevant in our own country, we can be also globally effective.

HD   It's precisely my point that this false binary opposition, that either you are making films for foreigners or you're making films for a domestic audience, and that these two are mutually exclusive, really doesn't hold. If you are making films only for the global market you will not be globally successful. This is really what I am suggesting. Conversely, if you make films only for the local market you will not be locally successful. The new term, which is a bit awkward but very accurate, is "glocal." The only way you can be global is to be local. And the only way to be local is to have a global vision. Does that make any sense from inside Iran?

BF   I think everybody starts with this idea of doing something in Iran and the fact that it goes beyond the border because of the technology and everything else is a bonus. The main prize is connecting with the people who are still not as sophisticated as perhaps my generation are because they have not read the same things and so on. Many of the classic books are not being reprinted or taught in schools anymore. Young people may not recognize the reference to Edgar Allan Poe in my film. They remember Vincent Price better than Poe's stories. Educating this huge young population is not my job personally, but I do my part, and I feel that Iranian cinema has done its share. But the fact that it has also succeeded globally—in Japan they screened Kiarostami's film in fifteen or twenty theaters—means that we have transcended our borders, our local thoughts, and now we are reaching a larger audience. And this allows a Minister of Culture as intelligent and great as Mohajerani, to say that Kiarostami is a great honor to our country. He not only says it, he emphasizes it. He dwells on it because he realizes that the only good picture that has been shown of our country in the last twenty years is that by Iranian cinema. Everything else is dark. Iran has become a black hole in the middle of the world; everything that is written about it by the media is dark, dark, dark, dark. And all of a sudden appears *Where Is the Friend's House?*, or *Gabbeh*, which is poetry in motion: out of this black hole comes poetry. This is the initial shock. And now, people are realizing the falseness of their idea that whatever is not American is backward, or whatever is not British is backward, because we're showing a new vision with this medium. It's not only Kiarostami. There's Makhmalbaf, Panahi, and so on, and all these people are uprooting a tree that for so long grew out of the illusion that Americans have dominated the motion picture industry. You can't have an industry unless you have distribution. When we succeed, we give our films to the Americans or the Europeans to distribute. We don't have the access that they have to the world market. But, perhaps the new technology, as it's forcing a reappraisal of the system of distribution, will give us access to the world market without going through European distributors.

HD   My point is that when a film opens in New York or in Tokyo, the people in Iran should know that this is not viewed by some fictitious foreigner. Massive demographic changes at the heart of European and North American cities have resulted in audiences that are very similar to those inside Iran. That's my first point. My second point is that the major film festivals, like Cannes, Venice, and New York, are really the conduits of contact with the rest of the world. The same way that we in Iran discovered Gabriel Garcia Marquez only after he was first translated into English and French, and then into Persian, people in Latin America or in Asia or Africa have discovered the Iranian cinema after it had been celebrated in Cannes or Venice. This is of course the indication of a relation of power. We all know it. The global reception of the Iranian cinema is mediated through its European and North American reception. But it does not stop there. There are unanticipated consequences of that reception which are beyond the control of those major film festivals.

BF   I can see that.

HD   But let's go back to your film. Your central character is an aging, mellowed intellectual. What is striking is a confidence and cultivation about him that is quite unlike anybody we see after the Islamic revolution. He is an intellectual with a certain familiar catholicity of learning and cultivation. Now, after the revolution we have a new group who call themselves "religious intellectuals." Having lived in Iran for the past decade or so, how do you view the character and mind-set of the intellectuals that have become prominent? For example, Abdolkarim Soroush and Mohsen Kadivar. They are extraordinarily courageous public figures. Do you see something constitutionally different happening to the figure of the Iranian public intellectual?

BF Well, intellectuals prior to the revolution were in general highly political. After the revolution, we have the same thing of course. But something else has also developed. Now, the whole nation is politicized. As a result, we feel much closer together. For example, I admire the characters of Shamsolva'ezin, Soroush, or Kadivar, and even Ganji, while I may have reservations regarding their past activities. But something has developed and the fact is that we have made a move. This move has forced us to reappraise the whole way that we look at our government, the way we have to function under it—are we going to accept everything that the government says or are we going to have our say in it? So, the intellectuals after the revolution have had the advantage of a public that is extremely receptive to what they say. Before the revolution they talked only to the elite. In my film, I have one of the right-wing papers, *Keyhan*, being read by the man in the mortuary, because in Iran this is like a bombshell. The young people notice. Why is this guy reading *Keyhan*? The same is true about the papers that are on the protagonist's coffee table in one scene. This awareness is something that has forced even the intellectuals to be a lot more up to date, foster a much wider connection. Nabavi's humorous column about what is happening in Iran, the banning of the liberal newspapers, etc., show how effective they have been in focusing the collective consciousness on a movement. I think the intellectuals of today have a much larger public that is responsive to them. The death of Ahmad Shamlu, for example, and his funeral. Ten thousand people showed up at the hospital when he was dying. They were reading his poetry, and singing the national anthem. Ninety percent of the people who were there were below the age of twenty-five. They needed three hundred buses to take all these people to the graveside. In the mourning procession on the third day after his death, everybody walked as if they were passing in Washington, DC, by the coffin of a statesman. Total self-restraint. Total respect. And this is the man who for the last twenty years had been in seclusion, whom the officials had never lauded publicly as our greatest living poet. Still everybody knows about him. Intellectuals today, even those of prerevolutionary days, have a much wider connection to the masses than before the revolution.

HD   I understand. Let me now go to the most striking feature of your character in *Smell of Camphor, Fragrance of Jasmine*, which is his sense of humor and his sense of self-deprecation. I don't know how consciously or subconsciously you have done it, but it is a very critical aspect of the character. Let me explain why. Like all Iranians of our generation, I adored Ahmad Shamlu. But on the occasions that I met him and during the few hours I was in his presence I was petrified. I couldn't even string together three consecutive sentences to say to him. I loved him. I admired him. I can recite miles of his poetry for you by heart. But he terrified me. I began to examine this fear later on and understood it in this way: when my generation were growing up, we created heroes because we were not a heroic generation, whereas this postrevolutionary generation is a heroic generation and does not need to create them. The death of Shamlu is a very critical moment in our history, which I think is amazing and is reflected by this character in your film. This mutation of the creative consciousness of the intellectual into the collective consciousness of his audience stops with Shamlu's generation. Suddenly, with your film, and, through a self-deprecation of your lead character, you become in fact the spokesman of the collective consciousness rather than imposing your own creative ego upon it. If you were to sit down and analyze this, where could we start to begin to undo this malady? We constructed this imposing character of a public intellectual who becomes virtually divine, as when I was in the presence of Shamlu, I felt I was in the presence of a divinity, a prophetic figure. However, your character's sense of humor, his self-deprecation, in addition to the weird angle of the camera showing his big belly and his constant smoking, enabling us see how the man is falling apart, is a phenomenal occasion of catharsis in our collective consciousness. Were you aware of it?

BF   Well, maybe not with the clarity with which you just expressed it. But, it is something about the way I look at myself. I have been battling being overweight for the last twenty-five years. I've lost twenty-five kilos three times and I've regained it with additional weight, and, like so many other people, I know most of the weight-loss books by heart and could write one myself. So, I'm always the first person to make jokes about my weight. Whenever somebody sends me a photograph of myself, the first thing I tell them is that if you take a long shot, you'll get a close-up! So that's my sense of humor. The falling apart of the character was very deliberate because I didn't try to choose angles that showed me in a better light or slimmer or anything like that. I just threw away the whole vanity part, and said this is the only way that this character is going to be believable—that he smokes, he's fat, he doesn't care about himself, and he has a death wish, and at the same time that's why he's accepted his fate. The first line he speaks in monologue is that he doesn't fear death, he fears a futile life, and that is the essence of what I think. I want to pass on what I know to the next generation, and I have to fight against anybody who tries to stop me. But acceptance of death makes it very easy to make fun of the way you live. And that's what I do. The humor is part of my character. This is something that I wanted to include in the film in order to undercut the serious events, and also to make people feel comfortable about the whole situation—we are talking about death, but at the same time it isn't a big deal. Everybody dies, so why worry?

HD   But, apart from the story, were you conscious that you're dismantling a type of public intellectual?

BF   Well, I think in order to reach the new generation, we have to dismantle the figureheads. I never believed in them. I loved Shamlu as well. I knew him well. But at the same time, he was a bore. I preferred reading his poetry to being in his presence. I am always against these idealizations of great writers, that whatever they write we have to approve. Bullshit. I don't have to approve of everything they write. I'm a person who questions. And where could I start this questioning? With myself. Because so easily in Iran, you fall into this trap of being called an *ostad*, a master, you know, that you start repeating yourself. I don't want to be called a master. I don't want to be called the great filmmaker. I want to experiment as much as I can until I can't do it anymore. Then I can rest my case. But before that, no. The dismantling has to start, and so much the better to start with yourself.

FIVE

ONCE UPON A FILMMAKER: CONVERSATION WITH MOHSEN MAKHMALBAF

Born in Tehran in 1957 to a staunchly religious family, Mohsen Ostad Ali Makhmalbaf grew up in southern Tehran and spent his early childhood in the loving care of his maternal grandmother and aunt while his mother, divorced by Makhmalbaf's father, worked as a nurse. He grew up in the religiously and politically charged atmosphere of the 1960s, and the June 1963 uprising of Ayatollah Khomeini is one of his earliest memories. Chiefly responsible for his early politicization was his stepfather, a religiously devout and politically active supporter of Khomeini, whom his mother married soon after Makhmalbaf was born. In 1972 Makhmalbaf formed his own urban guerrilla group; two years later he attacked a police officer, and was arrested and jailed. He remained in jail until 1978 when the revolutionary wave led by Ayatollah Khomeini freed him and he launched his literary and cinematic career. The following is a conversation I had with Mohsen Makhmalbaf in October 1996, when he was visiting New York during the screening of his film Gabbeh *in the New York Film Festival. We began by reviewing a three-volume collection of Makhmalbaf's writings,* Gong-e Khabdideh *("A Dumb Man's Dream") by way of a general introduction to his film and fiction.*

Mohsen Makhmalbaf   The first volume is a selection of stories. There are five stories in it: they make up more than 400 pages—about 45 percent of my published fiction. These are mostly dark in spirit, with the exception of the first two stories, which are gentler. The third story is an incredibly dark story, and the fourth and fifth stories, that is to say, *"Hoz-e Soltun"* and "The Crystal Garden,"

Mohsen Makhmalbaf and his daughter Hana on the set of *A Moment of Innocence* in 1995. Makhmalbaf's family became integral to his career as a filmmaker from the very beginning. Hana debuted at the Locarno Film Festival in 1998 with the short film *The Day My Auntie Was Sick*

both concern women. *"Hoz-e Soltun"* is about women before the revolution, and "The Crystal Garden" about women after the revolution. The second volume is a selection of my screenplays and writings for the stage. The plays make up about a thousand pages, of which only thirty have been previously published. Moham-mad Reza Honarmand made a 16-mm film of one play called *Marg-e Digari* ("The Death of Another"), which has been shown on television. It's a good work; I hope that you'll be able to see it some time.

Hamid Dabashi   Have you ever directed any of these plays yourself?

MM   No, although some of my plays provided the basis for my screenplays.

Shishomin Nafar (*"The Sixth Person"*) became the film *Este'zah* (*"Seeking Refuge"*). *Valeh* (*"Bewitched"*) became the film *Baykot* (*"Boycott"*). *Zangha* (*"The Bells"*) is another screenplay that someone else directed. *Boycott* was the most popular film that year [1365/1987], and *The Bells* was the second . . . They didn't let me direct *Madreseh-ye Raja'i* (*"The Raja'i School"*) myself, so Karim Zargar, the head of the Audio-Visual College, made it. But it ended up a somewhat weak film. *Bacheh-ye Khoshbakht* (*"The Lucky Child"*) was based on a story by Alberto Moravia, but I wrote the screenplay, and it became the first episode of my film *Dastforush* (*"The Peddler"*). *Tavallod-e Yek Pirezan* (*"The Birth of an Old Woman"*) became the second episode, and the screenplay *The Peddler* became the third. *Comedi-ye Ehtezar* (*"The Comedy of Death"*) is a short and very black screenplay that I was not permitted to film. *Bicycle-Ran* (*"The Cyclist"*) is of course the screenplay for the film of the same name. *Farmandar* (*"The Governor"*) was made into a film directed by Morteza Masaeli. This turned out to be a mediocre film which was subjected to censorship. Parts of it were changed and the end result was worthless. *Moftabad* (*"Gooodfornothingville"*), *Garmazadeh* (*"Heat-Stricken"*), and *Nazar-e Aghnia* (*"The Point of View of the Rich"*) have never been produced, and the same is true for *Seh Tableau* (*"Three Tableaus"*) and *Fazilat-e Bismillah* (*"The Virtue of 'In the Name of God'"*). *Nobat-e Asheqi* (*"A Time for Love"*) is the screenplay for the film of the same name. *Nan-o-Gol* (*"Bread and Flower"*) and *Khab-e Bi Ta'bir* (*"A Dream with No Interpretation"*) are also in the volume but have not been produced. *Mard-e Na Tamam* (*"The Unfinished Man"*) was made by [Moharram] Zaynal-Zadeh, the same actor who played the lead role in *The Cyclist*. *Naseroddin Shah, Actor-e Cinema* (*"Once upon a Time, Cinema"*) is the screenplay of the film of that title, as is *Honarpisheh* (*"The Actor"*). The more recent screenplays are not included here since this collection only covers the 1980s.

The third volume starts with the essay *"Qesseh Chist"* (*"What Is a Story?"*). Aside from "What Is a Story?" the other three essays, *Honar Hameh-ye Honar Ast* (*"Art Is All of Art"*), *Cinema Hame-ye Cinema Ast* (*"Cinema Is All of Cinema"*), *Realism Hame-ye Realism Ast* (*"Realism Is All of Realism"*), deal with the question of relativism.

HD   How's that?

MM   That is to say, they are an outline of the relation of art, cinema, and realism to the question of relativism. The last two are more technical. "What Is a Story?" also to some extent deals with relativism, and how it is impossible to arrive at description, since description can only apply to that which is dead—when the subject is living and ever-changing, how can we define its limits? *"Monhani-ye Keshesh dar Film"* ("The Arc of Suspense in Film") is a mathematical discussion about incorporating certain principles into the production of a good solid screenplay that will sell. I've done it this way two or three times myself, thinking "Well, now I want to make one that sells." So I used this method, and—

HD   And it was successful?

MM   Yes, it was successful . . . I think it's an essay that could have an application in university courses, for example in screenplay-writing classes. It might actually gain something in translation, and I think it's more use to Hollywood than—

HD   How do you mean?

MM   I wrote it at a time when I was making art films, and they would say "It won't sell," and so I decided to write something to show them, "See, I can make films that sell, and I can tell you how to do it."

HD   But it would not apply in making art films, would it?

MM   In some sense, certainly, you can use these principles and adapt them in making an art film. You can say, "I want to make a film that will sell in Iran," or "I want a film with a world market." But the question is how to devise a method that suits film production companies. The essay's been printed several times in various places. Anyway, last [in the volume] comes *"Gozide-ye Naqd va Barressi-ye Film"* ("Selections of Film Criticism"). It begins with *Seeking Refuge* and goes through *Once upon a Time, Cinema, Boycott, The Peddler, The Cyclist, Arusi-ye Khuban* ("The Marriage of the Blessed"), *A Time for Love*, and *Shabha-ye Zayandeh-rud* ("Nights on the Zayandeh-rud"). But you can also find discussions of *Tobeh-ye Nasuh* ("Nasuh's Repentance") and *Do Chashm-e Bi-Su* ("Two Sightless Eyes") here as well . . . These articles express my views and beliefs . . . And in discussing my films, this section really should be of use to you, especially the interview with me, which I still think is really the most important interview I've ever given—*Sorush* [magazine] conducted it over a period of five hours, and it was published as an issue containing only the interview, which is the only interview in the history of Iran for which an issue of a major magazine was republished because of the demand for it. Much of the controversy over my work began with this interview, although in this book it is greatly edited and condensed. In the interview I was asked about [Bahram] Beiza'i. I gave my opinion on most everything: the government, propaganda, the Left, the Right, moderates; I spoke of everything rather quickly. For example, I said that Beiza'i has no ideals, he only criticizes; for him everything is bad. He never tells us what is good. I also said that we should be very grateful to Kiarostami, who at least asks, "Where is the friend's house?" And now, many people ask, "How could you say that Beiza'i should be executed?" I always reply, "You fool! When have I ever said that Beiza'i should be executed?"

HD   Should be executed?!

MM   Yes! And I say, "What words are you putting in my mouth? I mean, now when something has been published and distributed, how dare you attribute something like that to me!" But I still say that Beiza'i is ideal-less; he has no vision for improving the world, not like Sepehri [Sohrab Sepehri, a major Iranian poet] does. He simply has no vision.

HD   But how could "has no vision" be turned into "ought to be executed"?

MM   Well, that's just it. Things get twisted around . . . Now, the original is published only in the magazine, and all of it is there. The version in this book is edited and only reprints discussion from the interview about more technical issues. But if you get your hands on that magazine, you'll get a good range of my opinions. What's interesting is that my beliefs have not changed, really, since then and I'm not much different from the person I was. My tone was sharp, certainly. For example, consider the question there about Kimiya'i: I called him a person who has been defeated, and who in vain tries to associate himself with this or that nonsense—and I still feel the same way. I just don't like his work! Again, that is why I've said that we should thank God for Kiarostami. Perhaps the only thing I've changed my mind about is Amir Naderi's film *Davandeh* (*"The Runner"*). I had said that *Saz-dahani* (*"The Harmonica"*) is better, and now I feel the opposite. But that isn't strange. Sometimes I feel as if people expect me to give my final views on everything from beginning to end. But if I did, what would I live the rest of my life for? So, this interview is important, in that it contains my views on cinema. And then, going back to the book, there are a series of critical essays concerning my films, but somewhat edited, among them another important article: "Director's Notes on *A Time for Love*." If I were to recommend two things for you to read about my work, one would have to be the interview for *The Peddler* and the other would be my notes on *A Time for Love* . . . These two pieces represent my present views . . . Then also my notes about *Nights on the Zayandeh-rud.* The book contains a summary of the six months' worth of insults published in Iranian newspapers concerning that film. And I was never permitted to defend myself against them. There are about thirty pages of insults written about me here, from a random statement from [the daily newspaper] *Keyhan* to everything else. There were even demands for my execution . . .

TO THE MANNER BORN

HD   Tell me about the circumstances of your birth.

MM   I was born on 28 May 1957. My grandfather is from Kashan; he had eight sons and two daughters. His sons all took several wives, and they each have several children from each wife, and so when I was released from prison, after the revolution, I found that I had 156 or 157 cousins, most of whom were total strangers to me. This was because my own mother was one of my father's wives for only six days, after which they separated, and we had no contact with my father's family.

HD   Your mother was married for only six days?

MM   Yes. From my father's side I have roots in Kashan; my grandfather was a baker, and he had an uncle called Seyyed Sagha. His story is told in *Nun va Goldun* ("*A Moment of Innocence*") and *Hoz-e Soltun.* And on my mother's side, my grandmother was the wife of a gravedigger in Tehran, who later became a mason. They had three daughters and a son. So, from my mother's side I'm Tehrani, and from my father's, Kashani. My mother was first married at the age of twelve to a man of about twenty-seven, someone within the family circle.

After three or four years, and having had two children, they separated. My mother studied and became a nurse and a teacher.

HD   What about your siblings?

MM   An older sister and a brother. So then my father becomes acquainted with my mother. He has a wife, with whom he'd had two daughters, and not having a son, he made some excuse about wanting a son, but, in fact, he'd actually fallen in love with my mother.

HD   Where did this all happen?

MM   They were more or less living in the same district. But my father was illiterate—

HD   And your mother was living alone with two children?

MM   No, the two children were with their father. And so my father comes along and marries my mother, and after six days his first wife appears, grabs him by the ear, and takes him back. I'm the outcome of those six days (laughs). If my father hadn't fallen in love, and they'd not spent those six days together, well, who knows what would have happened to the fate of Islam and blasphemy? After I was born, I lived with my mother. My grandmother looked after me as my mother worked at night in the operating room of the hospital. She paid our bills. My father refused to get a birth certificate for me, and the two of them fell into playing petty games of trying to humiliate each other and holding grudges.

HD   Their love was over?

MM   Well, yes. So, my mother paid our bills until she was suddenly dismissed. She got into an argument with the hospital administrator because my father had canceled her nursing certificate. She could no longer work as a nurse, just because he made a pen mark across her certification card. And so due to the situation she was forced to file a complaint and try to get child support from my father. She had him arrested—naked, from the bathhouse—and had him taken to the police station wearing only a loincloth. This episode humiliated my father (laughs) and he decided to kidnap me, since my mother had refused to let him be my guardian. And since I'd only seen my father once or twice, I only knew that he was really fat, I was afraid of him . . . and at this point he decided he would kidnap me.

HD   How old were you when this was going on?

MM   I was about five years old. My dad hired a thug to wait at the head of the alley, and paid his wages for two years for him to look out and kidnap me whenever I might venture out the door of the house and into the street. And so I spent two years imprisoned right there in my own house (laughs). I had an aunt who was a schoolteacher. She lived with us and loved me quite a lot. She taught me to read and write. My grandmother, since she couldn't leave me at home alone, would take me with her to the mosque. I became first a *mokkaber* [one who calls out *"Allah-u Akbar"* to alert people who are praying to change their ritual positions], and then a *mo'azen* [one who recites the call to prayer before every required prayer time]. Meanwhile my mother had met a lawyer while dealing with our legal problems. He was a young man recently arrived from Qum. He was a follower of Khomeini, a religious and political person, and she married him . . . Fear of my father had the effect of scaring me, isolating me from the life of the alley which was more or less the real world, and trapping me in a house where three important people tried to take care of me. One was my grandmother, who introduced me to religion. One was my aunt, who made me literate. The last was my stepfather, who made me political . . .

HD   And your stepfather, what was his name?

MM   Kamalian.

HD   Kamalian. However, you chose to keep your original name?

MM   Well, this is Iran, after all.

HD   Yes.

MM   So until the age of seventeen when I was arrested, I'd probably only seen my father a total of fourteen or fifteen times, that is, once every year or two, and that would be for no more than a minute or two at a time. Later, when I was in jail, he never came to visit me. After I was released, my son, Meysam, who was then four or five years old, demanded to see his grandfather. I tried to go and see him then, but was unable to. Two years before he died, I saw him briefly. He'd gotten diabetes and had lost a lot of weight. He completely denied our relationship. Imagine, two years before his death, even after I'd made *The Peddler*, he still had no idea what I did for a living. He said to me, "I hear that you work in a tobacco shop!" (laughs). He really had no idea. And he didn't care what or who I was. He was the father of a child who had come from a six-day marriage.

HD   Was he not at all political?

MM   No. He ran a public bath. He was illiterate . . . It's funny, when I look at myself in the mirror these days, I find that my appearance has come to resemble my father's to a great extent. As for my mother, she married three times. First, as a child; second, my father, which lasted for six days; and then her third husband, who was really a very good person. If you read *"Hoz-e Soltun"* there is a character, a mosque attendant, whom I based to a great extent on my stepfather.

HD   Were you very close?

MM   Very close. My politicization occurred entirely under his influence.

HD   And his political beliefs, what were they exactly?

MM   He was a follower of Khomeini.

HD   And was he in contact with people in Najaf, Khomeini or anyone else?

MM   Well, he wasn't . . . He was only a supporter, that's all.

HD   What I mean is, did he support the cause financially?

MM   Yes. However, after the revolution, he reversed his position. We had our disagreements then—the very same person who had politicized me during the revolution, one year later was saying, "I no longer accept these people" (laughs).

HD   While you still accepted them?

MM   I still accepted them.

HD   And you disagreed, politically, at that time.

MM   We were not on speaking terms then. But now—

HD   This is after you were released from prison.

MM   Yes . . . but enough about my stepfather . . . If I have been a religious person, it's because of my grandmother. My grandmother was a very interesting character—she was incredibly kind. I think that the greatest love of my life has been my grandmother, because at the very time when I was most afraid that my father would kidnap me, and I was caught up in this madness, when I slept beside her I felt more secure than any place in the universe. The stories she told me at night, all the bedtime stories, were tales of the prophets. In those conditions the tales of the prophets would give me such peace of mind that I would feel practically invisible to the world. She was so kind that God and my grandmother merged into one in her stories. When I think of God, I think that this is still the case—the God that rests in the depths of my heart looks like my grandmother. When I was young, there was a cabinet in our house, and when I opened it, there was a picture of my grandfather, and he had a hat on his head. I used to think that God was an old man. But later, God became an old woman. The affection my grandmother used to show me, and her religious talk, at that age . . .

HD   Other than the stories of the prophets, what else would she tell you?

MM   I went to the mosque with her for years . . . So imagine, one hundred clerics in the mosque, whatever they spoke of up there, of *fiqh* (jurisprudence) and *irfan* (mysticism) and history—it all settled in my mind. When I was to take the high-school entrance exams, I actually left school and became a seminarian for two terms.

PRECOCIOUSLY POLITICAL

HD   And you feel that now you've put your grandmother and stepfather behind you?

MM   Yes, the combination of their influence led me to jail, and to the political and religious concerns that filled me. But what has remained with me is the influence of my aunt . . . So, after leaving school, I worked a while—remember that this was the period of armed rebellion. I'd written a play, *Balal.* So when we formed an armed resistance group—all of us aged fifteen through seventeen—we named it Balal-e Habashi.

HD   Balal-e Habashi?

MM   The name was based on the title of my play, the protagonist of which was constantly under torture. Our goal was to increase political resistance. Slowly, from the mosques, a religious movement was also brewing. Some were arguing for rebellion against the government, another group—

HD   You're now about fourteen years old?

MM   Yes, when I began to pursue artistic work. And when Shari'ati was first becoming influential.

HD   Where did you first hear of him?

MM   He was being mentioned in our mosque—and there's an interesting story connected with that. When I had returned from studying in Qum, I thought to myself that it would be impossible to go as I was to Palestine, and that I should instead do cultural work. So I began to establish a public library with a friend of mine, and I collected about 100,000 tomans' [then almost $15,000] worth of books for free. In those days one could buy a house for 20,000 tomans. I would stop by bookstores, introduce myself, and give them my card, saying that I'd just started a library, and I would often be given a free book by the owner. So imagine how many bookstores I visited! And I would write letters to scholars, authors, and printers, and get complimentary copies of books from them. Eventually we had about 100,000 tomans' worth of books. And that's how we started our library—which we called the "Danesh Library"—inside the local mosque. And we soon had about 400 members. It was there that we began putting on our plays and performances—it was very popular. When Shari'ati's books began to come out . . .

HD   First, tell me, didn't the local Mullah have a problem with your putting on plays inside the mosque?

MM   No. But once we took a gramophone into the mosque and all hell broke loose . . . It was an issue solely about the machine. They said that we should only use a tape; they had a problem with the LP disk. We were playing Abdul-Baset [a famous Egyptian Qur'an reciter] on a record . . . the mosque regulars ran and got the clerics, and the mullah came and told us to play a tape.

HD   Even for Abdul-Baset?

MM   Even Abdul-Baset. They wanted us to play a tape recorder, not a gramophone. To them, we had committed sacrilege—and we argued against them. It was this very incident which brought about an epiphany for me. Just the idea that we were bickering over using a gramophone rather than a tape machine! (laughs). And so, it was around that time when Shari'ati was coming to be known. We were already beginning to think more seriously about armed resistance, and so when this person Shari'ati came along and was starting to undermine Shiite causes, it seemed crucial to find him and kill him. (Pause) I went with some of the other guys to investigate whether or not it would be possible to kill Shari'ati in Mehrab.

HD   Really? In Hosseini-ye Ershad?

MM   In Hosseini-ye Ershad. I went and listened to him speak, to hear what he was saying—I was thinking, who is this person they say is attacking Imam Ali? He spoke for four hours, and I never returned to that mosque. I became a devotee of Shari'ati. (laughs)

HD   (laughs)

MM   I mean, it was over! The next day I began distributing Shari'ati books, and they barred me from the mosque, from the library, people in the neighborhood began to avoid me, and I was treated like an infidel. But I kept on buying Shari'ati's books and giving them to my friends. But the effect was that, well, my status in the neighborhood was gone. It became clear that we would have to leave.

HD   "We" meaning who?

MM   Meaning myself and my entire family. Since we rented, we first moved from one part of the neighborhood to another, but then we eventually just left and moved to Meydan-e E'dam.

HD   Meydan-e E'dam?

MM   Yes, I just tore myself from that place . . . This was all between the ages of fifteen to seventeen, and I was by then very much influenced by Shari'ati's work. I read all of his books from beginning to end, twice over. I became a new person. Until then, of the religious authors, I had read Bazargan and Naser Makarem.

HD   Yes, I remember them.

MM   But with Shari'ati, the theoretical base which had made me revolutionary—

HD   Was destroyed . . .

MM   And with the armed struggle ongoing around me, I decided that I had to do something myself. I came to believe that I would not live for more than another two years. So I tried to put together another group—

HD   By now you're seventeen?

MM   No, this was when I was fifteen or so . . . So we started the group "Balal," and for about two years we were involved in underground activities.

HD   How many people were in this group?

MM   About seven or eight. There was a girl in the group, and after we were released from jail, one of the other members married her . . . Every time we considered joining up with the Mojahedin or other groups, we ended up not joining and remaining separate unto ourselves.

HD   They didn't accept you?

MM   We weren't worth their time. They didn't think we were serious—a bunch of kids.

HD   Since you were fifteen—

MM   It was not only my age—at that time I was still a short skinny kid.

HD   And how old were the others?

MM   The others were sixteen and seventeen.

HD   And you were the leader of the group?

MM   I was generally the leader.

HD   And what did you do?

MM   We would write leaflets and distribute them. We would rent a room in a boardinghouse claiming to be from outside Tehran, and we would rent one of those machines—

HD   A mimeograph?

MM   Yes. We'd print up leaflets—and when we'd distribute them, we'd hear comments in the mosque, such as "Someone's put out another leaflet and look how many grammatical errors it has!" (laughs). Like we'd misspell *Arz*, as if it were the Arabic word. And we were into sports—karate—and we'd spend some time on athletics, some time on political activities, and some time on fundraising. The last thing we did—and before that all we'd really done is distribute leaflets—was to attack a police officer. And during that attack, I was injured and arrested.

TO TAKE ARMS, . . . AND BY OPPOSING END THEM

HD   So why did you attack that policeman? Was that an idea of the "Balal" group?

MM   Yes. The three of us wanted to steal a gun from a policeman. Our plan was to take his gun and use it to rob a bank, so as to have funds to widen our activities. I had a knife, another had a Molotov cocktail . . .

HD   You had the knife.

MM   Yes, I was the more athletic one, and so I was to attack him. When I was young, I was so afraid . . . Mostly that my father would kidnap me. Anyone who wanted to would beat me up, even kids younger than me. By the time I was sixteen, I would take on five people at once. I still don't really understand how I came to change that much. In fights, even if they broke five wooden boxes over my head, I wouldn't even say "ouch" . . . So the plan was for me to take on the policeman in a fight, and for one of my friends to steal the gun, and for the third to block off the end of the alley with the Molotov cocktail. Those were bad days, and the police always patrolled in pairs, one armed with a handgun, and the other with a submachine gun. We had to look around to find a policeman who was alone. The one we chose was guarding two banks on Iran Street. Even though we had investigated all the routes and planned everything in advance, and had found out when the street was least crowded and when the policeman would be least likely to suspect anything, it turned out that on the day and time we went, the street was crowded, and the policeman was busy talking to some other person. We went back three times in the hope that the situation would improve, but then my friends began to get cold feet. And I was afraid that if we didn't do it that day it would be impossible to get them to try a second time. So I put pressure on them to do it that same day. By then my friend who had the Molotov cocktail was soaked with the gasoline out of the bottle, and I realized that if my friend tried to light the fuse he'd go up in flames as well, and so we decided against using that. We finally attacked the guy, and he began to put up a struggle, and my friend couldn't draw the policeman's gun out of the holster—he was afraid, and he didn't realize that he had to release it by pushing it down first. He thought that there was some kind of button somewhere. It was in the holster, and he needed to push it down before drawing it out, but he couldn't, and so he gave up and ran away. Then the policeman pulled his gun on me, so I began stabbing him, four times, with my knife. As I twisted the knife he cried out, and his cries still remain in my ears. They were the sort of cries I've only heard people under torture make. These are cries you'll never hear in a film . . . the cries of true pain. As I stabbed him, he pulled the trigger and shot me in the side. I was wearing some old army pants that were too big for me. I had tied them around my waist with an elastic band . . . When he shot, the band broke, and my pants fell to my feet . . .

HD   Cut by the bullet?

MM   By the bullet. (laughs)

HD   The bullet didn't hit you?

MM   It did. I was shot in the stomach. I grabbed my pants and began to run away. He shot at me again, and hit the wall beside my head. A bit of brick flew off in front of me. My friends saw that I was shot and tried to help me, and I told them run and leave me. I looked down at the knife and saw that the blade had broken off . . . I'd left it in his body. The policeman came forward, pointed the gun at my head and fired. I thought that I was dead. It turned out he didn't have any more bullets. So he swung his arm and hit me in the head, and broke my skull. But then he fell, unconscious, and I got up and ran. I'd gotten down about seven or eight alleys, but was caught . . . and this part is so important. Ordinary people took me and turned me over to the police . . . it didn't matter how many slogans I shouted—it didn't affect them: the people caught me beat me and then took me to the police. They even stabbed me, and as you can see, they cut my nerves to these fingers. I still can't bend them. They even stabbed my friend in the neck.

HD   Did they arrest all of you?

MM   No, they only caught two of us. One of us got away. He had been wearing a hat, and quickly took it off, and no one recognized him as having taken part in it, and he walked away.

HD   So you were arrested at seventeen.

MM   The old regime wouldn't execute anyone under the age of eighteen. So the maximum sentence was five years, which is what I was given. I was convicted in the first degree, and my comrade was convicted in the second degree, and was given fifteen years . . . He was eighteen at the time. The friend who got away got involved with the Mojahedin, became a communist, and bombed some place. He was arrested two years later, and it took two years for him to be convicted, and he was sentenced to death. They took him to death row to execute him, and he was due to be executed the next morning, and that night Carter became president and the government stayed all executions. And this person, who was very disciplined, on his last night—they would give a cigarette to the convicts on their last night—so he said to himself, "let me enjoy a cigarette, it's my last night." And the next morning, instead of executing him, they brought him back to the main prison and his death sentence was commuted. And two months later all the political prisoners were freed, so he was released too. But by then he'd become addicted to smoking! This same person joined the Peykar movement and then became a member of the Cherikha-ye Fada'i-e Khalq and was arrested again. He got mixed up, kept on switching his affiliations, and ended up a heroin addict. After I had made the film *Boycott*, I was walking down the street and I saw a heroin addict acting strange, it was him, and all he said was "Mohsen, you're still destroying the left!" (laughs)

IN PAHLAVI PRISON

HD   What was it like in jail?

MM   Looking back at my jail sentence, that period can be divided into two separate stages: During the first, I was enamored with the people who had ended up there . . . everyone—doctors, engineers, students . . . However, most of the people who had done work similar to mine had been executed, since they were mostly older, and had also been tortured quite a lot . . . After I was arrested, I was in the hospital for two weeks, and then I was beaten and ended up back in the hospital, this time for about a hundred days, with three rounds of surgery. I was torn up all over, especially the soles of my feet, which seemed never to stop bleeding. I still have backaches which I think are due to my having been tied flat onto the bed for three months. For about six months I was under medical observation, but once I entered the ordinary jail, I was treated like a hero . . . I was a young kid who had endured a gunshot wound, a stabbing, torture, and I also had a good memory, and I was very literate. In jail, books were few and far between. It's true that since I wasn't in the Mojahedin, I didn't have a place in the prison's social hierarchy . . . But back then, when one was put in jail, you were evaluated on the basis of the resistance you had been a part of, the importance of work you had done, and also on your memory. If, for example, there were three core decision makers, and they wanted to give a two-hour presentation, they were forced to set out all the information to three people, who each had to tell two others, who in turn had to tell another two people, and so on to the bottom of the organization. So they would start out giving a full two hours of information, but then when they checked with the last person, they'd find that a quarter of what he'd tell them had nothing to do with what they'd initially said. (Laughs) Because of this, they were forced to put people who were good at memorization higher up in the organization, to ensure that as much of their message got out as possible. And so I was quickly moved into the inner circle of the organization.

HD   Was this an organization of both Mojahedin and non-Mojahedin people?

MM   Yes. At that time, at first, everyone was in it together. Or at least it seemed that they were. Later, with the divisions that occurred within the Mojahedin, the religious prisoners separated themselves off from the leftist ones. But the organization itself, its structure, was still secret. Eventually the religious prisoners had one command and the nonreligious ones another. Later it all splintered: the Tudeh followers, the Maoists, the religious leftists, the religious rightists, the moderates. As we came into the Carter era, when SAVAK's pressure lessened, the divisions grew greater. However, in the earlier stages, I was part of this organization. But the organization I was a part of was fascist. And so in 1977 I separated myself from the Mojahedin. Earlier, I had had a very close relationship with them, but I didn't say anything for fear of SAVAK's taking advantage of the situation. But they themselves began spreading rumors about me, and so I was forced to speak out against them, and a series of successive divisions took place in the group, shortly after Carter was inaugurated. What I'm saying is that my years in prison should be divided into two periods: the time I was with them, and the time after I cut myself off from them because their behavior was fascist.

HD   Meaning what, exactly?

MM   Meaning that they would accuse anyone who didn't follow them exactly as having betrayed them and having joined up with SAVAK.

HD   You mean they would accuse you of being a stool pigeon?

MM   For them, any person who wasn't part of their organization was automatically considered to be associated with SAVAK. Art, culture, everything was suspect to them. In my last year there I remember I'd written my first long story, which after the revolution was serialized in seven issues of a magazine. It was the story of the people from Meydan-e Jaleh who had turned me in, five years earlier, to the authorities, and who now were under fire from those same authorities in that same street. It was about the change in popular sentiment. While I was in jail, I was constantly in conflict. I, who had gone to jail an enlightened person, was released a much more dogmatic one. There was nothing good there—from prison rapes to the suicides, fascism, lies, hypocrisy. I was completely fed up with it all. And when I decided to break with the organization, at first I tried simply to remain silent, but that became impossible. And when I began speaking out against them, of the fifty-six people who were in our section, about twenty-eight broke off from them in sympathy with me.

HD   Meaning that they joined another group?

MM   No, they just made their own. A group which was solely in opposition to the organization. This group later evolved into the Ommat-e Vahedeh ("Unified Nation"), who were about forty people, and who were one of the seven groups that joined the Mojahedin-e Enqelabi ("Revolutionary Mojahedin").

HD   Who were the Mojahedin-e Enqelabi?

MM   They were more or less based on this group. For example, Raja'i [the second president of the Islamic Republic] was one of these forty, as were Behzad Nabavi and Mohammad Salamati, who ended up being the minister of agriculture.

HD   You were all in the same section, then?

MM   It was always being mixed up. Every six months or so they moved everyone in the jails around. They were trying to break up the organizations, but instead this tactic actually helped strengthen and unify them.

HD   What is your worst memory of your time in jail?

MM   The torture was perhaps the worst. You see, we hear about torture . . . torture that is different from being beaten . . . but if you want to understand the feeling of being subjected to torture, perhaps the story I wrote called *Jarrahi-e Ruh* ("*Surgery of the Soul*") can convey some of that feeling to you. In a moment a person is put under so much pressure that all of his beliefs are lost to him—

which is only natural. Generally speaking, when you feel cold, you often feel angry. When warm, you might feel hungry or sleepy, and your inner balance may be out of kilter. Multiply all of that a thousand times and imagine the feeling. Still, even all of this pales in comparison to the pressure by the organizations in the jails, especially when the schisms erupted . . .

HD   Hold that thought . . . first, tell me, what is your worst memory of the torture you endured?

MM   The opposite of what you'd expect, burning and such things. The worst torture I endured was when they used cables.

HD   What do you mean, cables?

MM   I mean like telephone cord, the thick ones. You know, the sort you see in hardware stores. They come in different sizes, from 1 to something like 40 . . . Well, they had everything from thin wires to thick cables. When they started, they'd tie you to a bed and it would go one of two ways . . . one was a chair they called "Apollo." Consider, for example, this chair (points), or one more like a barber's chair—the wooden ones—sort of like a business-class seat in an airplane. They'd pull your hands back, tying down your right hand like this, and your left hand like this, just to the point of breaking your wrists. Then they'd put a motorcycle helmet on your head. And when they began to beat you, you start screaming . . .

HD   Where would they hit you?

MM   On the soles of your feet, with a whip. When they beat you, your screams would reverberate inside your head . . . but these details are not so important. When they'd whip you, they'd begin by hitting you here first, here next, here next, very accurately.

HD   By 'whip', you mean with those wires?

MM   Yes, the cables. They kept changing them. After a while you became numb to the whip, so they'd switch it to a thinner wire, which would hurt again. After that they'd make you run—you can see that part of it in *Boycott*, the running—so that the swelling in your feet would go down, and they'd start again. There was a doctor who came regularly to monitor your condition and give you serum. They didn't want your blood pressure to fall too much or to rise too much. All these "services," were to—well, when they first beat me, I felt as if a tree was being swung at my feet, not a wire. It hurt so much that you felt as if your eyes were about to explode out of your skull. They'd even tape your eyes tight shut. It was like—you know, when your hand touches something hot, the reflex the body has to that . . . Well, imagine that sensation in some part of your body every five seconds, imagine that going on from the morning to evening. You begin to feel as if you're on another planet, and just then they return you to reality . . . They wouldn't let you descend into numbness and unconsciousness. They would return you to reality, and then they would resume beating you. But the greatest pressure you would feel would be from within—the fear that you might give in, that you might let slip some information that they want.

HD   Were they interrogating you?

MM   They tortured me precisely because they'd heard that I had not given them any information. Since they captured us in the course of an attack, they didn't believe us when we said that there were just the three of us involved . . . At that point, the most important thing is not to turn anyone in. What I want to tell you is that the beatings, the torture in prison, these were not important. If you want to know about how all that felt, I've described it in *Surgery of the Soul*. Torture, after it's done, is meaningless—ten days later you're the same person you were before. But worse was the prison environment, the insults. If you dared challenge someone, question their ideology, they'd make you out to be a SAVAK informer—it was so childish—and then you'd be "boycotted." Imagine, living in a cell with thirty other people, and then suddenly all thirty of them are boycotting you. Imagine no one speaking to you for six months straight. And think of going to take a shower, and finding when you're done that they've taken all of your clothes so that you're forced to walk around naked, looking for something to wear. You go to take a bath and everyone leaves.

HD   They did these things because—

MM   Because you've stood up to them. These movements—it's like when Parajanov said that the Soviet government called him a pederast, and so he had to spend fifteen years in the company of an angel. You see, this pressure draws you inward, it takes you deep into yourself.

HD   During this time, was there any evidence of the opposite of what you are saying—signs of humanity, kindness, brotherhood, camaraderie?

MM   Certainly, there were occasions, as I've mentioned in my stories and films. There's the story I wrote of a schoolgirl who was in prison for distributing leaflets, having fallen in love with a boy who was a political activist. Her love was stronger than a political ideology, it was one of those loves that are based in the heart and are deep and strong in the mind. She would take a beating, but not give in, not give up her love. *Boycott* gives you a sense of the environment and feel of prison then—the factionalism, the party lines, that in the context of imprisonment inevitably lead to fascism. It's because under that kind of pressure, you can't have too many people making decisions. Democracy is impossible to institute in an oppressive environment. When it's necessary to speak in code, debating and voting are impossible. Under this pressure many resistance movements collapse of themselves. Even if they are committed to democracy, these movements are necessarily clandestine and centralized so as to operate quickly and elude detection. But this centralism is antithetical to democracy . . .

AT THE DAWN OF THE REVOLUTION

HD   Tell me what happened after your release from prison. Were you disapppointed with organized resistance, given these experiences? Were you a religiously devout person?

MM   At that point I was turned off to politics. It seemed to me that a revolution was happening, which was incredible, but worrisome also.

HD   You were released from prison in the course of the revolution?

MM   Oh yes, they released everyone who was imprisoned.

HD   While you were in prison, were your contacts with Khomeini and Shari'ati cut off?

MM   Khomeini and Shari'ati were completely unrelated to my imprisonment. Shari'ati was my religious ideologue, and Khomeini my childhood dream. But it was my own resistance that led to my imprisonment.

HD   And so, when you were released, did Khomeini remain your dream?

MM   Well, while I was in prison, the religious factions split in two, and I was associated with the second faction, the faction that was less organized and more independent, and closely identified with popular resistance. So when I was released, I was worried that the oppression I had experienced from the Moja-hedin in prison would be unleashed on the entire populace should they come to power. You might not believe it, but even with the worst conditions that I've observed under the ruling clerics, I'd still prefer their rule a thousand times to that of the Mojahedin. They're Stalinists! With these clerics, there is even an anarchy, a looseness of sorts . . . The Mojahedin are a catastrophe waiting to happen. So when I left prison, I started writing plays, thinking I might just become a writer. Do cultural work. I'd written my first short novel in prison.

HD   What was it called?

MM   It had an Arabic title, *Ya Muhawwil al-Hawl wa al-Ahwal* (*"O the Changer of Condition and of Conditions"*). When I left prison, I joined the Mojahedin-e Enqelab. You see, to prevent the leftists and the Mojahedin-e Khalq from impos-ing their program upon the people, in order to oppose them, all of us in grass-roots groups began to build organizations that would stand up against them. The revolution was still completely disorganized. So, to build up our opposition to them, we established the Mojahedin-e Enqelab-e Islami, which was made up of seven groups. One consisted of people who had returned from abroad. Another was made up of people from southern Iran. Mohsen Reza'i, who became the head of the Sepah-e Pasdaran [the Islamic militia], was originally from that group. Another group was the Safr group, which had blown up helicopters on US military bases. We worked to bring together these groups, which had done so much separately, so as to prevent any of them from joining forces with the leftists or the Mojahedin-e Khalq. The Mojahedin-e Enqelab was at first led by seven people, each a leader of a separate organization. After the revolution, there was a shortage of people to staff the governmental offices. Khomeini needed people who would be able to assume roles of authority: governors, ministers, military commanders. We began to fill these positions. I myself was one of the people who had to decide who was qualified for ministerial posts.

HD   You were independently in touch with Khomeini?

MM   No, you see, Bani-Sadr [the first president of the Islamic Republic] became the overseer of the organization, and he was in contact with Khomeini. After that Jalaleddin Farsi took over, and after him Behzad Nabavi. We had some 200-plus members in Tehran, and 200-plus members in the provinces. The six months after the revolution were spent first in liquidating the seven groups and amalgamating their members into a single organization, and second on strengthening the infrastructure of the revolution. We'd appoint a person to keep watch over things in a certain town, to make sure that there would be people there making decisions and taking care of any problems that came up. We would take those who were lower in the ranks of the organization and put them into high governmental positions: ministers, and governors and so on . . . But after six months, I began to fall out of step with this group. I realized they were becoming just like the Mojahedin-e Khalq. Fascism took hold. And I decided right then that even if we were to undergo thirty more revolutions—I think I'm well known for saying this—until our culture undergoes an essential change, nothing will be altered. The first thing that the Mojahedin-e Enqelabi decided to do was to set up an organization to control the people. This attitude was there right from the start. And then the hunger for power increased, and the internal strife followed. So I resigned and began working at the radio as a simple newsman.

THE POLITICS OF A POETIC TURN

HD   Who was in charge of the radio at that time?

MM   It was all in a state of confusion. Every faction, from the Hezb-e Jomhuri to the Mojahedin-e Enqelab, was involved in some way. [Sadeq] Qotbzadeh [one of Khomeini's earliest companions, who was put in charge of the national television network and was later executed for plotting to overthrow the Islamic

Republic] was in charge of the radio and television, but he was not involved in the daily running of the stations. And the radio productions themselves were done by twelve different people. I was in the production department for a few months and then moved over to the broadcasting department. Even a year after the revolution, I was the sole writer in the broadcasting division of radio. They'd have musical interludes for a couple of minutes, and I was supposed to write the next segment in that little time. And as soon as they'd finished that, it was another two minutes of music during which I'd write the next thing.

HD   This was the national radio?

MM   Yes. You see, they couldn't produce programs! Each day there'd be about three hours of programming, and the rest had to be live. Occasionally I'd be running around like a madman. In those days, there were three political factions involved in the radio. There was the Mojahedin-e Enqelab, from whom I'd disso-ciated myself. People who had been lower in the organization than me had by now become my superiors at work. No matter how hard they tried to convince me, I refused to rejoin them. I said that I'd cut myself off from all organizations, that I'd become an anarchist! So, every day, the Hezb-e Jomhuri had control of the radio for eight hours, Bani-Sadr's faction ran things for eight hours, and the Moja-hedin-e Enqelab took over for another eight hours. But I was the sole writer for all three factions. So I had to regulate my language, and say such-and-such during this group's period, something else during the next one's, and so on. But I'd always say what I wanted to, though I had to be discreet about it. Eventually they realized that "this guy's fooling all three of us!" and fired me. Then Mustafa Rokhsefat [a leading Muslim activist] decided to put together a group of talented people and inaugurate a center called Hozeh-ye Andisheh va Honar-e Islami.

HD   Were there any women in this group?

MM   At first there were only one or two. Later on, there were more. After I started working at the center, we began to publish some of these stories in a series called *Sureh*, of which perhaps a hundred editions came out.

HD   These were all young people you were working with? There were none of the established prerevolutionary writers?

MM   No, they were all young. When we began to work on screenplays, I wrote a script, and a group made a film based on it called *Tojih* ("*Explanation*"). It was very similar to Sartre's *Soiled Hands*. It's a story of a person who was going to detonate a bomb somewhere and suddenly notices that there are children nearby. Then SAVAK arrests him before the bomb goes off, and he tells them about the bomb so that the children won't be harmed. They are surprised and find respect for him. He says, "Well, I can't go through with it, I didn't mean to kill anyone." But the film was very badly made, and took a long time to finish. Meanwhile, I saw a very bad film by Iraj Qaderi. My friends wanted me to criticize it, but I realized then that I didn't really believe in criticism. I decided that whoever wants to should make the films they want to make, and instead of critcizing them I'll simply make my own films. A month later I began to make films. Iraj Qaderi inspired me to make films!

CINEMA SAVES

HD   Do you remember the title of Iraj Qaderi's film?

MM   It was called *Barzakhi-ha* ("*The Imperiled*"). A story of a bunch of roughnecks in jail . . . one of them had killed his own mother, another had raped his sister. These characters escape from prison and attack Iraq so as to defend the Iranian people! I found this really insulting, that all of us nationalists are no better than people who kill their own mothers. It was a Hollywood-like story with action and violence and lies. The film I made was called *Tobeh-ye Nasuh* ("*Nasuh's Repentance*"). It was the story of a banker who has a heart attack. His family think that he's dead, and prepare to bury him. But then his body moves, and they run away. He wakes up and realizes that his family, who he thought loved him so dearly, is more afraid of him living than dead. He decides that he didn't really feel emotionally attached to his family, and if so, why did he harass so many people to support them? He then begins to take account of all of his sins. For example, he refused loans for no reason. He asks forgiveness for this. He rebuilt his home taller, casting the house next door in perpetual shade. He asks for forgiveness for this. He realizes that he's committed so many small sins in his life that seeking forgiveness is useless. Better, then, simply to stop committing them. Remembering the film now, I see that it has the sensibility of an [Yasujiro] Ozu film, although it's still hard for me to understand my early works. Now I'd say that prejudice governs this film, although the perspective is very aridly religious. But it is still very much concerned with the struggle for the betterment of human relations. This is the result of two factors: the first is that my first screenplay was very poorly adapted to film, and that from a philosophical and political screenplay they tried to make an action film.

HD   Wait a minute. From the time you saw Iraj Qaderi's film until you made *Nasuh's Repentance*, how long?

MM   One month.

HD   And in one month you gained all you needed to know in terms of the technical aspects of filmmaking?

MM   Well, yes. I really think that it's possible to learn the technical side of filmmaking in two months, and that it's much more important to have an idea of what you want to say.

HD   And before you saw Qaderi's film, before you made *Nasuh's Repentance*, you'd never even handled a camera?

MM   Never. My grandmother's influence on me as a kid led me to refuse even to listen to music for religious reasons. If I passed by a store that was playing music, I'd even put my fingers in my ears so as not to hear it. I would occasionally go to the cinema with my mother and my stepfather, who was, as I said, very religious and political. But I'd argue with my mother about whether her *chador* was on right, and so on, and I'd tell her that she'd go to hell for going to the cinema. When I was taking part in political activities, at the ages of fifteen to seventeen, I did see a few films . . . One was *Tangsir* by Amir Naderi, which was considered a revolutionary film. Another was *Fahrenheit 451* by Truffaut, which I still love, but then I saw it as pertaining to SAVAK's burning of censored books. Now it seems to have more to do with the relationship of film to literature and whether film will do away with literature. Another film I saw then was *Madar* ("*Mother*"), but I don't know which film version of the story I saw. And in jail, well, we didn't watch films there, or even television, with the exception of the news. But in 1978, television started showing a series of very good films. Like that Bergman film—I forget its name now.

HD   *The Seventh Seal?*

MM   Yes. And I saw two Italian revolutionary films on television then, also. After the revolution, I may have seen another five or six films. One I already mentioned, *Barzakhi-ha*, and another by Amir Qavidel. So, by the time I set out to make *Nasuh's Repentance*, I had seen, in the whole of my life, less than fifty films.

HD   And so, after making *Nasuh's Repentance*, you—

MM   I made *Do Chashm Bi-Su* ["*Two Sightless Eyes*"], and *Este'azeh* ["*Seeking Refuge*"]. But remember that before I began to make films or write film scripts, I read short stories and novels and plays every day for about a year and a half. So even though I'd not seen many films, I was familiar with the literature behind them. And when I came to making them, I thought them through shot by shot. When I went to Ershad [the Ministry of Culture and Islamic Guidance] to get money to make a film, they were amazed that I didn't have any photographs to show them, or a super-8 film, or anything. They said, "How will you make a film with no cinematic background?" So I borrowed some money from my stepfather and a couple of friends. I bought a Tousi camera, the "Traveling" model, a projector, and some lenses—all for 200,000 tomans [then about $30,000]. I made twelve copies of the film, which brought my costs up to 700,000 tomans. The arrangement was that if the film came out well, I would give it to my stepfather. If it was bad, I'd have to live with it. He liked the film. So my first film was paid for by going into debt, like that library I started. The profits from this film financed a sound studio which we built in our arts center [*Hozeh*]. We bought a crane from abroad, and a few other cameras with scope lenses.

THE TOTALITY OF A CINEMATIC CAREER

HD   Tell me more about your films to date.

MM   I'd divide my films into four periods. The first is made up of *Nasuh's*

Repentance, Two Sightless Eyes, Seeking Refuge, and *Boycott.* This period was marked by my previous experiences—my run-ins with the leftists and the Mojahedin, my antifascism. I was moved by my belief that these organizations were confusing their ideologies, and that in the end all that was left were groups of people who believed that they alone held onto the truth, a conviction which, I think, naturally leads only to fascism. And although I know that these are cultural and social problems and I hate fascism, I still prefer it to communism and anarchy. I also know that very often religious activism has led to fascism. But this is what I felt, based on these early experiences. So these works were either moralistic, like *Nasuh's Repentance,* which essentially tells people how to live, or political, like *Boycott.* If you see *Boycott,* you'll realize that one can distill the entire film into a brief critique of fascism. These first works are also very influenced by my religious beliefs then, and they are clearly the works of a person without a background in film, as they are full of cinematic errors.

HD   How did the established filmmakers and film critics react to your films? These were dire circumstances. It was a privilege to be allowed to make films.

MM   When I began to make films, a wave of anger rose among those filmmakers who had not been able to make films after the revolution. They were jealous that a new generation of filmmakers had appeared, and so they began to attack me. And this attack was one of the most educational experiences of my life. Here was a director that everyone seemed to hate, but anyone who went to see his films liked them.

HD   They derided you because they associated you with the government?

MM   No, not at all. You see, these film people were quite reliant upon the government for their living. But they were jealous, I think, of my films.

HD   "Jealous'? How could Beiza'i, Mehrju'i, or Kiarostami be jealous of you? They were the acknowledged masters of Iranian cinema, and you were just beginning to learn their craft. Maybe you mean that politically and professionally they resented your having resources to make films while they did not?

MM   The leftists said that I was religious. The religious people said, "What do we have to do with art?" Every group had its complaints. *Ershad* [the Ministry of

Culture and Islamic Guidance] itself, which is the government, demanded, "Who are these people and why are they making films?" Everyone had insulted me. And I had become a problem. And so my fame, in this early period, was 90 percent due to my opponents. Some even began to say that my work wasn't really "cinema,"—which I have concluded is an idiotic charge—all of my work is cinema. Whose definition of "cinema" do the rest of us have to conform to? Each person has his own "cinema".

HD   I agree. Obviously you have placed your own stamp on your films. But you knew that you had no experience. You knew that this was an art and you needed to master at least its basic requirements. Whether or not they were "jealous," your critics certainly had some cause for their resentment. Don't you agree?

MM   Well, let me put it this way. After I'd made three films—in 1982, *Nasuh's Repentance*; in 1983, *Two Sightless Eyes* and *Seeking Refuge*—I decided to read books on the cinema for a year. I used the same method I had used in prison, something I'd learned from the other prisoners. It was to collect everything I could on a certain topic, read it all comparatively, and come to some conclusion. I assembled 400-odd books on the cinema—translations and edited collections, mostly. Those which were available I bought; others I borrowed or photocopied. Then I spent about six months reading these books from morning to night, taking notes on whatever I thought was interesting. I divided the material into various topics, like "camera operation," "directing," "acting," "editing," "sound," and so on. And then I further subdivided the topics; for example, I divided "camera operation" into the material on "lenses," "motion," "angles," etc. When I was done, I had a great deal of information. For example, on directing, one author argued against the use of the zoom; another stated he didn't use filters for such and such reasons. I took notes on all of it. And as I began to condense and edit my notes, I found that I could write all the information pertaining to, for example, camera lenses on a single page. Then I reduced all of what I had written until it fitted into a small notebook. So these 400-odd books were distilled into a pocket-sized notebook, with 100 headings. I made *Boycott* after going through this process. And everyone was surprised that the same person who had made those three earlier films had made something so different. I looked at it this way. Anyone who gets a high-school diploma has to read, say, 120 books; that is, ten a year. And how many books are needed for a college degree? Let's say 200 altogether. How about a doctorate? 300 books? Well, it's true that I haven't been to film school, but I've probably read more, or at least as much, on the subject, as someone who has gotten a doctorate. During this same time, you remember, those *komitehs* [revolutionary committees] would go around setting up archives of various videos and that sort of thing.

HD   No, I don't. I wasn't there.

MM   You're right. At any rate, there was a place with an archive of 400 videos of films, all of them bad. Features with Beik Imanverdi [a popular actor of mostly commercial films]—things of that sort. Some were Iranian, others foreign—all terrible. Among them there were some forty or fifty watchable films. So, in addition to my books, from which I learned most of what I needed to know, I also watched forty or fifty films. If I think about them, except for a handful, I wouldn't be willing to sit through any of them again, although at the time I did think that they were mostly worthwhile films. I should say that most of my technique comes from those books, not the films. For example, it was at that time that I saw Hitchcock's *The Birds*, which was one of the good films, *The Bicycle Thief* and *Citizen Kane*. The more I watch *Citizen Kane*, the less I understand it! I still think that people who say it's a great film are idiots who are afraid of being found out, and continue to parrot the idea that it's a great film. (laughs) I just don't see why people still say that about it.

HD   Let's go back to *Boycott*. How would you characterize its significance in the course of your filmmaking?

MM   *Boycott* falls between my first and second periods of filmmaking, my second period being made up of *The Peddler*, *The Cyclist*, and *The Marriage of the Blessed*. All three of these films deal with social issues . . . A few years had passed since the revolution and I'd by then come to believe that the new government was not going to do anything worthwhile either. I asked myself "What comes after these slogans?" The left had been beaten down—it's true I had been worried that they might take control—but then I realized that capitalism was beginning to pull the strings that controlled the revolution. These films are a critique of capitalism and its effects on our society. But, by now, the form of my

Makhmalbaf made *The Actor* to a formula intended to prove that he could make art films that did well at the box office. Fatemeh Motamad Arya emerged as one of the finest postrevolutionary actresses

films, from a technical standpoint, was beginning to be good. They were well made, and head and shoulders above the average Iranian film. This opened the door to the admission of Iranian films to international film festivals. These three films have done quite well on the festival circuit. Although the directors of Farabi [Film Institute] were worried . . . They did not officially submit *Marriage of the Blessed* or *The Peddler* to any international film competitions. This was because these two films aroused hostility inside Iran, from the right wing, and Farabi was afraid that if they won prizes it might seal the fate of the institute. So they gave permission only to *The Cyclist*, and even when I had proposed the project, they told me to shoot the film in Pakistan. I ended up filming 90 percent of it in Iran and about 10 percent in Pakistan. As for my third period, it comprises *A Time for Love, Nights on the Zayandeh-rud, Once upon a Time, Cinema,* and *The Actor.* The worst of these was *The Actor,* and the best, *A Time for Love* and *Once upon a Time, Cinema. Salam Cinema* and *A Moment of Innocence* are like *Boycott* in that they sort of fall into this same period—they do and they don't. But these films quite certainly constitute a single period.

HD   And how do you define the films of this last period?

MM   Well, they are illustrations of relativity. That is, the problem I have with the films of my second period is that while the films of the first period portrayed the leftists as evil and religious people as good—that is, one group is good and the other as bad—the films of my second period have the same flaw. But in these, the poor are all good and the rich are evil. That is to say, these films lack psychological depth. In the first period, truth is defined by religion, and in the second, it is defined by, let's say, social justice. In the end they're one-sided. Absolutist . . . In the third period what has changed are the characters. They've become more complex; one doesn't see good people and bad people. Everyone is simultaneously good and bad, everyone is gray. This is the most important change in this period. And also, in these films there is no center of truth . . .

HD   What do you mean by "no center of truth"?

MM   I mean that truth doesn't exist! In fact, the very focus of these films is exactly this question: what is truth?

HD   I am not sure if I follow you. You are now talking of "truth" in what specific sense, as an artist or as a believer? Or you hadn't made that distinction yet?

MM   Let me explain. In *A Time for Love* the truth is seen from three perspectives; in *Once upon a Time, Cinema,* from at least two. *Nights on the Zayandeh-rud* is the same; it looks at the revolution from both a prerevolutionary and post-revolutionary angle. It's the same with *The Actor,* which is the story of a person who wants to become an artist, but conditions will not allow him to. The third period of my films is very much defined by analysis of the conditions which govern our lives, represented through multiple perspectives. Each employs a form suitable to its own attempt to view these issues . . . It's in the fourth period that the light begins to enter. It's the worldly nature, such as that of Sohrab

Sepehri, of the first period to which I am attracted, but the worldliness of the fourth period has made the greatest impact on me . . . I've moved toward life and humanity, away from deadly serious subjects. But I can't really say much more about this fourth period—I can't judge just yet. It's as if I don't have the patience even for relativism. In this fourth period I'm looking at two general questions. One is the multiplicity of perspectives and the other is human sorrow. I am searching for an emotional perspective, and the warmth of my films comes from the joy of living in the frame of human sorrow—but not a flaky kind of sorrow. And I have been looking at the constitution of this sorrow, and I'm still looking for it. This past year was a year very similar to the one before I made *Boycott*, when I did nothing but read. These days I've been watching many films, having discussions, thinking about the future, which is to say I've been thinking about what I should preserve from my earlier periods, and how to move ahead.

THE LOSS OF A PARTNER

HD   Mohsen, now tell me about your wife, about your experiences of love, marriage, the birth of your children, and the tragic death of your first wife.

MM   After I came out of jail, as I've told you, for about three months I was caught up with the establishment of the Mojahedin-e Enqelab. When the revolution did occur, it took us by surprise—we had thought that we would need to struggle for two or three more years before we would see it succeed. Of the two of us who were arrested from my original group, one was Hassan Langarudi, who was related to the woman who was to become my wife. Just a week or so after the revolution began, he told me that he had decided to marry the girl who had been a comrade of ours. He then asked, "Don't you want to marry?" And I said that I did, why not? (laughs) He then told me he had a relative whom I might like. I asked him if he knew her well, and he said that he did, and that her family was relatively poor. Her mother was dead and her father, a shopkeeper, was remarried with seven or eight children. He told me that she was very active in the revolution, in demonstrations and so on.

Would you believe that I agreed to marry her without ever having seen her?

Makhmalbaf's surreal camera began making magic as early as *The Marriage of the Blessed.*
In this carefully choreographed scene, the deranged man startles the approaching woman,
who in turn spills the dish of pomegranate seeds

When they went to arrange for the engagement, I was too embarrassed to go and
didn't . . . I remember I was at the headquarters where we dealt with organiza-
tional matters, like arranging for Bani Sadr to come and speak, when I ran into my
friend and asked him for a picture of my wife-to-be. Just then gunshots rang out
from the roof and I was afraid . . . I thought that someone was being executed. It
turned out to be the warden of the jail I had been in—I just heard the gunfire, and
then it was announced on a loudspeaker that he had been executed. I was shocked;

it was a bad moment. So you can see what strange circumstances surrounded our union! When the marriage was arranged, all I owned was a pair of very worn army pants. When I went to my fiancée's house, her stepmother opened the door and we exchanged greetings, and she asked me to come in. I explained who I was, and that I'd come to make arrangements for the wedding. So I first saw Fatemeh then. She was a few days shy of eighteen. I was twenty-two. We spoke, and we decided that we'd be married even though she was a few days too young, and that we'd get the license afterward. And then her stepmother very politely asked if I could please not wear the same pair of pants to the wedding. I said, "Never! You can't change my beliefs!" I had a younger cousin who owned a suit, and I tried it on. It was too small for me, the sleeves were way too tight on me, and the pants were all wrong. Then I went to a barber thinking I should get my hair cut properly. Instead, he gave me a terrible cropping. So imagine, a half-bald groom in a weird suit (laughs) . . . What a wedding! I didn't want a license or anything . . . I wanted to be like Imam Ali and and his wife, Fatemeh. Of course, my wife's name was Fatemeh. That's what it was like, with these slogans in our heads . . . There's that scene in *The Marriage of the Blessed* when one character says, "It's impossible to live like Imam Ali and Fatemeh." At that point it was impossible to live without those slogans. So it was set that we be married a few days later. Remember that in those days everything was run by the *komitehs*. Behzad [Nabavi] asked me, "Where were you yesterday?" and I replied "I was busy getting married." He said, "Is this a time for that?" Then the two of us went to Refah School [the headquarters of the revolutionaries] and got two shovels and a broom. Then we went to the old Majlis building [the Iranian Parliament], which some civilians had taken over. We swept and prepared an office for military operations, which were being moved from Refah to the Majlis. In those days Bazargan was at Refah, the prisoners were kept at Refah, Imam Khomeini was staying at Refah, and it was also the place where people came to hand in the guns they'd captured during the revolution. It was crazy. So we cleaned up this place, and fixed up a telephone (laughs)— the next day that building became the Department of Foreign Affairs. So, in the midst of this hullabaloo, I was married. And then I realized I wasn't even interested in being married . . . and we still didn't have a license. So we got a couple of mattresses, a couple of lamps, plates, forks, and moved into a tiny room fit for a cockroach. It was just like [Ali Hatami's film] *Suteh-Delan* [*The Downtrodden*]. I saw *Suteh-Delan* later, and immediately fell in love with it because it so much resembled my own early married life.

When I left the political organizations and moved into radio, Fatemeh came with me. I wrote programming and she became an announcer. When Samira was born, we'd take her with us to the radio station. We worked and she was always with one of us. So when I went to work at the Arts Center, I borrowed some money and built a house on the other side of Vali Asr [Street] between a couple of brick ovens . . . When they extended the road to our house, the house sank because they'd built it on unsettled earth. We lived there until I made *The Peddler.* Fatemeh was with me when I made *Seeking Refuge* and *The Marriage of the Blessed*, but not so much during *Boycott* because we had another child by then. She was on the set of *The Cyclist*, but not during the parts shot in Pakistan. Somehow, until the end we worked together.

Then, in 1992, we were forced to move again . . . With my increasing fame, especially with my second-period films, which dealt with social issues, we'd find a group of people standing outside our door every day. People thought that since I'd made *The Marriage of the Blessed*, I would certainly give them a loan. People would come with their sick children . . . Sometimes we'd rent a house; other times we'd buy one . . .

The last place we bought . . . in Dolatabad . . . I don't like . . . telling this story . . . She was wearing plastic sweat pants, and went to light an oil-lamp we had, and some of the oil got on her . . . It caught on fire . . . The neighbors rushed in to put it out, but it was too late . . . It only took a minute. She was at home with her sister, the two of them were watching a film, and both of them were burned. Her sister got burned because as soon as she saw the fire, she reached out to help and her clothes caught on fire as well . . . Her clothes were also plastic, and as she ran from the living room to the kitchen upstairs, her entire body burned. It's . . . How can I describe it? Look at a burnt matchstick, and think of a human being in its place. Fire . . . They described how a spark landed on her clothes, and as she slapped at it to put it out, it only spread. So she tore her clothes off . . . And in the hospital, the poor thing . . . Those plastic clothes are the worst . . . Plastic clothing, as soon as it catches fire, sticks to your skin and burns you. All of this because of plastic clothing. In a second, a little oil, a spark flew and grew into a huge flame, and it took a minute. When she caught on fire she began to run around the room. Then the neighbors ran in and tried to put her out. I was at my mother's house . . . It took five days . . . clothes sticking to skin and . . . and I thought that if we moved from that house it'd become a tomb. (pause)

Well, as for my children, Samira was born a year after the revolution; Meysam was born two and a half years after it. Hana was born as I was making *The Marriage of the Blessed*.

HD   So your wife was very actively involved in your work.

MM   Yes, very much. She also acted in *Once upon a Time, Cinema*, in *The Actor*, and in a few others. Whenever I needed a role filled, she'd do it. When I needed a nurse, for example, in *The Marriage of the Blessed*, she put on a nurse's uniform and acted the part. She would play many roles, all bit parts. She was also involved in the screenplays, especially in writing the women's roles. My children are also in many of my films . . . That's how it was, which is to say, I didn't fall in love . . . Our love was a love that came after marriage. Fatemeh was a normal South Tehran girl . . . she was surprised when she saw that so many of my comrades ended up becoming ministers and holding other leading positions in the years after the revolution. She would joke that the revolution was a sham because so many of my friends became somebody. (laughs) She never took herself too seriously . . .

HD   Tell me about your second marriage.

MM   My second marriage coincided, more or less, with the making of *Salam Cinema*. I married Fatemeh's sister, Marzieh.

HD   And you've not had any more children?

MM   No. We don't want any more children.

ART AS A FUTURE

HD   It must have been difficult after Fatemeh.

MM   My introduction to filmmaking was as accidental as my meeting my wife. I married my wife and then later fell in love with her. When Fatemeh died, it took me two years to come to terms with it. I was unwell—I couldn't work. If you ask me what the worst experience of my life is, I'd say it was losing the person who was with me day and night. She was amazing. She would take care of the children, run the house, keep in touch with our relatives, help the wives of my friends—and suddenly, in a second, something was erased which had for me a million memories. I fell in love with her slowly, and my love for film was similar. I fell in love with it little by little. And there were other factors. My best-selling book sold 120,000 copies. As you know, in Iran, books are published in runs of 3,000. 120,000 copies of a screenplay is really a lot. But then *Boycott* had one million viewers in Tehran alone! One day's ticket sales of an unpopular film of mine is equivalent to five years' sales of a popular book. I couldn't get away from this fact . . . I don't make films for posterity, just for myself. Communication is important to me. Also, all of these things I was doing—writing plays and short stories, and so on—all of these are present in filmmaking.

HD   But in a more complete and mutually complementary fashion.

MM   Exactly. I even think about the music I use in my films, so I'm even somewhat of a composer! Photography is also important, as is theater. Film is simply a more complete art form. And the possibilities are greater. It's because of cinema that I've seen so much of the world that I no longer have the patience for travel. Last year I had forty invitations. This is due to cinema's international scope. Literature isn't like that—in Persian we have only a few books that have been translated into, say, English. But how many Iranian films have been sent to every corner of the world? Cinema is a more international art, and uses a more global language. These reasons made my decision to pursue film and forget all about writing for publication an easy one.

HD   Tell me about these forty or so countries you've visited.

MM   I didn't go to forty or so countries. I had that many invitations, and my films have been shown in some seventy countries. I myself haven't traveled that much. I don't like to travel. The most important trip was that first one to London, the first time I ever saw the West. I felt as if all the bad things I had been told about the West were lies. They had taken what was different between the East and West, distorted it, and had given me a vulgar notion of what the West was like. Seeing *Wings of Desire*, directed by Wim Wenders, and seeing Britain coincided for me. The shock was so great that I became ill, so much so that for fifteen days my head ached. At that time, no film had had such an effect on me as *Wings of Desire*.

HD   What did you like so much about *Wings of Desire*?

HD   All the religious slogans I used to chant were there in that film, and yet the film represented the West! But I had already begun to reach these conclusions on my own. You see, if I'd gone to London three years earlier, neither the film nor the environment would have had such an effect on me. People first reach conclusions, and then search for proof of them.

HD   You needed Wim Wenders to confirm your own conclusions?

MM   Exactly. First you arrive at a relativist position, and then—in Locarno you told me that when Ibsen was about to die, he said, "*az taraf-e digar* " ["on the other hand"]—and then it means something to you. Otherwise, you can't grasp it. Or else, you reach the conclusion that everything is absurd and strange, and a hidden force takes shape in your soul that brings everything in life into question. You feel that in all the happiness and beauty of life, there is a certain futility. That's why it's good to see the fun in things, not to take everything so seriously. Ozu asked that they not put his name on his tombstone, but instead write the word "nothing" upon it. And then you understand it, you see that Ozu is right. It's true that Ozu is not "nothing," that we find a million lives within his work. But all of that is still nothing before the enormous processes of life. And it's for that reason that I don't think I'd try to do anything but be a filmmaker from now on. Once or twice, after the tragic death of Fatemeh, and when the censors tried to stop me, I did think that I might give it up. But even if I was to change my work, I'd only consider doing the simplest sorts of jobs. I'd never take a position with any responsibility. For example, even if I had to run an arts center, I'd refrain from even going so far as to say that "this is so-and-so's desk". I love filmmaking because there is motion in it. I couldn't go to a certain location and work in the same place every day. My entire life is caught up in motion and constant change—which is why I work to simplify, to reduce, to summarize to the fullest extent possible everything in my life.

HD   On that premise, what animates your work most at the moment?

MM   Right now, as I told you, in my work only two things are of interest to me. Life and humanity. And I don't mean religion or ideology when I say "humanity." I mean "human" in the rawest sense. We are alive and therefore must live, and we are humans and so have to be humans. That's it. That's all. These are the most essential things we have.

HD   When you speak of issues indigenous to Iran in New York, Tokyo, or elsewhere, and a spectator you never could have imagined writes critiques of your work, what do you make of it?

MM   The color and flavor of my work are native to Iran, but its contents are not. My work concerns birth, life, and death. You see, *The Peddler* is in three sections: the first concerns a birth, the second a life, and the third a death. Now, it may take place in Iran, but it's the story of all of humanity! The story of arrival and departure, the story of love, of life. The meanings of these are the same for anyone, anywhere. And even if you make a film about Iranian nationalism, it will still resonate elsewhere for people who have experienced their own nationalism.

HD   But that's not what I mean. I, too, believe that unless an art is perfectly particular it cannot be entirely universal. The films of Satyajit Ray and Kurosawa are perhaps the best examples. Let me put it another way—have you ever come across a critic from either Europe, or Asia, or Africa, who has interpreted a film of yours in a way which you've found strange, or which has surprised you?

MM   Well, yes, I've been surprised by the comments people make. There have often been lies or rumours about me which have been picked up by various media, and which have influenced certain critics and distorted their opinions. For example, it was said that I had been a cleric in the ruling regime in Iran, and so these critics would see my work and try to understand how it was that I had come out of my clerical garb, when the very basis of their assumption was untrue. Another bit of misinformation spread about me was that I am an avid watcher of films. The truth is I don't have the time to watch films—that's my problem. (laughs) If only I really had a chance to sit down and watch films! I've told you about the effort I made to watch films during my first period. Somehow it got out that I had spent years in some obscure archives, studying films. You know, the biggest archive I've yet seen is Bahman's [Maqsudlou] right here in this house! Where is there an archive in all of Iran, especially after the revolution? There is no such archive. There is the National Film Center, but what can you get from them? What I've done is read books on film. Another rumor is that I'm completely self-taught—again, wrong. I've been greatly influenced by the books I've read on films and filmmaking. I've learned from books, from my life. Just the fact that I've not taken film courses doesn't make me strange! I studied on my own. For example, I love to read about Ozu, but when a film of his is shown they always say, "Let's invite him," but I really don't have the patience! (laughs) But give me an article about Ozu and I'll read it right away. And the next day I'll sit down and write a scene that captures the essence of what I'd gained from reading the article. The effect of these lies is that young people interested in my work think that they have to watch dozens of films to understand filmmaking. I argue that one can learn from books, or by speaking to people who are knowledgeable on the subject. One can learn so much more from reading than from watching! From watching, one can learn about living, that is true. But to understand the theory, one must read the theory. Another problem is the censorship imposed on us. It prevents us from telling the whole story. We can only say half of what is true. And so the way things are arranged must in the end represent what we are trying to say. Take, for example, that interview with me in *Sorush* [magazine]. In it, whatever I said, left, or right, or whatever—it was all true. But if you take what I said out of the social context in which I said it, the statements by themselves are misleading. It'd be as if someone took a sentence from this interview of my account of the attack on that policeman, and published it without explanation. People would say "What is wrong with that Makhmalbaf! He's still talking that guerrilla stuff!" But really I'm speaking critically about that event so that others will see it critically! You see what I mean? They always say afterward that the newspaper didn't have space, so they cut the beginning, they cut the end, and you're left with these out-of-context statements.

HD   Someone once said that every poet has a poem from which all of his poems are derived, but that essential poem is never uttered. Similarly, there may be a film in your mind, one that you feel you must make, and believe that someday you will make it. All of the films you make until then will in some way be attempts to realize that film.

MM   Well, let me tell you that for a while I lived with my aunt in her home, along with my grandmother and my stepfather and mother. You can see this house in the film *Boycott.* It's the home of an old woman. Intense interactions and relationships developed in this small house with only four rooms. It seems to me that I am always trying to make that film. Everything goes back to my childhood, then. We are always saying only half of what we mean. In a society which is full of official and self-censorship, I can never fully say what I mean. For example, can I even begin to speak about how I think I've confused the essence of my grandmother's religion, how I think my emotions toward her were intermixed with religious feelings?

HD   Well, that's not such a strange thing. One of our greatest living poets told me that once, as he was watching his grandmother comb her hair, a ray of light struck her silver locks. "I saw God at that moment," he said. And he is an atheist.

MM   True . . . So anyone who told you he was related to your grandmother you took in and received, only to find that he was like the father who abandoned you. You see? My story is a story of periods of infatuation and disillusionment; first an infatuation with political activism and then disillusionment; then an infatuation with philosophy followed by disillusionment . . .

THE POETICS OF A VISIONARY

HD   Let's speak about poetry. Do you prefer classical poetry or modern?

MM   Oh . . . I have a lot to say about Persian poetry. It's something I have no expertise in, but feel very strongly about. Of Iranian poets, I personally prefer Forough [Farrokhzad] and [Sohrab] Sepehri. [Ahmad] Shamlu's use of words is sublime! But I don't really like his poems. However, strangely, when I want to summarize a thought or idea—for example, when I want to explain that despite not being a nationalist, I have certain feelings linked to Iran—I always say that "in Shamlu's words 'my light burns in this house'" although I have to admit that

I don't really like that poem myself. Of the others, I have no great love even for Nima [Yushij]. But I do like Forough. But one has to read all of Forough's work to understand why it is that I despise parts of it, and think that parts of it are unparalleled. But, in general, I am moved by Sepehri. In my opinion, people are of three sorts. The first are those who have baseless miseries, but they have a million tiny miseries. One morning I woke up thinking that I must disgrace myself. I had been trying to sleep, but realized that a statement a person had made about me six years ago was suddenly bothering me. I lay there for a couple of hours before I got up and told myself that I must disgrace myself, because I was letting myself be distracted by this tiny misery. I said to myself that I need to become infamous because I'm supposed to be better than to be caught up in this sort of thing—to care who said what about me so many years ago. Thus, some people are preoccupied with tiny miseries. Another type of people are those who, like children, live for and in happiness; they delight in living. Those with tiny miseries are generally romantic people, and have any number of maladies. Those who delight in living are at ease with themselves. They don't allow themselves to be held back by troubles. The third type of people are those who are burdened with human misery. Forough, in her first three books, is filled with tiny miseries.

HD   Which of these three types are you?

MM   In my films I find that I'm searching for that simple delight in life, and I am also a little concerned with that human misery I mentioned. I hate tiny miseries, although some of my films are filled with them. *The Actor* is filled with tiny miseries. For me, then, Sepehri is more and more a model for what I would like to express. He has his roots in Khayyam, in childhood. I believe that art, when it returns to two things, is most effective. For example, think of Picasso, in his early cubist period, when he was painting portraits influenced by African art. All those forms that he adopted from African portraiture, which are both simple and engaging, are familiar to everyone. Or think of artists who take us back to the state of childhood, the infancy of mankind. My theory about actors is that the most effective are those who seem to us both innocent and charismatic. Charlie Chaplin is of course the epitome of that. We dislike passively innocent people. The ideal protagonist is a guiltless person who is active in life. That is why we enjoy watching well-spoken, talented children. We accept them as innocent because they are children, and we are attracted to their energy. For me, finding characters who fit this ideal becomes a treasure hunt. Because the charisma of these characters comes from their lives, and their innocence from their humanity. Sepehri has a good deal of innocence, but his charisma is low. Forough is very charismatic, but less innocent. Of other authors, I really dislike Sadeq Hedayat, really . . . But these days, for me, Sepehri is like a prophet who loved life. Most ideologies are based on messages of death—even Marxism. Marx is concerned with social justice, it's true, but more than anything he was a prophet of death. If I have come to terms with Sepehri, it's because of two lines of his poetry: "I am a Muslim, I pray towards a rose, my prayer mat is a river." Sepehri, with a certain naturalism, is criticizing this country of ours.

HD   Let me ask you this: You say that you used to see things more darkly than now. What made you change?

MM   It's as if a man is upset, shouts and curses, throws the door open, and is angry at everyone sitting in a room. It may even be that he has something to say that they should pay attention to. But after he gets it off his chest, what's left for him to do? He either has to leave, or sit down and say, "OK, someone bring some food for us to eat, let's drink some tea together." The darkness, you could say, might have been there in society, but was more in the way I looked at things. The other thing, I'd have to say, is a more simple event: fatherhood. A father wants nothing more than for his children to live in peace and with hope. After my wife passed away, I found one million poems to read to my children to keep them hopeful. You see, you constantly fear the idea that your child might grow up a revolutionary, or even become the leader of a great world revolution. And slowly you begin to see all of humanity as being similar to your children. You begin to feel that you don't have the right to stand in the way of their peace. This is fatherhood. Especially when they are adolescents, you worry that they might become political activists, that they might lose their lives for some cause. Fatherhood influences you to work for their peace, their hope. So one reason I've changed is fatherhood, and just the process of aging. Another is social reality. If society is colorful, then so am I. If I can't say anything, then I have to say it with colors. You see, I saw that although they were making society black, I myself was talking about nothing but its blackness. And then I slowly came to accept that I believe in nothing but the simple fact of existence—living. And living is white. So my ideology is white. And this was brought home to me on a trip I made to India.

HD   When was this trip?

MM   The first time I went to India, I had written a rather black screenplay, called *Bread and Flower*, which has some white parts, but basically is black. From the airport, the taxi ride to the hotel took us about an hour and a half. We went past a wide walkway full of people. It seemed a million beggars of all ages were camped there. They didn't have even a bowl to beg with . . . and they were of every sort—men, women, children, cats . . . torn clothing and all. It was around dusk. But you know, every one of the million beggars was dancing! Every one of them, like Amir Naderi's characters, was dancing. And I thought to myself that these people are crazy! I kept waiting for our car to pass them, but the street would not end. For the whole hour and a half of the ride we did nothing but pass people like them.

HD   What city was this?

MM   Bombay, in 1990 or 1991. At first I thought that it must be a religious holiday, or that some superstition had moved them all to hysteria. But it seemed that this was a normal thing, that they did this every night. I couldn't stop wondering what is driving these people to dance like this? And then the Indian cinema—one should never forget about Indian cinema. Of course, something like one half of the world's films are made in India, and the cinema is such an important part of society there. These same beggars first ask for a coin to buy a bit of food, and then will ask you for money to buy a movie ticket. They lose themselves in dreams in the cinema. And why not? This is a country with pretensions to socialism, but that has never had the economic basis for it. They had revolutions that were meant to bring about social justice, but then it became clear that progress was oriented only toward technology and science, that these things were supposed to help the people. So are they going to watch my films, or those of Satyajit Ray, to decide that they are poor and destitute? Let them dream! The infrastructure necessary to help them simply doesn't exist. It's like the sick child who is waiting for the cure to his illness. They medicate him until then to ease his pain! The economic demand for the Indian film industry is entwined in the spirit of the Indian people, who, on the one hand, are Hindu, and cherish the joy of living, and, on the other hand, have not come to grips with the fact that the source of this joy is the Indian cinema. That is why this cinema keeps selling dreams and the people keep buying them. They have confused the dream with the reality. And so if you subject them to a dark film, you've committed some sort of treason against them, because a dark film won't change anything but will make life less endurable for them. That is why I came to accept these beggars of India as my teachers. It's why I've been constantly writing screenplays since then. I've written dozens, and set aside most of them. You know how many times I rewrote *A Moment of Innocence?* For years I've been struggling with it. And then I read somewhere that after Sepehri had visited India, his work was changed immensely by that experience.

HD   [Sadeq] Hedayat traveled to India as well, but he ended up committing suicide in Paris.

MM   But it was a different experience for him—a bad experience. But I—well, I had moments of enlightenment, almost mystical ones, whether visually inspired, or from books and conversations. I wrote a piece which, in short, is a sort of comparison between three kinds of mysticism: Islamic, Buddhist, and Hindu. I contrasted them, and tried to see why it is that Hindu mysticism is more open. It's a mysticism that is close to the people, available to them, and has immediate results for them. Why is it that Buddhist mysticism, despite bringing peace to its adherents, is still idealistic; and Islamic mysticism, well, is just sick. (laughs)

SOURCES OF CULTURAL MALADIES

HD   What, in your opinion, is our worst cultural trait?

MM   Of Iranian society?

HD   Or of Iranian culture?

MM   There are a few films that have made an excellent critique of certain

The last frame of Makhmalbaf's *A Moment of Innocence* freezes with
the camera gazing at the open face of a woman in love, with a piece of
bread and a flower pot substituting for a potential gun and a knife

cultural or social traits of Iranian society. One of them is the serial *Dear Uncle Napoleon* [based on Iraj Pezeshkzad's satirical novel], in which the character Da'i Jan Napoleon suspects that his servant Mash Qasem is a British spy. Mash Qasem denies this—I don't know if you remember?

HD   Oh yes, I do very well. I have read the novel. Never saw the serial though. It started when I had already left Iran.

MM   Right. My point is that when Mash Qasem sees that his idol believes him to be a British spy, he begins to think that he really is one and confesses! (laughs) That to me is a metaphor, really, of a condition of Iranian society. I mean, to doubt yourself to the extent that you begin to believe accusations against yourself, even that you are a spy. Iranian society is, unfortunately, immature in this way. Rather than working hard toward a certain goal, people instead work harder to make sure that others never reach it. We excel at wrestling, rather than soccer, because we're individualists! Soccer must be taken seriously as a team sport before a team spirit emerges. Piety must be serious before we can have true religious leaders. But, with us, even piety is a kind of self-aggrandizement. Unfortunately, as I said, we are a people who are more concerned with what others are doing than with our own work, and so if we notice that someone is doing very well, we work twice as hard to prevent that person from reaching their goal.

Another thing is that we're a nation of pretense and hypocrisy. Even the sickliest heroin user pretends that he's a wrestler. In appearance we're all wrestlers, but behind the scenes we're all opium and heroin addicts. It's the same in our political life. These are national traits.

Not to mention that Iran is also an extremely sexist society. Look at our parliament. What percentage of it are women? How many voters are women? How many companies or offices have women directors? The government should take the initiative in addressing this, but it has blocked progress for women. Remember how Reza Shah by force instituted certain freedoms for women—he had to use force against society itself to institute these changes, because sexism is an Iranian cultural trait. While in Pakistan it is possible to imagine a woman as prime minister, in Iran such a thing is still impossible. And it's not only because of Islam. In comparison to Pakistan and India, we're more like Afghanistan in how we view women.

But in my opinion Iran's greatest problem is our belief in absolute truths. Everyone believes himself to be absolutely correct. That's why democracy has failed in Iran. Democracy, before being a political issue, is a cultural issue. We all think that we are the only holders of the truth, and believe that everyone should bend to our own views. We have no tradition of public discourse. Instead we have the mullah's pulpit from which a monologue is issued. Remember, you pointed out to me the difference between a round table and a pulpit. Now, it doesn't make any difference whether the pulpit is occupied by Shamlu, or Jalal Al-e Ahmad. Can one enter into a dialogue with Shamlu? Is this possible? Or Al-e Ahmad? Or Samad Behrangi? These would be one-way conversations.

We can't achieve democracy because everyone sees himself as being *the* holder of *the* truth, and cannot conceive of the truth as a many-sided thing spread out among the people. And so we cannot enter into real dialogues. Why is this the case? Because we can't escape our belief in the prophets of a single book. One ends up a follower of Shamlu, another follows his opposition. But the fact is that truth is not found in a single place! Since our scientific knowledge is quite low, we argue over whether this or that book will give us all the answers. Ignoring the possibility that they both may have some answers. This fundamentalism distracts us from perceiving the reality, and leads us down the path to fascism. When all truth is unified and held within the pages of a single book, and only one person can interpret that book, it becomes a fight between absolutes. And everyone else becomes fighters for whatever sect they follow. So we end up with either Shari'ati or Motahhari, and not simply two opinions. Two figures argue, and the rest pound their chests.

In the book on *Salam Cinema*, I claim that Iran never had intellectuals. Intellectuals are people who think, consider, discuss. We have people who make statements, who argue. For us, discourse is not valuable. What has value is choosing a leader to follow. These are among the greatest problems in Iranian society. For me, everything else relates to these cultural problems which have held us back. As the world moved on from the classical era, we did not progress. We are still in a state preceding humanism, much less modernism and realism.

People do sometimes travel around Iran, but those who leave the country and see beyond the borders do not return. How many people do we have who have lived abroad for a period, and then returned to play a significant role in society?

None. If the two million Iranians who live outside the country were to return, it would certainly change the nature of Iranian society. Two million can certainly influence sixty million. Traveling is so unheard of in Iran, even domestically. Iran, stuck as it has been in a previous era, has in recent years even begun to regress. We are still oriented to our ancient past. To be progressive, then, for us, is to be oriented towards an era four hundred rather than six hundred years ago. This fundamentalism, this hatred of relativism, leads to sexism and the other problems I've mentioned. Some believe that we need to influence Iranian society, and think that, by publishing books and making films, we cause cultural change in Iran. But that's not so. The work of cultural change would be to bring about a revolution wherein all people would arrive at decisions that may or may not be related to the aspirations of the revolution, but that would naturally result from the event. Instead, the atmosphere we live in only confuses people. Since the door to dialogue is closed and we are deprived of basic freedoms, people are left with little to consider.

HD   What would be the basis of this revolution that you would like to see?

MM   What I'm saying is that this revolution has already occurred, and the goals of this revolution and the experience everyone had led to certain conclusions. The results are around us; this is what we have to show for it. And these results haven't been assessed, or rather, they have been assessed incorrectly. In every person's life, these factors exist, but not the conditions that would have allowed them to be assessed collectively.

HD   Can't it be said that *Gabbeh* and *Salam Cinema* are a sort of assessment?

MM   No. These are my own assessments, not a collective one.

HD   OK, setting aside our ignorance of where we stand in the world, what traits in Iranian culture itself strike you as positive and could be used to reform the overall cultural conditions?

MM   (Long pause) I'm not sure exactly. In our culture, the tendency toward cheating and lying has its roots in people's fear of the powers that be, and this has led to our late arrival at even very basic ideas of fairness. Even in everyday matters, everything has been polarized, and results in the perception that cheating is a

Throughout *Gabbeh* Makhmalbaf uses close-ups for showing the face of a woman in love and long shots for the man she loves—a radical reversal of the primacy of the masculinist conception of love characteristic of the entire history of Iranian culture

necessity of life. In my opinion, not only does the government deceive the people, but also the people deceive one another, and even the government. When I was in prison, one day in 1978 we held a group prayer and the guards marched us to solitary confinement. In this group, I was with Raja'ian. Then they put Raja'ian into a normal group cell with nonpolitical prisoners. How long is it from 10 June 1978 to 10 February 1979? [the day of the final ascendance of the revolution over the provisional government]. When I saw Raja'ian again I asked him what had happened to him. He replied, "I was put in a cell and they brought in a group of new prisoners who told us that their goal was to oust the Shah by the end of the year. There were thirty or so of us already in there, and we all began to laugh for several minutes. Then the new prisoners began writing confessions on scraps of paper so as to be released. We told them to have some self-respect, to stay in jail for a few days. They looked at us as if we were crazy and said 'We want to get out as soon as possible so as to overthrow the Shah! Don't you have anything better to do than to rot in jail?'" Raja'ian then began discussing with the older prisoners how shallow and disappointing the new political activists were, and how their hopes to overthrow the Shah quickly would lead to their ultimate failure. You see, even the Shah had no idea what was coming. Do you know why none of us could have predicted the revolution? Because the Iranian populace is so caught up in chest-beating that they are likely to change their loyalty in a moment en masse. Since all political movements are based on deceit, they all run the risk of being overthrown in a moment by a new lie. One day the people will pour into the streets to support you, and the next week the same people will be in the streets demanding your ouster. And so the public has thus become deceitful even to itself. It has an outer and an inner life. You can only get to know Iranians by visiting them in their homes. This is especially true in the cities—

HD   Wait a minute. When I asked you what the most negative trait of Iranian culture was, you came up with a list of things. When I asked you for ideas about its emancipation, you first said that you don't know, and then began to speak at greater length about the negative characteristics. As an Iranian filmmaker, as an artist—

MM   I know, I am pessimistic.

HD   Listen, as a filmmaker who has just made a film like *Gabbeh*—

MM   Emancipation? From what?

HD   From itself! From deceit, and lies, and misery, and this vicious circle of stupidity and hypocrisy—

MM   From itself? And forget about the political dimension?

HD   No, not at all, precisely in, through, and against those conditions.

MM   And set up a framework which ignores the political?

Makhmalbaf visually celebrates the colorful life of nomadic migration in order to challenge the theocratic state's militant assault against beauty

Gabbeh is a love story told in colors, shapes, forms, all woven together in a narrative that plays with the borderlines of sur/realism

HD   Let me restate my question. What *does* morally and intellectually nourish you as an artist who is obviously concerned with the fate of our society? For example, in *Gabbeh*, which is a film in celebration of life, what provided the moral and intellectual energy for that work?

MM   It's hard for me to say—I'm too much inside the matter itself. I can't offer you some manifesto with a list of my demands. I can only give you a summary of my feelings about our predicament. I think that the Iranian people must, on their own and for themselves, pursue a more rational end, not an emotional end. The duality, the schizophrenia of Iranians, in being one thing in public and another in private, exists because our national character has not yet been fully constituted. We can be happy, but one cannot yet be sure that we are happy because of the envy of the rest of the world, or because of an innate inner joy. I see happiness as a right. I think that it is a human right to be joyful. The person who makes a dark, realistic film in India is wasting his time. Gandhi, in the large scheme of things, did very little. Socialism has also failed. Many things must yet change in India before the people's lives become better . . . So why should the people be depressed by movies like that? They must be allowed to have some pleasure in life. The person who has had to sell his body for a morsel of food—you want to make a film for him about social justice? What is he supposed to do after seeing that film? Kill the guy sitting next to him? It's far too simplistic to see films as answering these larger questions. These problems are so complex. I am moved by the problems of humanity, you know, and the meaning of life for me is not just in living for oneself, but in living for everyone else. That's called humanity. However, these problems don't have clear-cut answers—one of the things I am trying to do is speak of relativism in a society that has individualistic and fundamentalist tendencies. As for those who want to follow me instead of someone else, I will do all I can to dissuade them from blindly following me. I teach thinking, thinking for one's self, and I don't want any followers.

In conclusion, in choosing from among religion, politics, and art, I choose art. In the same sense that art has instructed and educated me, I feel that my own responsibility is to continue to educate myself through art, since I thereby become more knowledgeable . . . My hope is that the viewer of my work for an hour and a half will during this time, to a small extent, breathe in an air which is somewhat different from that in which he or she lives. If successful, this will be no more than a very small, almost insignificant, achievement. I don't believe that I am doing anything very significant. But I can do nothing else, and I must do something. But the significance of what I do is not very important to me. Its nature, its quality, is what is important to me . . . My influence is small, and I influence no one more than I influence myself. But, naturally, some people are affected by what I do, in the same way that I am affected by Sepehri. And perhaps some people will be influenced by those whom I affect. But I don't think that I am in any way changing the world. Any person who has tried to take the responsibility of the world upon himself has done nothing but corrupt it in the end. Instead, I criticize myself every day, I try to break myself every day. I am a filmmaker, and I hope that nothing I say will ever lead to an assassination, or to someone being killed in defending what I have said. A single human life is still more valuable to me than all of cinema.

We filmmakers are here only to illuminate, to bring joy to life. All I seek is that, after seeing a film of mine, a person feels a little happier, and acts with a little more kindness towards the world. I don't think that cinema can hope to do much more. But even this little is enough to fulfill my ambitions, which are to a great extent due to historical circumstances. I aspire to be a real person, rather than to represent some ideal, and that's why my films tend to be more realistic than idealistic, although idealism is certainly part of the reality of life, its joys and pains. As for religion, I accept God, in my heart. But I would never want to try to persuade someone else to accept him. This is a personal matter. The things which attract us to the world are the details of living. The prophets of religions all have come to tell us just that.

When, as a child, I started going to the mosque, I wanted to save humanity. After growing a little older, I wanted to save my country; now, I think, I make films in order to save myself. With films I can create a representation of myself that I can then examine, and say "Where have I come to now?" I can see where I have problems, what things I wish to change. I make mirrors, then, to see myself. For example, when I watch the scene in *The Peddler* in which a sheep is slaughtered, I become enraged at myself. I begin to wonder whether the film was worth the life of that one sheep. Or in *Boycott*, someone plucks the wings off a butterfly. I go mad when I see that. I hate it. I've edited it out. Not that I'm not committing injustices every day. By simply walking, I may kill numerous ants. What I'm saying, though, is that I'm interested in changing myself rather than anyone else—not that I'm against others changing. I just don't know what the truth is, so how can I play the soothsayer and try to convince others to change?

There is a wonderful fable that the truth is a mirror that shattered as it fell from the hand of God. Everyone picked up a piece of it, and each decided that the truth was what he saw reflected in his fragment rather than realizing that truth had become fragmented among them all. In my opinion, everyone is confronted by their own particular truth, but there is no need to be too worried about that. People who live under all sorts of stress and tribulations get by and go on living. I simply want people to have hope while they live. And we can all choose our own way of living. Shamlu writes in a poem, "This long road . . . with all of this faith in one's own road." We should have faith in our own road. I don't want to tell anyone to follow mine, to waste people's time with my opinions. A friend of mine once said that certain poets waste the time of words. I replied that certain clerics waste the time of knowledge. And revolutionaries can waste the time of the people. People will find their own ways. There is a peddler you can hear when he calls out his wares in the street. He sells trinkets. Occasionally, he swindles a few people, and he is swindled from time to time. At night he goes home bringing food for his children, and sleeps beside his neighbors. He lives in the depths of reality. For him, life is about washing a dish. About being a small shopkeeper, or working for a pittance. It's all those things that are worth living for. That's all.

SIX

IN THE SPECULUM
OF THE OTHER:
THE FEMININE FIGURE OF
MODERNITY

Iran was ushered into modernity with a bang. After the two successive Russian defeats of the Qajars that resulted in massive territorial losses and the two humiliating treaties of Golestan in 1813 and Turkmanchai in 1828, two facts were simultaneously evident: Iran was in the full grip of colonial powers, and the medieval Qajar polity could no longer resist their encroachment. On the premise of this political predicament, throughout the nineteenth century, a succession of infrastructural developments and institutional changes prepared the Iranian people for their fateful confrontation with modernity. Chief among these were the dispatch of a number of Iranian students to Europe by Abbas Mirza early in the nineteenth century, the introduction of the printing press, the radical simplification of Persian prose, an extensive translation project from European sources, publication of the first newspapers, and the formation of voluntary cultural associations.

Upon the success of these groundbreaking initiatives, we witness the gradual formation of various forms of resistance to the onslaught of colonialism and its categorical denial of historical agency to the Iranian subject. These modes of resistance were instrumental in restoring an active historical agency to the Iranian subject. Had it not been for these forms of resistance, the Iranian subject would have been either historically denied or colonially modulated. Iranians, like most other people at the receiving end of capitalist modernity, confronted European culture through the gun barrel of colonialism. Had Iranians been left in their colonialist predicament, they would have had no choice but to retreat to a fictive "tradition" created as a shield from the colonially militated "modernity" they faced, or "become Western from head to toe," as one reformist particularly enamored of "the West" had suggested. These modes of resistance emerged as the sites of the assertive cultivation of a restored Iranian subject, and the retrieval of historical agency.

By far the most influential form of resistance from the earliest moments of the encounter with colonialism was the emergence of a powerful narrative of *social criticism*, which was the defining moment of Persian cultural production throughout the nineteenth century. From Mirza Saleh Shirazi's *Safar-Nameh* ("*Travelogue*," 1819) to Haj Zeyn al-Abedyn Maraghe'i's *Siyahat-Nameh ye Ebrahim Beik* ("*The Travelogue of Ebrahim Beik*," 1894), an avalanche of critical treatises mapped the contour of constitutional changes in the history of the Iranian encounter with modernity. The critical treatises of Mirza Fath Ali Akhondzadeh (d. 1878) and Mirza Aqa Khan Kermani (d. 1895) were chief among these social critiques. The principal function of these treatises was to slap Iranian political culture out of its feudal slumber. These treatises were in effect the growing pains of a new body politic.

In the wake of the constitutional revolution of 1906–11, *poetry* expanded into a labyrinth of creative insurrection. It is impossible to exaggerate the critical significance of the kaleidoscope of modernist poets who revolutionized the Persian imagination. Taqi Raf'at (1889–1920), Mirzadeh Eshqi (1894–1924), Iraj Mirza (1874–1926), Aref Qazvini (1882–1934), Malek al-Sho'ara Bahar (1887–1951), Ali Akbar Dehkhoda (1880–1955), and Abolqasem Lahuti (1887–1957) are chief among the revolutionary nationalist poets who effectively gave birth to the very idea of *Iran* as a creative and critical source of collective consciousness. From the dawn of the constitutionalist movement in the first decade of the twentieth century forward, Persian poetry was the principal cultural medium through which the hopes and aspirations of a newborn nation were creatively constituted.

It is not until well into the 1930s that modern Persian *fiction* surfaces as the next focal point of Iranian cultural modernity. Although the publication of Mohammad Ali Jamalzadeh's *Yeki Bud Yeki Nabud* ("*Once upon a Time*") in 1921 is generally considered the commencement of modern Persian fiction, and although the beginning of modern creative prose in Persian can even be traced back to the nineteenth century, it is not really until the appearance of Sadeq Hedayat (1902–1951) and particularly the publication of his *Buf-e Kur* ("*The Blind Owl*") in 1937 that we can seriously talk about a modernist movement in Persian literature. If the "constitutional" poetry of the 1900s to the 1930s marked the birth of the very idea of Iran as a creative source of a collective consciousness, Persian fiction of the 1930s through the 1960s maps and surveys its topography. It is impossible to imagine the restoration of historical agency to the Iranian subject without these two groundbreaking developments.

From the 1930s onward, modernist Persian poetry and prose were the twin peaks of cultural confrontation with a rapidly changing reality. While in the first three decades of the twentieth century *poetry* was the sole defining moment of Iranian cultural modernity, during the next three decades, from the 1930s to the 1960s, Persian *fiction* secured an equally illustrious position. From Nima Yushij (d. 1959) to Sohrab Sepehri (d. 1980), a monumental revolution took place in Persian poetry in the first half of the century, and from Sadeq Hedayat (d. 1951) to Houshang Golshiri (d. 2000) an equally important spectrum of creative fiction coalesced.

It is only during the 1960s that *cinema* rises as the third, equally important, form of cultural creativity. Although the origins of Iranian cinema stem from the earliest decades of the twentieth century, it was not until Daryush Mehrju'i's *The Cow* in 1969 that Iranian cinema became a contender in the definition of cultural creativity. There are obvious antecedents of Mehrju'i's masterpiece, such as Farrokh Ghaffari's *The Night of the Hunchback* (1964), but it is with *The Cow* that Iranian cinema could stand on its own and demand to be taken seriously. Although late in joining forces in the battle to garner a sense of national dignity for the Iranian subject, the contribution of Iranian cinema has been trans-substantial and qualitative. Inherently verbal and audile, Iranian culture has had a blind spot in its creative constitution. The function of Iranian cinema, which is predicated on an array of medieval and modern visual and performing arts, has been to restore the vision to that verbality. It is thus quite critical to note that the first serious Iranian film, Mehrju'i's *The Cow*, is the cinematic adaptation of a story from one of the masterpieces of modern Persian fiction, Gholamhossein Sa'edi's *Azadaran-e Bayal* ("*The Mourners of Bayal*," 1964).

Something utterly strange happens after the Islamic revolution of 1979, and it will be some time before Iranian cultural critics will be able to account for it. While prominent poets like Shamlu (d. 2000) and writers of fiction like Golshiri (d. 2000) were still active, both poetry and fiction lost their significance after the Islamic revolution, and effectively relayed all their creative energy and prominence to cinema. After its auspicious commencement in the 1960s, Iranian cinema has never slackened in momentum; it has taken full advantage of the other two creative modes, weathered a revolution and a catastrophic war, and yet emerged stronger than ever, not only to be *the* defining moment of Iranian cultural modernity but also to capture a global audience. What has happened during the last two decades of the twentieth century when Persian poetry and fiction effectively yielded their creative effervescence to Iranian cinema, and what the creative consequences of this development would be for the future of the Iranian subject, are very much tied to yet another twist of this extraordinary tale.

SUCCESSIVE SITES OF RESISTANCE

By far the most critical aspect of the long history of Iranian cultural modernity is that its principal architects have been men. The masculine nature of the Iranian encounter with modernity is impossible to disregard. But to the rule of that masculinity there are crucial feminine exceptions, which ought to be taken equally seriously. Unless we view this rule and its exceptions in each other's speculum, we will mistake the true texture of Iranian cultural modernity.

To begin to see and read that texture, we must begin in the middle of the nineteenth century when Iran was facing the full force of colonialism. The Babi revolutionary movement marks the last premodern social insurrection of the century, and it is in this context that the spectacular figure of Tahereh Qorrat al-Ayn shines like a brilliant star. Fatemeh Beygum Baraghani, honorifically called Tahereh Qorrat al-Ayn (1814–1852), appeared like a comet and advanced the revolutionary cause by measures and modes far beyond anything achieved before or since. Deeply cultivated, and a poet of an exceptional versatility, the critical cast of her intelligence staggered the leading revolutionary figures of the Babi movement, who gave her the honorific titles of "Solace of the Eyes" (Qorrat al-Ayn) and "Pure" (Tahereh). She was a radical theorist of monumental talent, morally courageous and a revolutionary strategist of uncommon brilliance. "Radical in her interpretations of Babism," one historian of the period reports, "Her assumption of leadership split the Babi community in Karbala between the more conservative Babis and her own circle of devotees."[1] Tahereh Qorrat al-Ayn led a radical faction of the Babi movement in Iran and Iraq and helped her comrades to rattle the foundations of the Qajar dynasty to the bone. Her radical ideas ultimately resulted in her "being expelled from Iraq by the Ottoman authorities after sparking off disturbances in Karbala by her unorthodox and challenging behavior."[2]

Tahereh Qorrat al-Ayn's moral courage matched her political audacity. In the course of her insurrectionary career she refused "to have any dealings with her husband," because "cohabitation with her unbelieving husband was no longer possible." Of course, this aroused "the enmity of non-Babis and controversy with Qurratu'l-'Ayn's more cautious co-religionists."[3] Qorrat al-Ayn "defied and scandalized social convention with the freedom with which she spoke and traveled."[4] But that was not all: she found the practice of veiling unnecessary, and at a public gathering she suddenly unveiled. Even that was not enough. Separated but not divorced, she openly lived with her revolutionary comrade Molla Mohammad Ali Barforush, known as Qoddus.

As a result of her subversive activities, Qorrat al-Ayn was executed in 1852. The effective presence of a feminine character at the dawn of the Iranian encounter with modernity thus begins with the figure of a revolutionary whose poetic talent and cultivation matched her political acumen. Qorrat al-Ayn was audacious and imaginative in both her poetry and her political actions, one feeding on the other.

While Tahereh Qorrat al-Ayn is a heroic figure of the Babi movement, the last premodern revolutionary uprising, there are two far less illustrious, yet still extraordinarily critical, female figures whom we encounter in the course of the ideological foregrounding of the constitutional revolution of 1906–11, the first large-scale insurrectionary encounter with modernity. Both Bibi Khanom Astarabadi and Taj al-Saltaneh were members of Qajar aristocratic families who broke rank with their class and wrote valiantly on behalf of women's rights. They both used the dominant genre of the critical treatise as their mode of social criticism.

Bibi Khanom Astarabadi wrote her *Ma'ayeb al-Rejal* ("*The Vices of Men*") in 1895 and published it a year later in Tehran in the heat of ideological preparation leading up to the constitutional revolution. The book is ostensibly a polemic against an anonymous misogynous tract, *Ta'dib al-Niswan* ("*On the Admonition of Women*"), published in 1880.[5] Reminiscent of Christine de Pizan's *The Book of the City of Ladies* (1405) and Mary Wollstonecraft's *A Vindication of the Rights of Women* (1792), Astarabadi's *The Vices of Men* is a scathing attack on the arbitrary rule of men in family life and the abuse to which they subject their spouses. With a great sense of humor and remarkable literary prowess, Bibi Khanom Astarabadi unleashed a biting criticism of the behavior of men and held up a full-size mirror before them. *The Vices of Men* is a rare and priceless account of the patriarchal traits endemic in Iranian culture, examined with a piercing intelligence. Bibi Khanom Astarabadi is no Tahereh Qorrat al-Ayn, and there is not a trace of revolutionary zeal about her, and yet she was totally aware of not only the responsibilities but also the rights of women. "Certainly, certainly," she exhorted women, "try to emancipate yourself as soon as possible. Before you know it you are old and surrounded by children."[6]

Almost two decades after the publication of Bibi Khanom Astarabadi's *The Vices of Men*, another Qajar princess wrote an equally astute reflection on the status of women in her homeland. Taj al-Saltaneh's *Memoir* was written in 1914 while Iran was in the heat of constitutional fever, and her reaction to the idea of the constitution reveals the vision of a future in which women will have a share.[7] In response to a questionnaire sent to her by an Armenian from Caucasia, she wrote:

> The restitution of its people's rights is the duty of every progressive nation. When can it have its rights restored? When the country functions under constitutionalism and a proper system. What brings forth progress? The rule of law. And when are laws implemented? When despotism is overthrown. Therefore, we see from this that constitutionalism is preferable to despotism.[8]

If Tahereh Qorrat al-Ayn established a feminine *presence* in the Iranian polity during the course of her revolutionary activities in the middle of the nineteenth century, and Bibi Khanom Astarabadi gave that presence an eloquent and critical *voice*, Taj al-Saltaneh's *Memoirs* expressed a feminine *vision* of Iran in modernity.

Thus, when, after one hundred years of struggle against colonial aggression, under the corrupt and incompetent Qajar rule, Iran entered the twentieth century, the country had been strengthened by successive insurrectionary movements and a liberating discourse of resistance, principally in the form of social criticism. Together, Tahereh Qorrat al-Ayn, Bibi Khanom Astarabadi, and Taj al-Saltaneh had given presence, voice, and vision in an active feminine participation in this encounter with modernity. The towering figure of Tahereh Qorrat al-Ayn showed the dual aspect of that feminine character, at once poetic and political, imaginative and pragmatic, dreaming of an alternative and acting out its interpretation.

As constitutional poetry gained momentum at the beginning of the nineteenth century, amidst a legion of men poetically imagining the new nation, one feminine voice was heard, that of Shams Kasma'i (d. 1961). The singular distinction of breaking the tyranny of classical Persian prosody once and for all would remain for Nima Yushij to claim, but it was Shams Kasma'i who for the first time composed poems in free verse. At a time when Mirzadeh Eshqi (1894–1924), Iraj Mirza (1874–1926), Aref Qazvini (1882–1934), Malek al-Sho'ara Bahar (1887–1951), Ali Akbar Dehkhoda (1880–1955), and Abolqasem Lahuti (1887–1957)—a rainbow of revolutionary poets—were at the center of a poetic uprising,[9] it was the singular voice of Shams Kasma'i that began to conceive of freedom from Persian prosody. Shams Kasma'i "is one of the earliest Iranian women to use the composition of modernist poetry as a means of personal expression."[10] She was a talented, multilingual, and courageous woman. "When she came to Tabriz with her family, she did not wear the *chador*, and was the first Iranian woman to appear unveiled in the streets and bazaars of Tabriz. For this very reason she suffered much at the hands of ignorant people. [Nevertheless] in Tabriz, her home was the gathering place of writers and other learned men."[11] As early as 1920, she composed and published free verse in the leading literary journal of her time, *Azadistan*.[12]

What Shams Kasma'i achieved with her unprecedented daring imagination was to break the poetic tyranny of Persian prosody, which had so rigidly limited the creative boundaries of Persian poetry that monumentally talented poets never even thought of defying it. Kasma'i's creative courage wedded the critical intelligence of her age with the emancipating forces of poetry and cut a creative aqueduct from the political drives of her turbulent time into the poetic needs of her nation's language. This creative conduit was by far the most transgressive act of poetic rebellion and had palpable political implications. The corrective aesthetic curve that Kasma'i gave to the constitutional formation of the prosaic idea of Iran as a nation was to have an enduring effect throughout the Iranian encounter with modernity. She gave a poetic depth to the flat political masculinity of the nation and put a paternal speculum in front of its face. In siding with the poetic to correct the political, Kasma'i was in judicious resonance with Tahereh Qorrat al-Ayn's tilting toward the poetic side of her politics.

The transgressive move of Shams Kasma'i in daring to imagine Persian poetry otherwise and compose free verse, which was the poetic equivalent of going out in public unveiled, was the final preparatory step towards the creation of the Iranian feminine subject by one of the most gifted poets of the twentieth century, Parvin E'tesami (d. 1941). Parvin E'tesami's principal achievement in this crescendo building to historical agency was to evidence the creation of poetic consciousness by a woman. Her poetry came to full fruition during the first three decades of the twentieth century. She was a contemporary of Shams Kasma'i but did not follow her example of revolt against the tyrannical prosody, though no doubt she was aware of this defiance. Instead, what Parvin E'tesami achieved was to bring the whole spectrum of creative outbursts from Tahereh Qorrat al-Ayn, through Bibi Khanom Astarabadi, Taj al-Saltaneh, and Shams Kasma'i to a solid formation of the feminine subject: fully active, vocal, visible, and insurrectionary in its moral disposition.

The publication of *The Blind Owl* in 1937 by Sadeq Hedayat marked the birth of modern Persian fiction, and the publication of *Savushun* in 1969 by Simin Daneshvar gave that fiction its enduring feminine perspective. In *Savushun*, Simin Daneshvar takes a clear, perceptive, and confident stand, and in the central character of Zari gives panoramic expression to one of the most enduring feminine characters in modern fiction. *Savushun* is set in Shiraz during the Allied occupation of Iran in World War II. The central character of the novel is Zari, a woman devoted to her husband and children, who maintains a simulacrum of order in her home as her husband is increasingly drawn into the political chaos around him. By far the most significant aspect of *Savushun* is the confidence with which Simin Daneshvar crafts the universe of Zari's imagination. Never before had a feminine character been given such a towering presence in a modern work of art in Persian.

By the time of Parvin E'tesami's death in 1941, the historical memory vested in the constitution of the feminine subject stretched from the inaugural moment of Tahereh Qorrat al-Ayn to the subversive creativity of Shams Kasma'i. A fully active, vocal, visible, and insurrectionary historical agency was thus prepared and available to Simin Daneshvar when she created Zari as the central character of *Savushun*. Daneshvar inoculated the shape and dimension of that agency and the flat platitude of the singularly patriarchal, at times even misogynous, topography of the Iranian subject became narratively pregnant. Without her intervention, the Iranian subject would of course have flourished on the solid ground of the creative consciousness that Nimaic poetry had given it and thrived on the rich soil of Hedayat's fiction. But the fruit of that historical agency would have never ripened to perfection had it not been for its necessary feminine component.

Groundbreaking as these developments were, something far more radical took place in the 1960s that would forever cast the character of the Iranian feminine subject in the frame of defiance. The modernist poetic diction that had taken root in the first three decades of the twentieth century bloomed in the following three. It claimed Parvin E'tesami as its crowning achievement, and moved full throttle into the 1960s. By then modernist Persian poetry had six decades of effervescent impetus expanding its creative boundaries into one of the most aggressive determining forces of the Iranian subject. From Nima Yushij to Ahmad Shamlu, Mehdi Akhavan Sales, and Sohrab Sepehri, we witness the critical constitution of the Iranian subject, fully alerted to its historical agency. It is impossible to exaggerate the significance of the 1960s, a decade in which the celebrated memory of Nima Yushij was reflected in the poetry of Akhavan Sales, Shamlu, and Sepehri. These poets were the visionary theorists of Iranian modernity freed from its colonially militated reception. It was possible, and that possibility was actively materialized, to be born in this poetry with a singularly self-confident historical agency and no false dichotomy between so-called "tradition" and "modernity." In an enduring act of creative imagination, this poetry gave birth to the Iranian subject and made possible a historical agent.

However, this birth was conceived and delivered only by men. How can one sufficiently acknowledge Forough Farrokhzad and what she achieved in a career that lasted only from 1955, with the publication of her first collection of poetry, until her tragic and untimely death in 1967? She was in poetic rebellion what

Tahereh Qorrat al-Ayn was in revolution. She delivered Iranian women to her confident place in modernity. A political pregnancy that began with Tahereh Qorrat al-Ayn in the middle of the nineteenth century came to full, fruitful delivery almost a hundred years later in Farrokhzad. Without her, a century of creative effervescence would not have sublated into full historical agency. She was the daughter that Qorrat al-Ayn had conceived in the speculum of her insurrectionary imagination, a conception at once out of wedlock *and* immaculate.

It is not just the formation of a feminine subject that Forough Farrokhzad delivered but the completion of a dialectic constitution of the subject as such, both masculine and feminine, that would not have coalesced had it not been for her poetry. She resolved not just the *feminine* subjectivity to modernity but the *Iranian* to history. Without Farrokhzad's poetry something far more important than the historical agency of Iranian women would have remained in a state of expectation. There was something lacking in some two hundred years of creative struggle to render the Iranian subject independent of colonially militated modernity. Farrokhzad was the "other" of the Iranian "same," so far as it was formed as a site of creative resistance to colonialism. We can thus categorically state that it is only after and in Farrokhzad's self-assuredly feminine poetry that the Iranian subject was born and fully bred in a creative modernity in opposition to and defiance of the one that was colonially constituted.

From the 1960s, Iranian cinema joined poetry and fiction in this collective creative constitution of the Iranian subject and its restoration of agency. On the premise of a few earlier works, such as Farrokh Ghaffari's *Downtown* (1958) and *The Night of the Hunchback* (1964), Ebrahim Golestan's *The Brick and The Mirror* (1965), Fereydun Rahnema's *Seyavash in Persepolis* (1967), and Daryush Mehrju'i's *The Cow* (1969) finally brought to Iranian cinema a critical distinction, with enduring consequences for the fate of cultural modernity in Iran.

Was it an auspicious accident or by deliberate design that the brilliant film inaugurating contemporary Iranian cinema was by a woman poet, in fact *the* poet of her time. Forough Farrokhzad's *Khaneh Siyah Ast* ("The House Is Black," 1962) precedes and surpasses anything that happened in her age. In this documentary about a leper colony, Farrokhzad gracefully narrates one of the most beautiful treatments of a horrific disease. Why leprosy? In less than twenty minutes, Farrokhzad detects and unveils the poetic souls hidden inside these ravaged bodies and does so with a quiet elegance that has never been matched. It would be long before Iranian cinema had another woman at the helm of its visionary imagination, but with *The House Is Black* Farrokhzad set the stage.

IN THE CURVATURE OF THE SPECULUM

By the time Rakhshan Bani-Etemad stood behind the camera to make her first documentary, *Farhang-e Masrafi* ("*The Culture of Consumption,*" 1984), the feminine voice and vision constitutional to Iranian cultural modernity was well in place and at her disposal.

If Kiarostami and Makhmalbaf's cinema are two visual modes of rereading Iranian culture in order to tease out its virtuality and thus negotiate a creative emancipation from it, the cinema of Bani-Etemad is a visual assault on that culture's Achilles' heel, namely, its conception of femininity. Nothing better holds and conceals the symbolic force of Iranian culture more than this metaphysical violence. Her work has a much wider spectrum of implications than the condition of Iranian women. What is at stake in her project is the constitution of femininity as the weakest and most vulnerable point of a much wider pathology of power, culturally constituted, socially institutionalized, economically based, and metaphysically theorized. Bani-Etemad's cinema is a visual theorization against that violent metaphysics.

The difference between Bani-Etemad's realism and that of Kiarostami and Makhmalbaf is that her subversive jolting of sexuality is something exclusive to her cinema, an extraordinarily powerful component almost pathologically absent from the work of those two great male colleagues. Her realism is of an entirely different sort than Kiarostami and Makhmalbaf's. She is not trying to tease any *virtuality* out of reality. She wants to overemphasize its *actuality*. It is only after observing Bani-Etemad's realism closely that we notice that Kiarostami and Makhmalbaf share this optimistic design of remodulating the real. Bani-Etemad harbors no such illusions and opts for an entirely different perspective. By putting her documentary social realism squarely at the service of a morally destabilizing confrontation with sexuality she attacks from an angle that is, we suddenly realize, almost completely absent in those two great male filmmakers.

Bani-Etemad's reconstitution of feminine sexuality is not done via a shallow feminism. Unlike generations of a supercilious middle-class feminism,[13] she wages a war on patriarchal readings of the body so powerful that no other visual theorist comes close. The key to her dismantling of patriarchally constituted femininity is a detailed reading of the Iranian working class, the material evidence of her realism. She then turns her documentary camera to the most subversive destruction of the patriarchal constitution of culture. From Tahereh Qorrat al-Ayn to Forough Farrokhzad, material evidence has been cast into a categorical reconstitution of the Iranian subject. Bani-Etemad's reconstitution of femininity against the grain of the metaphysical violence perpetrated against it is critical for the final delivery of the Iranian subject from its patriarchal entrapment. Unless we understand Bani-Etemad's cinema, which means rescuing her vision from her culturally blinded audience at home and abroad, we will never understand the long and arduous road that Iranian creative resistance to colonialism has traversed, leading, as it does in Bani-Etemad's cinema, to a fully integrated and complete historical agency, defiant and affirmative in its rebellion against both the patriarchally constituted femininity and the colonially militated subject.

To see Bani-Etemad's work in full gear, we should concentrate on her three successive moves in *Narges* (1991), *The Blue-Veiled* (1994), and *The May Lady* (1998), and then rest our case with *Baran and the Native* (1999).[14] But before we do that, we need to address a critical aspect of Bani-Etemad's cinema: the link between her documentary and her feature films, a significant aspect of her career.

DETERRITORIALIZING THE IRANIAN SUBJECT

Rakhshan Bani-Etemad is the beneficiary of all that has happened in the history of Iranian cultural modernity. The commencement of her career as a documentary filmmaker reflects the rise of social criticism as the singular narrative of resistance from the mid nineteenth century onward. In this, she carries the historical recollection of Tahereh Qorrat al-Ayn, Bibi Khanom Astarabadi, and Taj al-Saltaneh in her critical memory. She brings all these scattered elements to cohesion in her later films. Her career began with a staccato of social documentaries and culminated in a succession of feature films.

Since 1984, Bani-Etemad has made a series of documentaries that are critical commentaries on social malaise. She has focused on the plight of social pariahs, the collateral damage of the material changes at the core of her society. *Farhang-e Masrafi* (*"The Culture of Consumption,"* 1984) is an examination of rapid urbanization in the absence of productive forces and of those completely lost in consumption. *Eshteghal-e Mohajerin Rustay'i dar Shahr* (*"Occupations of Migrant Peasants in the City,"* 1985) examines urban population growth, the destruction of the agricultural economy, and the catastrophic consequences of labor migration. *Tadbirhaye Eghtesadi-e Jang* (*"The War Economic Planning,"* 1986) traces similar problems in the context of the Iran–Iraq war (1980–88). *Tamarkoz* (*"Centralization,"* 1979) is a critical commentary on the nature and disposition of bureaucratic centralization. *Gozaresh-e 71* (*"The 1992 Report,"* 1992), *Bahar ta Bahar* (*"Spring to Spring,"* 1993), and *In film ha ra beh ki neshun midin?* (*"To Whom Do You Show These Films, Anyway?"* 1993) constitute a documentary trilogy on the Fatemiyyeh neighborhood, illustrating one of the most devastating consequences of rapid urbanization and the staggering state of urban poverty. *Akharin Didar Ba Iran Daftari* (*"The Last Visit with Iran Daftari,"* 1995) is a loving tribute to the veteran Iranian actor, Iran Daftari. *Zir-e Pust-e Shahr* (*"Under the Skin of the City,"* 1996)[15] is an exposé of drug addiction among the youth in the heart of the Islamic Republic.

Bani-Etemad's creative vision is poised outside the territorial boundaries of her society, documenting the plight of the outcast, the derelict, the vagrant, the downtrodden, and the forgotten. Her attention to the excluded side of the civic center—the poor, the afflicted, the jobless, and the drug addicts—circulates around the territory in which the moral measures of society are constituted. By going "off limits," as the title of one of her earliest documentary-based features suggests, she defines those limits, reminding us that the deliberate amnesia of the material is the epistemic foregrounding of the dominating domain of the moral. Her social documentaries are a checklist of our forgotten material memories. She brings them to the forefront of our attention, reminding us what we have deliberately forgotten in order to make the moral possible.

In her earliest experiments with feature films, Bani-Etemad extended her documentary angle on social issues. *Kharej az Mahdudeh* ("*Off Limits*," 1987) is a satirical commentary on municipal bureaucracy. In *Zard-e Qanari* ("*Canary Yellow*," 1988), Bani-Etemad explores the nature of labor migration between the rural and urban areas. *Pul-e Khareji* ("*Foreign Currency*," 1989) brings into full view the disorienting paralysis of postrevolutionary inflation, the fixation on foreign currency, and the schizophrenic confusion of reality and fantasy which results. These are transitional films, in which the moral and the material begin to inform each other, and in which Bani-Etemad begins to be confident in her critical use of the camera. *Off Limits*, *Canary Yellow*, and *Foreign Currency* are all comedies. "Do not think that one has to be sad," she would have agreed, "in order to be militant, even though the thing one is fighting is abominable."[16]

Bani-Etemad's creativity culminated in her most accomplished feature film, *Nargess*, in 1991. But in the fate of Morteza Olfat, the protagonist of *Foreign Currency* (made about two years earlier), is a very crucial link between Bani-Etemad's documentary and her feature films that allows us to grasp the singular vision which distinguishes her cinema. Like millions of others, Morteza Olfat is a wretched bureaucrat trying to make ends meet in a highly inflationary economy. He stumbles upon a stash of fifty thousand dollars smack in the center of Tehran. This is the commencement of the calamity that ultimately leads him to an asylum. Confusion inundates this film, and we never know whether this fifty thousand dollars is real or just a figment of Olfat's perturbed imagination.

When we compare Bani-Etemad's documentary and feature films, we perceive the remarkable way in which she balances the moral and the material aspects of her society against each other. Bani-Etemad inches toward a persistent re-imagining of the moral. Her initial attraction to societal peripheries, the down-trodden and the forgotten, circumambulates and thus locates the center and reveals its territoriality, and the fact that we have deliberately opted to live and locate it as the territory of our moral imagination. Bani-Etemad exposes the concocted nature of that territoriality. In awakening our conscience, she alerts us to its insidious tendency to fall asleep. The same strategy is evident when in her early comedy features she begins to juxtapose the serious and the frivolous. In her last comedy before *Nargess*, she delivers what she had promised and with surgical precision grafts the schizoid element of Olfat into the Oedipal order of the familial ordinary.

Bani-Etemad's films, documentary and feature, are a singular reminder of the material brutality of the present, a brutality which is violently suppressed in order to make our morality possible. In effect, Bani-Etemad's cinema is the return of the Iranian repressed. To dismantle the power bases of the dominant morality, she exposes the material misery of the dominated, a misery that has to be collectively denied in order for that collective amnesia to begin to authorize itself. Her strategy of emancipation thus works from the bottom up, from the suppressed material toward the celebrated moral, from the active forgetting of material misery toward the passive remembering of a moral superiority. By exposing the denied material, Bani-Etemad dismantles the acknowledged morality. To attack the moral jugular, she takes an ax to the material base. By exposing the denied and concealed material that the dominant morality must suppress, she aims high at the narrative visualization of the alternative.

Bani-Etemad detects the breaking point of the dominant morality. First, it sweeps under the carpet of denial the material misery on which it stands; second, it normalizes its materially based morality by an aggressive act of Oedipalization. The mommy-daddy-baby triumvirate triumphs, the organic body is constituted, and the presumption of the Oedipal complex sets the family unit on an economically productive course compatible with capitalism and the instrumentality of its reason. Bani-Etemad's creative impulses aim at precisely these concealed blind spots, exposing the denied material misery in her documentaries and jolting the morality that has to deny that material basis in her feature films. Of course, Bani-Etemad's critics have so far carefully noted the peculiarly creative nature of her documentaries and the documentary nature of her feature films. But they have failed to see the thematic cohesion of the two as a unique exposure of the link between capitalism and Oedipalization. Bani-Etemad's critique of the catastrophic consequences of the reign of capital in her documentaries throws a schizoid monkey wrench at the normalizing of Oedipalization, while her dismantling of the bourgeois morality is based on blasting open its concealed and denied material misery. This strategic double bind collapses the very foundation of bourgeois modernity.

Bani-Etemad's cinema is at once diagnostic and emancipatory, critical and creative. By exposing the material misery in her documentaries, she dismantles the metaphysical authority of the morality that has to authenticate itself by denying its basis, and then jolts the sexual blind spot of the dominant morality. We are thus cured of both the historical amnesia of the material misery and of the Oedipalization of the psyche that instrumentalizes our historical agency. No other filmmaker has dared imagine the Iranian subject so radically otherwise, so constitutionally emancipated, from the external tyrannies of the Traditional and the internal imperialism of the Oedipal. Against generations of "territorialization," in Deleuze and Guattari's term, of the colonized body and the desubjected psyche, Bani-Etemad's films, both documentary and feature, are a defiant act of deterritorialization. From the individual to the family, religion to nation, each is now exposed in its inherently fascist collaboration between the suppression of the material misery and the constitution of a morality on the basis of that cultural amnesia.

A THREESOME ARRANGEMENT

In her daring depiction of a *ménage-à-trois* in *Nargess* (1991), Bani-Etemad reconstitutes the very nature and disposition of sexuality. The love affair between the young thief, Adel, and his visibly older lover, Afagh, is narrated with such dark and passionate intensity that with this single stroke Bani-Etemad counters generations of both the over- and the desexualization of women in Iranian cinema. Between the paralyzing chastity of the ever-virgin, would-be bride, and the pathological investment of all promiscuous sexuality in the whore—two staples of the *Film jaheli* genre, those of Kimiya'i in particular—Bani-Etemad introduces the character of Afagh. Afagh is fully self-aware and confident in her sexuality, without ever being either frivolous or prudish. She has a quiet dignity, a subdued awareness, and a factual realism. Next to Afagh's rugged but assertive dignity, Adel is reduced to an emotional wreck, his dull sexuality contingent on Afagh's generosity. What is successfully shattered and dissolved by Bani-Etemad's confident camera is the presumption of the primacy of masculine sexuality. Afagh is in fact at the center of both the sexual and the textual tension of *Nargess*. Bani-Etemad achieves this reversal of the primacy of masculine sexuality despite the fact that it is Afagh who is being abandoned by Adel for a younger and more "respectable" woman. While steadfastly maintaining her sense of

In this dark portrayal of an older woman in love with a younger man, Bani-Etemad tells the story of a *menage-à-trois* with haunting precision. *Nargess* confirmed Bani-Etemad as the most piercing feminine vision of her generation

realism, Bani-Etemad both sexually and narratively holds Afagh at the center of events. *Nargess* is characterized by a powerful erotic tension although there is (for obvious reasons of censorship) not a single explicit sex scene in the film.

Bani-Etemad constructs Afagh from the very heart of the Iranian underclass. She is a professional thief who has employed Adel as both her accomplice and her lover. She is a moral pariah, a social outcast, a renegade from the culturally con-stituted norms of respectability. By dwelling on Afagh and all her moral indices of rejection, Bani-Etemad approaches her society from an oblique angle that exposes its anxieties. The constellation of all these transgressive elements in a woman strips the culture naked. But that is not all. Bani-Etemad restores dignity to Afagh and all that she represents: she is by far the most powerful character of the story. In comparison to Afagh, her lover Adel is unstable, childish, and dull in his pathetic attempt to attain what he considers to be a more "respectable" life. The more he is drawn to "respectability," the more indecent he appears and the nobler Afagh. If we recall the year of this film's release, 1991, a decade into one of the most brutal theocracies in history, the minutiae of its medieval morality and puritanical ethics fixed in statute law, we may grasp the significance of *Nargess*.

To see how Afagh is central to the sexual tension in *Nargess*, let us examine the moment when she volunteers to ask for the hand of Nargess for her lover Adel. This single move dismantles the patriarchally constituted roles of both men and women and the relationship of power they entail. Afagh suffers all the miserable consequences of having facilitated the marriage of her lover to a younger woman. But the dark entanglement of suffering emphasizes her presence at the very heart of the narrative as the defining catalyst of sexuality, shattering all the myths of feminine passivity. As such, she is the acid test of a whole reconstitution of gender and sexuality, challenging the holy trinity of mommy-daddy-baby. Conspicuously absent from the triangle of Afagh, Adel, and Nargess is a child. The de facto identification of the nuclear family as the coagulated institution of patriarchy leads to the preliminary move to disentangle the moment of the Oedipal crisis. The triangle of the two women and one man is blatantly marginal in society, in the realm of social rejection and abject poverty. This narrative simplicity, which on the surface just creates more room for dramatic tension, does something far more crucial: it traces the patriarchal order to its primal moments with a dangerously transgressive urge. The strategy is directly anti-Oedipal because here all we see are a woman/mother and a man/son experiencing strictly instinctual, transgressive, raptures. In the presence of Afagh, Adel is triumphantly de-Oedipalized, conquers his absent father by having his mother, and with him the entire constructed history of gender constitution is vicariously de-Oedipalized. What makes this rather revolutionary counter-subjection of both the masculine and the feminine possible is Bani-Etemad's dedication to factual realism. With a transgressive urge rarely seen in any other Iranian artist,

Bani-Etemad transforms the sexual encounter between Afagh and Adel into a radical dismantling of the Oedipal and an equally radical critique of the economic foregrounding of Oedipalization.

Bani-Etemad's de-Oedipalization of the nuclear family and the culture it reflects is achieved not by the mere visual evidence of the absence of a child in the mommy-daddy-baby triumvirate.[17] The substituted triangle at the center of *Nargess* is completely unproductive, negating the very productive logic of capitalism that legitimates and substantiates the Oedipal constitution of the nuclear family. The *ménage-à-trois* at the center of *Nargess* is almost rhetorically unproductive, as the two thieves, Adel and Afagh, incorporate Nargess into a triangle that is peripheral to the instrumental rationalism of capitalist modernity that disenfranchises them. As character types—the root of Bani-Etemad's sexual psychoanalysis being predicated in her sociological realism—the three figures arise out of the material evidence of her documentary films. As a documentary filmmaker, Bani-Etemad has gone deeply into the predicament of the urban poor and the social pariah. In *Nargess*, she draws from the material evidence of that record to create counterproductive forces that, in their triangulated simulacrum of the bourgeois Holy Family, in effect negate both capitalism *and* its material production of the Oedipal. She borrows from the material evidence of the catastrophes of capitalism in order to deconstruct the cultural constitution of the family as the social nucleus of that inevitable conclusion.

Barring the moment of Oedipalization, *Nargess* is the site of the dismantling of what Deleuze and Guattari have called "the imperialism of the Oedipal."[18] "Oedipus restrained," Deleuze and Guattari assert, "is the figure of daddy-mommy-me triangle, the familial constellation in person."[19] Bani-Etemad breaks that triangle by replacing it with a far more real coagulation, drawn from her already extraordinary career as a documentary filmmaker. The *ménage-à-trois*, here, replacing what Deleuze and Guattari call the Holy Family, comprises a thief, his older lover, and his younger wife. By breaking the implications of all those possessive adjectives, Bani-Etemad launches her destruction of the patriarchal constitution of sexuality from the depth of her documented reading of Iranian society, intending nothing short of the total dismantling of the empire of Oedipus and the tyranny of Oedipalized psychosis. The result is a cinematic cosmovision that renegotiates the whole colonially militated culture of capitalist

The final scene of *Nargess* in a suburb of Tehran put the director and her entire camera crew in danger of being run over by a truck

modernity and its colonial consequences. The imposing edifice of patriarchal order, from its symbolic ordering of the culture to its metaphysical transparency, is thereby visually desubjected by dwarfing the figure of the father by the overwhelming logic of capitalism and its catastrophes.

Disentangling the Oedipal by dismantling the Holy Family is done through Bani-Etemad's unrelentingly realistic gaze. She does not *invent* that revolutionary dismantling via an ideological manifesto, a fact that many of her Iranian critics have failed to understand, and as a result have accused her of antifeminism. She proclaims this dismantling through her firm attachment to the factual realism of her camera. It is the poverty and misery of Afagh and Adel that bring them together, their being socially rejected, financially disadvantaged, culturally demonized, and, more than anything else, economically unproductive. And it is because of Adel's pathetic attempt to become socially mobile by marrying a "respectable" young woman that they are separated. That is not a revolutionary manifesto, but a piece of brutal realism that Bani-Etemad confidently, through the experience of decades of involvement with the plight of the poor and the disenfranchised, has achieved. The kind of hope that Bani-Etemad cultivates has to emerge from the most unshakable fixation with present reality. This is what ultimately distinguishes her realism from that of Kiarostami and Makhmalbaf, who seek to liberate through an entirely different modulation. Bani-Etemad intends precisely the same sort of liberation by in effect overemphasizing the economic factor, underlining its social consequences, and then dismantling the most powerful institution of its perpetuation, namely, its strategies of gender formation via the sanctification of the Holy Family. What Bani-Etemad in effect exposes is the brutal economic forces that successfully disguise themselves as "traditional family values" in one of the most tyrannical institutionalizations of power.

Bani-Etemad's realism is far from being transgressively mute. It is not just by an unproductive parody of the Holy Family that Bani-Etemad exposes the catastrophic consequences of capitalist modernity and its violent Oedipalization of the psyche. She has something far more effective up her sleeve. She has an uncanny ability to plant the seeds of a vertiginously transgressive jolt in the soil of a perfectly realistic narrative. Central to the formative cast of *Nargess* is the active dismantling of the Oedipal via a *suggestion* of incest. It is crucial to note, before anything else, that Afagh and Adel's is primarily an amorous relationship between an older woman and a younger man. That Afagh had initially "adopted" Adel is a powerful reversal of what in the language of prostitution in Iran is called *neshandan* (literally, "to sit someone down"). In bordello slang, this word denotes a man's exclusive claim to a prostitute, to which she consents. Afagh's relationship with Adel is the precise reversal of *neshandan*; that is, she makes an exclusive claim to the man. This practice is also common, and the invariably younger lover of an older woman is called a *faseq* (literally, "the man with whom she sins"). In such cases, the woman is usually wealthier and more powerful, and the man poor

and inexperienced. Within this doubly transgressive suggestion, further emphasized by the fact that both Adel and Afagh are thieves, the liaison intimates an
incestuous relationship. Adel is not *really* Afagh's son; he is *like* her son—to feel
the full power of Bani-Etemad's vision, we need to remain on the border of that
transgressive suggestion. If we lose sight of this suggestion, we lose her realism.
The active imagination of an implicitly incestuous relationship between Afagh as
mother and Adel as son shatters the cultural constitution of the Oedipal, above
and beyond its economic basis, and forces it to regress to its culturally formative
stage.[20]

The suggestion of an incestuous relation between an older mother/woman
and a younger son/man adds a dangerous implication to Bani-Etemad's dismantling of the Oedipal, and the result is an insurrection against the metaphysical
violence of the culture and the active de-Oedipalization of the nuclear family in
both its material basis and its cultural construct. While the absence of a child
and the substitution of a *ménage-à-trois* for the Holy Family (Deleuze and Guattari's mommy-daddy-baby) disrupt the Oedipalization of the psyche as an
instrumentally beneficial mode for capitalist productivity, the suggestion of an
incestuous relationship attacks the moral supposition of the nuclear family. The
former attacks the colonialist consequences of capitalist modernity, and the
latter its mutation into presumably "traditional family values." The strategy is
ingenious, its consequences revolutionary, and its premise deeply rooted in the
material reality of marginal elements on the periphery of social mores.

Bani-Etemad's visual confrontation with the patriarchal paradigm and its
simultaneous release works through transgressive suggestions that do not violently challenge the metaphysical ordering of reality, but effectively dislodge it.
The strategy works precisely because it is aesthetically predicated on a visual
challenge to reality and deauthorizing of its regulating grammar. The place of
inarticulate visual suggestion is central to her project of resubjecting the politics
of femininity and gender formation. By the time she had made *Nargess*, some
two decades into her career as a documentary filmmaker, Bani-Etemad had come
a long way from her earliest attempts to translate visually her preoccupation
with documentaries into a richly realistic cinema. Her command of the camera;
the depth of the emotions she evokes; her sense of mise-en-scène, motion, and
camera movement; and, ultimately, her brilliant sense of light, shadow, and

darkness all reach a rich maturity in *The Blue-Veiled*. Here, her sense of alignment in long shots reveals her impeccable awareness of proportionality in the
range of sentiments they generate and sustain. Trains, train tracks, roads,
highways, and high chimneys are among the vertical and horizontal lines that
Bani-Etemad visually invokes in order to suggest the range of rigid sentiments
operative in a repressive culture. To remain factually faithful to that culture and
yet visually intimate a radical rebellion against its repression is the particular
genius of Bani-Etemad's cinema. There is thus a transubstantial movement in
her cinema from visual negotiation with reality in order to tease out its alternative resistance to the thematic imposition of the dominant culture. The result is
a shock that questions not only the grammatical ordering of reality but also, and
far more crucially, its presumed metaphysical inevitability.

What we see in Bani-Etemad's cinema is thus a transgressive suggestion that
visually challenges the verbal constitution of power. To see that strategy in full
operation, we should consider the narrative composition of *The Blue-Veiled*.
Echoing the central theme of *Nargess*, *The Blue-Veiled* is a story of forbidden love
between a rich and powerful widower and a poor but dignified young woman. To
tell this story, Bani-Etemad reaches deep into the most recent and distant memories of her culture. There is detailed attention to the semiotics of names in *The
Blue-Veiled*. The widower at the center of the story is Rasul Rahmani, whose name
means "the Messenger of the Merciful," thus evoking the memory of the Prophet
of Islam. Like Muhammad, Rasul Rahmani lost his pious and dignified wife half-
way through his life. The prophetic figure of Rasul Rahmani is emphasized by his
evident concern for his employees and customers. He is driven to his tomato fields
in a white car, the color visually recalling the ancient tales of saints and heroes.
The woman who acts as a messenger between the two lovers is named Kabutar
("dove"), recalling an important motif in classical Persian stories. Bani-Etemad's
semiotic exploitation of names, shapes, objects, and colors again assumes mythical dimensions when moments of sexual and conjugal intimacy are visually suggested in the film. All such features are geared toward a visual assimilation of the
audience into the culturally familiar, where the most subversive suggestions can
be generated and sustained.

Before we explore what precisely those transgressive suggestions are, we
ought to remember one more critical factor. Even more important than what

happens in front of Bani-Etemad's camera in this and all her other films is what occurs behind it. Paramount in the telling of this story is the question of how exactly a woman director is to present a love story in an Islamic Republic. The sheer fact of a woman's presenting a love story on a public screen in a land of veiled faces, denied sexuality, concealed bodies, and distorted sensuality is perhaps the most significant aspect of Bani-Etemad's cinema. That such transgressive suggestions are being shown by the camera of a female filmmaker increases the danger of the territory we are about to traverse. Bani-Etemad's camera is an extraordinarily destabilizing instrument. She is reflecting a society that is so petrified by the feminine gaze that it forces that gaze behind a veil. Her disquieting camera strips the patriarchal culture naked and thus adds a far more risky twist to whatever story she is about to tell.

In *The Blue-Veiled*, what that destabilizing camera reveals is a love between two people that is forbidden by both society and morality. Through the semiotic suggestion of names, colors, and shapes, Bani-Etemad mythologizes the story. The result is rather ingenious: the immediacy of the story makes it real, while its mythologization makes it culturally destabilizing. On the surface, we see very familiar, almost documentary, reality: factories and workers, fields and farm machinery, familiar urban settings, the hustle-bustle of routine life. But Bani-Etemad's mythologizing narrative transforms these daily realities and gives them subtextual signification. The result is a visual destabilization of power on a peculiar border between social criticism and symbolic reconstitution of the culture.

How, exactly, is this remodulation to move from one creative occasion to another, as it oscillates between the semiotic possibilities of the culture and its symbolic ossification, to follow Kristeva's distinction?[21] The semiotic realm is the zone of libidinal energy, the domain of the mother, where, following Plato's *Timaeus*, Kristeva locates a haven she calls the "semiotic *chora*". The *chora* is the space of the subversion of the subject, where libidinal energy is not yet regulated by the cultural mandates of propriety and normality. Beyond the semiotic and into the symbolic, the Oedipal is inaugurated and the law of the father imposed. The dominance of the symbolic over the semiotic is, however, precarious. Kristeva has demonstrated how the triad of subversive forces—madness, holiness, and the poetic—produces the counter-institutional rupturing of the symbolic.

Fatemeh Motamad Arya's stunning performance in *The Blue-Veiled* gave dignity and credibility to a younger poor woman in love with an older rich man. Bani-Etemad's directorial precision turned a potential melodrama into one of the most successful postrevolutionary films

Poetry, as the semantic suspension of the symbolic, points to specific moments of the transgressive shattering of the dominant semiotics of power. Now, if the constitution of gender occurs precisely at the moment of entry into the symbolic, any aesthetic strategy of arresting the Oedipal forces the symbolic authority of cultural institutions back to the open-endedness of their semiotic origins. Kristeva associates the pre-Oedipal with the polymorphous erotogenic zones that existed before culture carved its authority upon the body.

There is always a tense relationship between the body as the repressed reservoir of the semiotic and culture as the (almost) successful symbolization of its controlling mechanisms. The tension between the body and culture, and between the semiotic energy of the visual and the symbolic grammar of the forbidden, is nowhere more evident than in the nooks and crannies of cultural taboos. In Bani-Etemad's cinema, the suggestion of the incestuous in *Nargess* (1991) recurs in *The Blue-Veiled* (1994), but it is strategically reversed. Here, we have an older lover/father and a younger lover/daughter becoming entangled in a love affair. The complete reversal of roles here is crucial: in *Nargess*, Afagh is older, wealthier, and more powerful, and Adel is younger, poorer, and weak, but in *The Blue-Veiled*, Rasul Rahmani is older, richer, and more powerful, while Nobar Kordani is younger, poorer, and weak. Like two bookends, *Nargess* and *The Blue-Veiled* complement each other; one suggests an incestuous relationship of the mother-son type, the other that of the father-daughter. Whereas in *Nargess* we have an active dismantling of the Oedipal as the son possesses the mother, in *The Blue-Veiled* we have a seduction of the father by the daughter that results in a radical deauthorization of the father figure.

What the incestuous suggestion entails is a critical confrontation between the body, which is semiotically defiant, and culture, which is symbolically tyrannical. The love between Rasul Rahmani and Nobar Kordani, a much older man and a much younger woman, opposes the semiotically defiant body against the symbolically tyrannical culture. The seduction of the father/lover by the daughter/lover in *The Blue-Veiled* is done in the absence of the mother, Rasul Rahmani's dead wife, as well as in the absence of her surrogate, the daughter whom Rasul loves most, and who is abroad. We only hear them talk to each other on the telephone, which is placed on a small table by the dead mother's picture. The other two daughters hate Nobar because she is going to have what they desire most and cannot have, a suggestion emphasized by their two extraordinarily feeble husbands. Thus, Rasul is completely surrounded by seductive daughters, three of his own, in addition to Nobar, to whom he is allowed to be attracted, and even Nobar's younger sister Senobar.

On what is intimated as Rasul and Nobar's wedding night, Senobar symbolically acts as sexual intermediary when she sleeps with her head on Rasul's lap, while Nobar, true to her name (which means "fresh fruit"), offers fruit to her husband. Seated, wearing a white shirt, his back against the wall of the softly lit courtyard, Rahmani seems like a figure in a painting by Titian. On his lap lies the youthful head of his wife's very young sister. As he gently caresses the hair of the sleeping girl, Nobar offers her husband a tray full of fresh fruit (herself). In this tableau, the linear alignment from the vertical Nobar to the horizontal Senobar to the seated Rahmani is mediated by the roundness of the tray of colorful fruit. Rarely are we offered a scene so innocent and yet so provocatively sensuous. When we see Nobar the following morning, her beautiful face radiating happiness, the empty pool at the center of the courtyard is now full of fresh water, and around the pool are vases of bright red geraniums, one of which her younger sister accidentally drops into the pool. In this sequence, Nobar's body magically morphs to embrace her entire household, into which she has welcomed her husband.

The complete absence in *Narges* of the father figure by which de-Oedipalization can effectively take place is mirrored in *The Blue-Veiled* by a deauthorization of the father via a collective seduction by all his daughter figures. The result, though, is the same. Bani-Etemad captures the moment of Oedipalization right before the pregnant energy of the semiotic is to yield to the grammatical order of the symbolic. It is impossible to exaggerate the transgressive force that Bani-Etemad intimates by sacrilegiously invoking the Prophet of Islam in the name of the father figure, Rasul Rahmani. Transfiguring that memory in the father figure of *The Blue-Veiled* involves much more than the immediate material surroundings of the story. Through that very name, and the succession of other suggestive names, such as Nobar ("fresh fruit") and Senobar (which can be read as *Se-Nobar*, i.e., "thrice fresh fruit"), an entire sacred memory is invoked to charge the remissive jarring of the culture at large.

To understand the revolutionary nature of what Bani-Etemad has achieved here, we must keep in mind the sheepish tributes to Shiite sacred tradition abundantly evident in Iranian cinema. Consider, for example, invocations of classical Shiite leitmotifs and variations on the Karbala story (the martyrdom of the Imam Hossein and his supporters) that have provided many Iranian filmmakers with themes of tragedy, sacrifice, and redemptive suffering, all subservient to the reigning patriarchy. Kiumars Pour-Ahmad's *Beh Khater-e Hanieh* ("*For the Sake of Hanieh*," 1995) is a good example of this genre. The Karbala martyrdom leitmotif in *For the Sake of Hanieh* reveals itself in the visual celebration of sacrificial themes. When the father of a southern family in Bushehr dies while playing the dammam (a drum hung around the neck and beaten on both ends), his young son aspires to take his father's place as the drummer in the Muharram ceremony. The boy, Bashiroo, must now also support his family by doing odd jobs. Returning from one of these jobs, he throws the money he has earned on the ground where his mother is sitting. Offended by this disrespectful gesture, she slaps his face and tells him that he must offer his earnings respectfully, "like a man."

Pour-Ahmad relies heavily on the theme of thirst, central to the story of Karbala, as Bashiroo's repeated attempts to drink are thwarted. Bashiroo has a handicapped sister, Hanieh, for whose sake and in the hope of a miraculous cure he has vowed to beat his father's drum throughout the night of the tenth of Muharram, the most sacred night for Shiites, as it was on that night that Imam Hossein was martyred. But the elder in charge of the Muharram ceremony refuses to allow Bashiroo to beat the drum lest the older and more eligible members of the community be offended. Finally, the tired, thirsty, disappointed, and heart-broken Bashiroo is accidentally locked in a cellar. About to pass out from exhaustion and thirst, he is stung by a scorpion. He kills the scorpion, and in desperation uses a piece of broken glass to cut the wound in order to suck out the venom. He then tries to drink water from a well that proves to contain bad water. Just before losing consciousness, he notices the drums in the cellar. In the quiet darkness of the night outside, the people of the community, including Bashiroo's mother and sister, are awakened by the muffled beat of a drum. The elder and his wife trace the barely audible sound to their cellar. They open the locked door and out comes Bashiroo, moved by a spirit of inexplicable force and gravity. His visage is pale, ashen, and livid; his eyes are mesmerizing; his completely white lips are parched like the barren surface of land ravaged by drought. With the drum hanging from his thin neck, Bashiroo walks from the cellar, the old man and his wife having no choice but to make way for him. As he marches through the village beating the drum, we hear the sudden, bounteous downpour of rain.

The timing of Bani-Etemad's films, their conception and production in the midst of one of the most brutal theocracies in history, is extremely critical. At a time when the sacred violence of metaphysical certitude had wrapped an entire culture in a sacrificial shroud, Karbala write large, as an army of artists, both convinced of and hired by a republic of fear, slavishly served that sacred violence, Bani-Etemad began to turn the symbolic tyranny of the edifice against itself.

The character of Forough Kia in *The May Lady* became the most daring cinematic portrayal of a divorced woman breaking the social taboos by falling in love while pursuing her career and raising her young son. Bani-Etemad never shows the face of the man Forough loves

In *The May Lady*, the suggestion of incest is extended even further and brought to a radical conclusion. Here, Forough as mother and Mani as son live together in the complete absence of Mani's father, and the visual absence of Forough's lover. The absence of Forough's husband replicates the absence of Rasul's wife in *The Blue-Veiled*, while the visual absence of Forough's lover, Amir Rahbar, duplicates the absence of Rasul's youngest daughter. The oral construction of Amir Rahbar in *The May Lady* has an antecedent in the oral construction of Rasul's younger daughter, which is also characterized through long-distance telephone conversations. The suggestion of incest between Forough and Mani exists on a purely semiotic plane and is launched ferociously against the monumentality of the totally symbolized culture of suppression Forough and Mani both face. Forough's attempt to make a documentary about the "ideal mother," while trying to raise a teenage boy in the suffocating atmosphere of the Islamic Republic is the heavily symbolized and consolidated cultural context against which the raw semiotic energy of the perennially pre-Oedipal subjection of Mani has taken place. Mani is palpably androgynous, and his barely hidden and visibly suggested homosexuality is the strongest sign of the arrest of the Oedipal in this fatherless environment where the Oedipal moment has been kept at bay. The visual absence of Forough's lover, Amir Rahbar, allows the libidinal semiotic of Forough as mother and Mani as son, as substitute lovers, to remain at the explosively suggestive level and never fully collapse into the abyss of raw libidinal energy. The orality of Rahbar's character, which is always exclusive to Forough's ear, makes him at once absent—so that Mani's pre-Oedipal homoeroticism is suggested—and yet present, so that Forough's own sexuality has the potential to burst out in the very last shot of the film. Bani-Etemad has prepared visually for that sexual encounter with the double voice-over of Forough and Rahbar, when his letters begin to be narrated by Rahbar's voice and then Forough's voice joins in, as in his initiating the sexual encounter and Forough responding.

By the time she made *Baran and the Native* (1999), Bani-Etemad had paved the way for a de-Oedipalization of the culture. Baran is on vacation on the island of Kish in the Persian Gulf with her mother. There Baran meets a native boy. A raw, inarticulate, sexual attraction brings them together. The boy is a pearl diver, and he shows Baran the island. They go out in a small boat. He dives into the sea and she stays in the boat, watching in excitement. He surfaces with a basketful of oysters, and then plunges back into the sea. She waits in despair— the boy does not come back. Baran and the native are on the threshold of their sexual awakening. Bani-Etemad narrates their emerging sexuality on the eve of purgatorial adolescence. On the paradisiacal island of Kish are thus born two new versions of reality, unencumbered by either the name of a father or the identity of a culture. Baran ("rain") pours over the native's soil. The two are thus reversed in their subjectivity: Baran will impregnate the soil of the native. The native has to remain at the depth of the sea in search of yet another basket of possible pearls. Baran is already pregnant with a basket full of pearls, the oysters the native has given her. As the boy says, she may get a pearl and if not she will have the pleasure of eating the flesh.

Baran and the native are a symbolic Adam and Eve, born out of the juridical wedlock of a culture that can no longer claim them. It is far more than coincidental that *Baran and the Native* was shot on Kish island, off the mainland that constitutes the culture that this outlandish transgression defies. The native plunges into a sea that is the oceanic extension of Baran's womb, right under her lap, as she sits in the boat suspended between heaven and earth. The inauguration of a counterculture of de-Oedipalized freedom, *Baran and the Native* is Bani-Etemad's last testament. With this film, Bani-Etemad's semiotic destruction of Oedipalized culture comes full circle. In her last feature film, *Under the Skin of the City* (2000), her camera has lost its touch. The plight of the urban poor, once her strongest cry for freedom, now becomes routine reportage. The magic of the possible has left her caring camera, and numbing impossibilities suffocate its movements. In Iran, *Under the Skin of the City* was one of the most successful films at the box office. Hundreds of thousands flocked to the theaters to see it. However, *Baran and the Native* is scarcely seen outside film festivals. Just like the hidden pearl for which the native plunged into the southern sea—in vain.

SEVEN

WHITHER IRANIAN CINEMA?
THE PERILS AND PROMISES OF
GLOBALIZATION

To see the current and future trends in Iranian cinema, we need to visit three distant but contemporary sites. We begin with Tehran where the old masters are aging gracefully, then move to Cannes where the new visionaries are daring the elements, and finally pay a visit to the United States, where the best and the worst in Iranian cinema have made it difficult for its audience to say which is which. On these premises, we witness the graceful decline of an older generation of filmmakers who saw the world as a reflection of their creative ego, and the equally graceful rise of a new generation who see the world from the material basis of their organic roots in reality. The transition marks a moment of the rapid globalization of Iranian cinema, and the ultimate question that faces both these generations is how well they will weather this challenge.

TEHRAN

In his summation of the Eighteenth Fajr International Film Festival in February 2000, the distinguished Iranian film critic Houshang Golmakani informed the Iranian audience that since the recent democratic developments in his homeland many were concerned that cinema was losing its public immediacy to the critical eminence of the Iranian press.[1] About a month after the festival, I flew to Paris to spend a week with Mohsen Makhmalbaf in order to catch up with the latest news about him and his family. Among other things, a major line of conversation between us during that week was also the most recent political developments in Iran. He agreed that cinema was now taking a back seat to the heroic efforts of the Iranian press in shaping the future of democracy. Indeed, Makhmalbaf told me that he had just finished shooting a short film on Kish island, *Testing Democracy*, in which he had also acted, and which was entirely devoted to this very intersection of cinema, democracy, and the press.

There was a ring of truth in what these veterans of the Iranian cinema were asserting. Over the last two to three years, reformers such as Saeed Hajjarian, Akbar Ganji, Abdollah Nuri, Mashallah Shamsolvaezin, Shahla Sherkat, Mehrangiz Kar, Shahla Lahiji, and Alireza Alavi-Tabar had come to supplant Kiarostami, Makhmalbaf, Bani-Etemad, Mehrju'i, and Beiza'i. In fact, the last time two of these great icons of Iranian culture had been in the press was over the embarrassing dispute about the *Kish Stories*, when Beiza'i and Makhmalbaf argued about whose episode had been accepted or rejected at Cannes and who was to be blamed. This public display of self-absorption happened when the entire country was preoccupied by the student uprising for democracy. It was clear that some major Iranian filmmakers had lost their public credibility and, as a result, did not have a moral stance from which they could participate in the events of that fateful summer.

In his summation, Golmakani had announced that social and political issues were soon to dominate Iranian cinema, and that in fact they were already evident in some of the best films of the Eighteenth Fajr Film Festival. He also concluded that the authorities in charge of cinema in the Ministry of Culture and Islamic Guidance had cautiously kept Iranian cinema nonpolitical during the last two decades in order to safeguard it from the vicissitudes of politics under the Islamic Republic.

To Golmakani and his colleagues, the difference between the Iranian press and the cinema is one of *timing*. The press can respond *instantly*, whereas for cinema *it takes some time* to do so. This assessment, which disregards the nature and disposition of a work of art, stems from the peculiar fact that engaged intellectuals in Iran one day function as journalists, another day as filmmakers, and yet another day as poets, novelists, etc. Matters of immediate public concern do of course appear as integral forces in making possible visions of alternative courses. But the nature and disposition of those conceptions are not reducible to their constituent elements, immediate or distant. The reason that Iranian filmmakers are concerned about the rise of the press is quite obvious: in Iran, engaged intellectuals are always wary of losing their discursive ground to the next bidder. What is lost in the midst of this territorial dispute for the creative ego is the nature and disposition of a work of art, particularly in a time of need. Iranian artists have had a critical role in the making of historical agency almost despite themselves.

The difference between the cinema and the press is much more than timing. But Iranian filmmakers' feeling that they have lost the center stage to journalists reflects the interchangeable nature of the functions that Iranian public intellectuals have felt obliged to assume. The instrumentality to which they thus subject their creative imagination completely escapes them. The singular predicament of these intellectuals in modernity has been the inadvertent substitution of their creative egos for the collective consciousness of society at large. There has been an overwhelming sense of responsibility on the part of Iranian intellectuals to secure freedom and democracy for their society. That they have failed to do so has, paradoxically, led to one inevitable and barely noted conclusion: the expansive bloating of their creative egos to embrace the universal reality of their society.

No other film in recent memory shows this pathological state of affairs better than Daryush Mehrju'i's *Derakht-e Golabi* (*"The Pear Tree,"* 1998), in which the central character shuts himself in a room to brood on his personal cum political failures. The fusion of the intellectual's personal ego and his social persona is best represented by the parallel between the protagonist's personal failure in his love affair and his subsequent political failure. When his teenage love for a girl was unrequited, the lead character in Mehrju'i's film turns to politics, only to be similarly disappointed. The personal ego thus mutates into a public psyche, extending the logic and failure of the one into the other. *The Pear Tree* is thus the story of a personal failure metamorphosing into a public defeat and resulting in a complete moral collapse. The collapse, however, is that of the personal ego and public persona falling into each other, the Iranian intellectual thinking himself at the center of a collapsed universe.

Iranian cinema has achieved its most glorious moments and suffered its greatest failures on the basis of this universal predicament of Iranian public

Mehrju'i's career as one of the most brilliant Iranian filmmakers took a dramatic turn after the untimely death of his friend and collaborator, the dramatist Gholamhossein Sa'edi

intellectuals. The future of Iranian cinema is now being charted in a singularly transformative moment when the very nature of the role of public intellectuals is being reconstituted, and we see the emergence of a new generation of film-makers whose commitment to a new form of organicity has made them far more other-centered than self-absorbed, so that the public is thus spared the megalo-mania of their creative egos. In no longer imagining their egos to be the public persona of their nation at large, the new generation of Iranian filmmakers are actively desedimenting the figure of the Iranian engaged intellectual back into the material forces of a new organicity. This new generation has arisen from the unexpected horizon of disenfranchised segments of society that find their subterranean ways into international film festivals, and then shine forth and back at their nation. Before we can see and measure the range of their light, we need to look at the father figures they have overshadowed.

Four major films were critically acclaimed at the Eighteenth Fajr International Film Festival, each illustrating the specific perils and promises of Iranian cinema. By both official recognition and collective critical judgment, Bahman Farmanara's *Bu-ye Kafur, Atr-e Yas* ("*Smell of Camphor, Fragrance of Jasmine*," 2000) was the best Iranian film of the festival. Farmanara had returned to his homeland and joined the ranks of his celebrated generation of filmmakers after more than two decades. With a few exceptions, Farmanara was joined by the best in his generation of filmmakers at this festival. Also featured were Daryush Mehrju'i's *Mix* (2000), Abbas Kiarostami's *Bad Ma ra ba khod Khahad Bord* ("*The Wind Will Carry Us Away*," 1999), and Mas'ud Kimiya'i's *E'teraz* ("*Protest*," 2000). This was a historic occasion. Four of the most renowned Iranian filmmakers had entered four of their best films. The spectrum of Iranian cinema, both in its glorious achievements and its catastrophic failures, was there in full view.

SMELL OF CAMPHOR, FRAGRANCE OF JASMINE (2000)

Bahman Farmanara's *Smell of Camphor, Fragrance of Jasmine* is the first film this veteran director has made for two decades, almost exactly as long since the Islamic revolution, after which he had temporarily left his homeland. But much had changed in Iran since Farmanara (b. 1941) made a permanent impression on Iranian cinema with his *Prince Ehtejab* (1974), based on an outstanding Persian work of fiction by Houshang Golshiri (d. 2000). The most critical aspect of Farmanara's *Smell of Camphor, Fragrance of Jasmine* is its personal texture and narrative.

Personal, in fact, is a key term for many of the films featured at the Eighteenth Fajr Festival. *Smell of Camphor, Fragrance of Jasmine* presents the story of Bahman Farjami (read "Bahman Farmanara"; Farjami means "at the end" or "toward the end," and Farmanara plays this role himself), a middle-aged filmmaker who is mourning the death of his close friends and colleagues Sohrab Shahid Sales, Bahram Reypour, and Ali Hatami (all actual directors recently deceased).

Farjami has a congenital heart disease and is very conscious of his own mortality. As a result, he decides to make a film about his own funeral, a scenario which transforms *Smell of Camphor, Fragrance of Jasmine* into a universal, long-shot reflection of Iranian society, politics, and culture, taking full advantage of the recent democratic developments in the Islamic Republic.

From the 1960s onward, Iranian filmmakers joined poets and novelists as the principal figures cultivating their public moral and cultural authority by expanding their creative egos to embrace society at large. But history does not stand still. Yesterday's cultural heroes are today's museum artifacts. The question is, do they know how to age gracefully? Farmanara does not recognize that he is making a public spectacle of his private mourning for his friends and colleagues precisely at a historical juncture when the mutation of his personal creative ego into a public wake is no longer acceptable. He remains a great filmmaker but a belated reader of the emerging terms of the dialogue. He does not recognize that a nation born by cesarean section into modernity through colonial midwifery, a country traumatized for two decades by war and revolution, a people held in an arrested adolescence by a puritanical theocracy, a locality brutally globalized beyond its control, is no longer interested in a director's private mourning and cannot allow its public space to be occupied by a universalized personal matter, however well-intentioned. There was a time when Farmanara's creative ego *was* the site of that public concern. But that collective consciousness has long since abandoned Farmanara's generation of public intellectuals; it has sought and grown into a much more creative, much more responsive thing. There was a time when a nativist intellectual was *the* thing to be. But the rapid globalization of all national interests no longer tolerates old-fashioned public intellectuals that have successfully mutated their creative ego into collective will.

MIX (2000)

The second celebrated film at the Eighteenth Fajr Festival was also by an established master. Since his groundbreaking *The Cow* (1969), Daryush Mehrju'i has remained one of the major forces defining contemporary Iranian cinema. *Mix* is a parody of the film industry in an Islamic Republic. In this production, Mehrju'i (played by his alter ego Khosrow Shakiba'i) and his crew are frantically finishing a film in order to enter it in the Fajr Film Festival, which opens in three days. This satirical set-up becomes the vehicle of Mehrju'i's critique of not just the Iranian film industry but the entire prospect of making a film for an audience with whom the director shares no aspirations.

Like Farmanara's film, Mehrju'i's *Mix* is really a funeral, but masked as a parody. Mehrju'i is the most unfortunate cinematic loss to the Islamic revolution. The greater his stature appeared before the revolution, the more tragic is his postrevolutionary decline. We owe our very public persona, our claim to any agencial authority in our modernity, to his generation of engaged intellectuals and their ability to transform their creative egos into the site of our collective identity. Mehrju'i's generation of poets, writers, dramatists, and filmmakers imagined us otherwise than as desubjected colonials. The Shah and his entire American-equipped army were no match for the confidence that Mehrju'i's generation inspired in us by turning their creative egos into our collective character. Had it not been for Mehrju'i's *The Cow*, Iranian cinema would not be what it is today. He created the very confidence with which every Iranian filmmaker after him looked from behind a camera. But the success of the Islamic revolution was the complete collapse and moral failure of the creative vision of his generation. He, too, like his closest ally and creative counterpart Gholamhossein Sa'edi (d. 1985), "died" in exile and yet continued to spew out bitter effusions of his paralyzing anger, films that are epileptic seizures of his moral authority, seismic measures of his creative collapse, a systemic mendacity he could not control.

PROTEST (2000)

If Farmanara's *Smell of Camphor, Fragrance of Jasmine* and Mehrju'i's *Mix* are two complementary funeral wakes for what was best in Iranian cinema, Mas'ud Kimiya'i's *E'teraz* ("*Protest*," 2000) is the convulsive persistence of what is worst. The first full-fledged encounter of a major filmmaker of the older generation with the predicament of the new generation's youth, Kimiya'i's *Protest* could not tell its misbegotten story without once again reviving one of the director's oldest character types, a man jailed for committing a crime to protect his "honor" (*namus*), and placing him vis-à-vis the tumultuous developments of the country at the threshold of the twenty-first century. Against the backdrop of the July 1999 student uprising, Kimiya'i puts two brothers, the older Amir, with his lumpen principles, and the younger Reza, with his post-ideological fixation with nonviolence, face to face. At a time when the most progressive filmmakers, like Mehrju'i and Farmanara, were constitutionally incapable of escaping their debilitating categorical imperatives in order to see what was happening in their homeland, Kimiya'i, by far the most reactionary director in the history of Iranian cinema, could not but demonstrate his constitutional inability to read those groundbreaking events.

THE WIND WILL CARRY US AWAY (1999)

While, at the same Eighteenth Fajr Film Festival, Farmanara and Mehrju'i screened the best museum pieces of Iranian national cinema and Kimiya'i the worst, the now globally celebrated Abbas Kiarostami presented *The Wind Will Carry Us Away*. It was shown outside the competition since he had premièred it the year before at the Venice Film Festival.

Kiarostami's long and illustrious career is unlike any other in Iranian cinema. He taught us an anti-ethics, the morality of never asking functional, instrumental, questions. Kiarostami has never surpassed his best work, the Rostam-abad trilogy. It was principally through this trilogy, predicated on his career before the revolution, that Kiarostami gave his camera over to the most radical onslaught opposing the metaphysical violence perpetrated against the nature and disposition of the real. At a time when our entire culture was inundated with the most pernicious consequences of metaphysical violence, he made the sensual simplicity of the real shine through every distorting layer of metaphysics superimposed on its evident matter-of-factness. The ingenious eye of his camera taught us the virtuous, audacious, glorious nakedness of reality. His was a journey from the metaphysical phenomenality of the real back towards its palpable noumenality, which needs no explanation. In the long and illustrious history of Iranian cultural modernity, from poetry to drama, from fiction to every kind of performing art, no one came close to what Kiarostami ultimately achieved in teaching us *to be* otherwise. At his best, Kiarostami showed us, not how to *talk about* the real but how to *show it*, to converse with it, to dwell on and in it.

It is critical to remember that in the decade that lasted from the 1960s to the end of the 1970s, during the early stages of his cinematic career, Kiarostami was not a prominent public intellectual. He was an entirely tangential and peripheral filmmaker at a time when Beiza'i and Mehrju'i were defining Iranian cinema. It is precisely for this reason that his camera works in a strategically unobtrusive and quiet manner rather than pursuing the universalization of his creative ego. He became the Iranian postrevolutionary filmmaker par excellence not because Gilles Jacob discovered him for Cannes, and *Cahiers du Cinéma* proclaimed his genius to the world, but precisely because of the unobtrusive corner in which his camera is positioned.

It is from that corner that Kiarostami's career has been constitutional to a visual modulation of *sign* as hermeneutically resistant to cultural *signification*.[2] This is the singular achievement of Iranian cultural modernity that has come to full creative fruition in Kiarostami's films. If, before Kiarostami, we had poetically shattered the word to dislodge the metaphysical claim of signification to it, with Kiarostami, we have visually mutated the very contention of signification back to its glorious stage of *signation*, sensual *sign* before any metaphysical insistence on it to *significate*. The reason that Muslim ideologues in Iran have so violently attacked Kiarostami's films is precisely this disturbing stripping of the real from all its violent metaphysical claimants, which has visually allowed for the *sign* simply to *signate*, palpitate with its semiotic sensuality, without ever collapsing into habitual modes of *signification*.

This has been by far the most enduring significance of Kiarostami's cinema. But he, too, finally exposed his own Achilles' heel. By the time he directed *Taste of Cherry* (1997), it was evident that he had achieved his best and did not know quite where to go with it, and with *The Wind Will Carry Us Away* (1999) he has sealed his own doom in a most unfortunate way. With *The Wind Will Carry Us Away* Kiarostami finally joined the rest of his generation in mutating his creative ego into the collective psyche of what he thinks is his nation but is not. Kiarostami has now reached the limit of his *universalization* of the Iranian *particular*. With this film he showed that when he achieved the universal he did not know quite what to do with it, and he failed in the face of a global deauthorization of the real, of which, alas, he has not a clue.

Every day, the lead character in *The Wind Will Carry Us Away* climbs a hill outside the Kurdish village of Siyah Darreh in order to be able to use his mobile telephone to report to an anonymous authority in Tehran that the old woman whose funeral they are there to film as a documentary has not yet died. After each splendidly repetitious Kiarostamiesque report, he walks to the edge of a ditch being dug by a man whose voice we can always hear without seeing his face. On one such occasion, he notices a young woman secretly coming to visit the worker and bring him fresh milk (a substance with mischievously sexual connotations in the film). From then on, the protagonist is determined to drink the same milk from the same cow milked by the same hands. By hook and by crook, he finally inveigles his way into the milkmaid's home. From the moment that Kiarostami's camera leads us into the dark, dungeon-like stable where the girl is milking a cow until the moment the protagonist leaves with a bucketful of milk and a satisfied grin on his face, we pay through the nose for every pleasure we took in Kiarostami's not showing the private moments of souls exposed in his previous films, for every ounce of joy in not hearing Tahereh and Hossein converse at the end of *Through the Olive Trees*, for every lesson we gained in humility by not hearing what Sabzian tells Makhmalbaf in *Close-Up* while riding on the back of his motorcycle and embracing him from behind. We are punished for all these past delights and uplifting moments by having to watch this ghastly sequence of Kiarostami's camera seducing the mutely innocent peasant girl. To add insult to injury, Kiarostami chooses this hideous instance to introduce one of the most glorious poems in modern Persian poetry. Never has Forough Farrokhzad's "The Wind Will Carry Us Away" sounded so silly, so graceless, as in this recital by a vulgar man intruding into the private passions of a young woman.

Kiarostami's mise-en-scène is a brutally accurate picture of dehumanization. From the vantage point of Kiarostami's voyeuristic camera, all we see is the backside of the cow, with the girl squatting to milk her in the dim, dungeon-like depths of an ocular masturbation. What a contrast between this cold scene and the melodious sweetness of Mehrju'i's *The Cow* when Mashdi Hasan lovingly caresses and eats with his cow. Betraying every principle of visual decency that Kiarostami had honored in all his previous films, the stable sequence in *The*

Wind Will Carry Us Away is the nightmarish negation of every film he ever made, the return of all that his cinema had repressed, negated, and defied.

How did Kiarostami allow himself this collapse? It seems that the global celebration of his genius has finally gone to his head and corrupted his miraculously caring camera. After three decades of making one masterpiece after another, Kiarostami has belatedly fallen into the trap of his generation of public intellectuals and allowed his creative ego to metastasize into the presumption of a collective psyche, claiming the authority to do just about anything. The dark stable scene sheds a new, unfortunate, light on the rest of *The Wind Will Carry Us Away*. Now everything makes horrific sense. A gang of Tehrani filmmakers have invaded this remote Kurdish village to see one of its elders die and make an ethnographic documentary of the event. Totally ignorant of the moral paralysis of ethnographic anthropology, Kiarostami becomes an ethnographer and a native informant at one and the same time. The village of Siah Darreh ("Dark Valley") welcomes the ethnographic crew and puts its youngest inhabitant at their disposal as their guide. They partake of the villagers' hospitality, pry into their private quarters, condescend to their elders, flirt with their young women, and ultimately perpetrate the final insult of visually copulating with one of them. The anonymity of the faces of the intruders, the fact that except for Kiarostami's own alter ego we do not see any of the crew members' faces, adds to their overwhelming power. In view of this slanted relation of power, we no longer care that between the director's outrageous treatment of defenseless subjects and the documentary that he has not made he has come to a new and fuller grasp of life. But of course the "documentary" *is* made, and it is called *The Wind Will Carry Us Away*, a documentary depicting something quite atrocious.

What is particularly disturbing about the stable sequence is that Kiarostami's camera is so overwhelmingly powerful that it is not even aware of its power, and in this oblivion he exerts this power against the weakest, most vulnerable, and mutest subject. The stable sequence is one of the most violent rape scenes in all cinema. Kiarostami fails in this film because he ceases to universalize this particular Iranian village. Over the last three decades, but particularly since he achieved international prominence, Kiarostami's has been the spectacular success story of a Third World filmmaker turning the particular of his native location into the global parameters of an emancipating rereading of reality. If he has richly deserved comparison with such great masters as Satyajit Ray and Akira Kuro-sawa, it is precisely because of this universalization of the Iranian village. They, as indeed had Kiarostami until this film, restored a universal dignity to the people they redrafted for the world at large. But in this stable scene Kiarostami does precisely the opposite of universalizing Iranian dignity; he begins to particularize a universal indignity. The blank-faced, wide-eyed, imitation-cool, made-in-Tehran protagonist, who may think that his unbuttoned shirt, dirty blue-jeans, unlaced boots, Japanese station wagon, and Tehrani accent tellingly distinguish him from the Kurdish villagers, does not realize, in the depths of his own depraved nativism, that, for the global audience, he is as much part of the Third World as the villagers.

Kiarostami rescued the Iranian particular from the violent disease of its universalizing metaphysics, and then, just when it was about to breathe and signal its emancipating defiance of all empty signification, he cast the deadliest, power-basing global gaze on it, the gaze of the First at the Third World, of the powerful at the powerless, of the center at the periphery, of the metropolitan at the colonized, of the Tehrani at the Kurd, imitating the Europeans at the height of colonialism. It is as if Kiarostami rescued the naked Iranian reality from its countervailing layers of native metaphysics only to subject it to a more debilitating globalism.

But why would he do that? A number of reasons suggest themselves: in an unfortunate turn of events, Kiarostami finally caught up with the principal predicament of his generation of public intellectuals and aggressively mutated his creative ego, taking it for the collective consciousness of the nation at large, but he did so remissively, in full view of the world, for everyone to see. If this transformation at one time helped restore dignity to a nation by creatively sustaining the development of its historical agency, it is now not only historically late but morally outdated. It is in front of a global audience that an ahistorical, bloated creative ego has turned Kiarostami in his last film into the simulacrum of a First World anthropologist doing an ethnographic study of a village.

What becomes evident in *The Wind Will Carry Us Away* is that the global attention has distorted Kiarostami's concentration by confusing him about his audience. The fact that recently he has been even more assertive than before of his preference for a cinema of enigma, which the audience participates in solving, is more than anything a refusal to engage in a critical reading of his own cinema, because he wants his domestic and global audience to sort out their differences so that he can remain aloof. The result is that the *universal* recognition of his cinema is distorting his vision of the *particulars* he has always addressed. There is nothing enigmatic about Kiarostami's cinema. It is very simple. His domestic viewers think it enigmatic because they are pathologically accustomed to conspiratorial readings. His foreign audiences, the critics in particular, think it enigmatic because they are always afraid they are missing something. The visual presence of Kiarostami's cinema, however, has nothing to do with those two modes of hermeneutic paralysis. Its destruction of the successive generations of Iranian and Islamic metaphysics does not mean that it is "enigmatic." Kiarostami's cinema is manifestly, and as a matter of an aesthetic manifesto, launched against interpretation. That Kiarostami himself now promotes this bizarre claim to be enigmatic is the most serious sign of his complete confusion of the nature and disposition of the global audience facing his cinema. He wants to leave it to the audience to decide, which in and of itself is a bogus democratic gesture, because who else is to decide other than the audience? His diverse audiences have completely bewildered his creative impulses, as now shockingly evident in *The Wind Will Carry Us Away*.

The cause of the hermeneutic paralysis that Kiarostami encourages is an insecurity in his own artistic disposition, which is squarely rooted in the catastrophic predicament of Iranian intellectuals throughout the last two centuries, the same difficulty of intellectuals throughout the Third World. Turned into nativist sites of creative resistance, they have become globally blinded. Kiarostami is no exception. A peculiar combination of awe and *ressentiment* has characterized this blind spot. For much of the last two centuries, though, this nativism has been necessary and constitutional to the modes of ideological and creative resistance to colonialism and its cultural hegemony. But it no longer corresponds to the blurring speed of globalization that endows every *locality* with a fully organic awareness of *globality*. While the Iranian intellectuals of Kiarostami's generation are still caught in the presumed spheres of "East" and "West," and while the new generation is threatened by yet another entirely futile concoction, "the religious intellectual," Kiarostami's triumphs at film festivals have given him the false impression that Cannes, Venice, and Locarno are the real world, the world of which he remains dangerously unaware. It is unfortunate that Kiarostami's generation of Iranian intellectuals is constitutionally nativist. There was a time that this limitation was aesthetically creative and ideologically potent. It is now catastrophic.

Kiarostami cannot tell the frying pan from the fire. His greatest strength throughout his career has now finally caught up with him and regressed into his weakest trait. He dismantled the received Iranian metaphysics by being so deeply and creatively embedded in it. He knew it so well he could undo it. But it is precisely this thorough familiarity with Iranian metaphysics that has made him so utterly unfamiliar with the larger global relation of power that engulfs the violence of that metaphysics. We have to remember that Kiarostami is of the same generation as Jalal Al-e Ahmad, whose most influential contribution was coining the term "Westoxication."[3] Al-e Ahmad considered fascination with the West a disease. Since then, Iranian intellectuals have been divided into two groups, one agreeing and the other disagreeing with Al-e Ahmad. Thus, a constitutionally flawed argument, entirely blinded to a global logic of capital and culture that could not care less about the West, the East, or any other geo-political sphere so long as economic systems were stable, divided Kiarostami's generation of engaged intellectuals into apparently opposing but essentially similar camps. Both credited the idea that "the West" was an autonomous entity, and that it was either good or evil. This catastrophic analytic failure has been singularly responsible for turning generations of Iranian public intellectuals into militant nativists. And this nativism, once essential to the restoration of a sense of national dignity to the colonial subject, is now unforgivable and artistically harmful.

Nativism not only blinds Kiarostami's generation of engaged intellectuals to the global configuration of power, but also makes them ignorant of subnational, domestic colonialism. The result, so horribly evident in *The Wind Will Carry Us Away*, is that the relation of power between national center and ethnic periph-eries simply replicates that of the presumed metropolitan center and its implicit colonial periphery. There is not much difference between the Iranian cultural colonization of ethnic minorities like the Kurds and global relations at large. Tehran simply replicates what London, Paris, and Washington have done to their satellite peripheries.

No Iranian intellectual, filmmaker or otherwise, can afford to remain ignorant of the global context of their work. Homogenizing institutions that exoticize the globe to presume moral ascendancy for "whiteness" are on the lookout for indigenous nativists like Kiarostami. The Eighteenth Fajr International Film Festival lacked one great filmmaker: Bahram Beiza'i was conspicuously absent. But he did appear on the cover of none other than *National Geographic*, directing a scene from one of his films, a catastrophic event, of the significance of which Beiza'i remains blissfully ignorant.[4] His generation of Iranian engaged intellectuals are totally unaware that *National Geographic*, published in Washington, DC, is principally devoted to turning the rest of the world into a zoo so that the white American may look civilized. Catherine A. Lutz and Jane L. Collins have brilliantly dissected the editorial policies of *National Geographic* in its representation of the exotic and the foreign.[5] Why is it that major Iranian intellectuals like Beiza'i and Kiarostami know nothing about the groundbreaking deconstructive works that have dismantled the authority of these journals and their long-standing interest in authenticating "Western" civilization and consigning things *Oriental* and otherwise Third World to earlier stages of human development?

Ignorance of the global picture is no longer a matter of artistic choice or creative disposition. By virtue of its universal celebration and global audience, cinema is a particularly public art. The abundance of detail about the local predicament of a community and a culture are now in the grip of the globalizing logic of material production. It is no longer possible to retrieve the mythological force of the Iranian or any other culture and creatively negotiate for the possibility of local emancipation. That negotiation is, *ipso facto*, a claim to *authenticity*. Such a claim has always characterized Beiza'i's cinema. But he fulfilled his function best by alerting his Iranian audience to the mythological condition of their perception of reality. He revealed that pathology by being part of it. But, today, the globality of our condition has left Beiza'i behind; as a result, in his own lifetime, he has turned into a museum piece precisely because he has persistently museumized his culture. Beiza'i is one of the giant figures of the old generation who successfully mutated his creative ego for the public persona of the nation. By being part of that generation, Beiza'i's singular contribution was to explode like a mine carefully planted in the depths of our archeological imagination. He explored the depth of our pathological fixations with culture. But he himself remained deeply buried in that archeological site and never surfaced to realize that he had taken the myth for the real thing. The next generation must now teach Beiza'i a new lesson.

CANNES[6]

Like most other countries in the full and tightening grip of globalization, Iran is at a critical juncture. What the older generation of Iranian filmmakers has brought to global attention is a mode of artistic production in which the creative ego subconsciously modulates itself as if it were the collective conscience of the nation. There was a critical moment in the course of cultural colonialism when, without this subterranean conversion of the personal to the public, no creative resistance to the aggressive desubjection of colonialism would have been possible. But inherent in that mutation of the personal for the public was the native and nativist disposition of the Third World intellectual. That nativism is no longer viable. The rapid globalization of capital and culture no longer allows for it. The principal predicament of the Iranian filmmakers of the last generation is that they have brought the nativist disposition of their creativity to global attention. If those who control the international film festivals at Cannes, Venice, and Locarno favor aggressive exoticization of the so-called Third World, so that these festivals become the cinematic version of *National Geographic*, that nativism can obviously be as politically catastrophic as creatively effervescent. But if their cinema is to have a public function beyond the film festivals, that nativism needs to be remodulated toward a critical awareness of globality. This ultimately becomes a generational matter: the creative disposition of the older generation is not supple in its responses to globalization. It does not even understand the process. But the younger generation need not even consciously comprehend the phenomenon, because it is creatively a part of it. To witness that generation in action, we need to go to the most international venue in world cinema.

For reasons that have nothing to do with the dawn of the third millennium, because Iran follows its own version of the Islamic calendar, the year 2000 marks a spectacular achievement for Iranian cinema. Three young film directors, their ages ranging from twenty to thirty-seven, won some of the most coveted prizes at Cannes. The youngest of them, Samira Makhmalbaf, "the Mozart of Iranian cinema," as the French have dubbed her, was born in the year of the Islamic revolution. The oldest of them, Hasan Yektapanah, was sixteen when the revolution shook his homeland to its moral and material bones. The third, Bahman Qobadi, experienced that cataclysmic event as a ten-year-old boy.

The cinematic world watched in admiration when twenty-year-old Samira Makhmalbaf, the eldest child of Mohsen Makhmalbaf, received the Jury Prize for her *Takhte Siah* ("*Blackboard*," 2000), while Hasan Yektapanah (b. 1963) and Bahman Qobadi (b. 1969) shared the *Caméra d'Or* for *Jom'eh* (2000) and *Zamani bara-ye Masti-ye Asb-ha* ("*A Time for Drunken Horses*," 2000), respectively. Samira Makhmalbaf has won even more fame and recognition for her father's name, but the names of the other two award-winning filmmakers were completely unknown, not only in the international film circuit but even in their own homeland. These are the courageous young souls who have dared the elements and imagined otherwise.

Letting things come to presence in their world, beyond metaphysics and ideology, is the singular defining moment of this new generation of Iranian filmmakers, the first since the Islamic revolution. In view of their reception at Cannes, and judging by their global celebration, these films are indices of a new postmetaphysical phase of Iranian cinema, the dawning of a whole new day of hope predicated on no categorical covenant. Their phenomenal appearances are all that is put forth: they make no claim to any noumenal authenticity, thus collapsing the bifurcation between reality and appearances. They are the true offspring of Kiarostami at his best. A poetic pulverization of the creative ego in a unprecedentedly democratic manner is the principal texture of what we see in the cinema of the first generation of postrevolutionary Iranians.[7]

JOM'EH (2000)

Is it accidental that in his *Jom'eh*, Hasan Yektapanah opts for a close examination of the nature of solitude? The other of the Iranian self, the young Jom'eh becomes the tabula rasa of a critical cleansing of memory, starting from scratch, a migrant laborer—both young and alien in a land of pathological fixations with identity-celebrating alterity, though not in a jaundiced neglect of the real but in the factual evidence of being an other. Yektapanah represents the first generation of a postrevolutionary poetic pulverization of the creative ego. He has collaborated with a host of prominent Iranian filmmakers, including Ali Hatami, Ja'far Panahi, Tahmineh Milani, and Abbas Kiarostami. Inspired by those eminent filmmakers, he seeks greatness in small things. *Jom'eh*, his first film, is about two Afghan migrant laborers in Iran. The younger one, Jom'eh, develops a close relationship with his employer, who owns a dairy business. The film is centered on Jom'eh and his hope to feel at home (Yektapanah had originally entitled his film *Relationship*) with his new surroundings.[8]

A TIME FOR DRUNKEN HORSES (2000)

Bahman Qobadi, a Kurdish Iranian at the ethnic and sectarian margin of Iranian Shiism, has made a number of short films, many of them acclaimed outside Iran. *A Time for Drunken Horses* (originally entitled *Arbaba Chestnuts*) is about a young Kurdish boy and his sister, who, in the absence of their parents, must care for their sick brother. The sister finally marries an Iraqi, whose family cheat her out of her bride price and instead give a mule to the younger brother. The film was shot entirely in Iranian Kurdestan, and Qobadi is reported to have waited a year to shoot the final sequence because he needed a harsh, snowy setting.[9]

Yektapanah and Qobadi, respectively, come to Iranian cinema from two opposite borderlands of the "Iranian" center, the Afghan east and the Kurdish west, thus challenging the official claim to national authenticity. It is not just the Iranian identity that they bracket with their alterity. They now represent the full poetic pulverization of the creative ego that defined their artistic mentors. Qobadi collaborated closely with Mohsen Makhmalbaf while Samira Makhmalbaf was making *Blackboard*, and acted in it. He believes that working with Makhmalbaf was instrumental in launching his cinematic career. "What I intend to do is to learn more about the cinema. Right now I would love to assist Mohsen Makhmalbaf in his next film, because I learned much from him. During the two months I spent with Makhmalbaf I have learned as much from him as if I had studied for a degree in the cinema."[10] There is a palpable sense of continuity from one generation of filmmakers to another. But the critical difference is that Tehran is no longer the center of the creative universe. It has been displaced by Cannes. But because Cannes is an outlandish place that is capital to no nation and is merely the annual mecca of filmmakers, its displacement is not substitutional but disorienting.

Qobadi has been a protégé of Kiarostami, too, having closely collaborated with him in his last film, *The Wind Will Carry Us Away*. But he insists that Kiarostami has had no influence on him: "I came to the conclusion that I admire Mr. Kiarostami greatly but I can never make calm films as he does. I love winter and harsh atmospheres and I believe that all my films ought to be made in severe climates. Although Mr. Kiarostami had given an idea [for a film to be] called *Honeybee* for me to work on, after some considerable reflection I came to the conclusion that I cannot make films like his. That's why I say the influence Mr. Kiarostami has had over others he has not had over me."[11] He goes on to say that he made absolutely sure that "not a single shot" of his film was similar to Kiarostami.

Killing the creative father in public is the singular sign of coming of age. The poetic pulverization of the creative ego tears the aesthetic urge to pieces and pushes it in uncharted directions, a rite of passage that must authenticate the creative vision. The result is far more communally palpable than egotistically satisfying. Communally, things begin to develop in their own world without the intermediary of the metaphysical grid, which invariably disguises itself as the creative ego. The creative ego is the principal force in authenticating the metaphysical ordering of the real, particularly when it appears to oppose it. The verbal and visual pulverization of the creative ego is not just the first sign of a rising democratic spirit. It is also the harbinger of the destruction of the metaphysics that sustains tyrannies.

THE APPLE (1998)

For the real spirit of the new generation of Iranian filmmakers, we need to look at its heart. Samira Makhmalbaf was born to Mohsen Makhmalbaf and Fatemeh Meshkini in 1979, the year of the Iranian revolution; this was a year after her father had been released from Pahlavi prison, where he was serving a five-year sentence for attacking a policeman. She grew up under his shadow as he was emerging as the most vociferous and visionary of the postrevolutionary public intellectuals.

Raised on the set of her father's films, it is impossible for Samira Makhmalbaf to imagine life outside cinema. She has had minor acting roles in many of her father's films, and at the age of eight played an important role in *The Cyclist*. Before she made *The Apple* (1998), she had made two films, *Sahra* ("*The Desert*," 13 minutes) and *Sabk dar Naqqashi* ("*Style in Painting*," 53 minutes). In 1995, at the age of fifteen, Samira abandoned formal education to devote herself entirely to cinema, studying primarily with her father at home. Her defiance of an educational system inundated by theocratic indoctrination is symptomatic of a larger predicament more than two decades into the Islamic revolution. Not only Islamic ideology and its immediate antecedent Persian monarchy, but also any ideologically mediated approach to reality was defied in this refusal to be educated in and by a theocracy. Samira's is a post-ideological generation that, in its defiance of the institutional foregrounding of abstract idealism, reaches for a kind of virtual realism, the most brilliant manifestations of which are to be seen in Mohsen Makhmalbaf's own films. The active defiance of one particularly powerful ideological institution is the symbolic defiance of ideology itself as the meta-narrative of salvation. The aesthetic opposite of this indoctrination is a direct reading of the real and the kind of virtual realism that it entails.

To Yektapanah and Qobadi's marginal take on Iranian national identity, Samira Makhmalbaf has added the most powerful cultural alterity. Put together the solitude of an Afghani migrant laborer, the marginality of a Kurdish film-maker, and the alterity of a young Iranian woman and you have the glorious orchestration of all the major cultural others that will no longer allow the Iranian same to remain as it was. It is not just Samira Makhmalbaf but her entire generation that is reaching beyond the violent metaphysics of their parental culture toward a virtual realism that will renegotiate every aspect of that culture. The poetic pulverization of the creative ego as a way to let things manifest themselves in the world and against all metaphysics is thus no mere artistic manifesto. It is rooted in the material existence of Samira's generation.

Two critical factors underlie Samira's artistic disposition: the influence of her globally renowned father and the tragic death of her mother in 1992, when she

This picture changed forever the image of Iran in the world media. After the stark and ascetic features of Ayatollah Khomeini in the 1970s, suddenly a young and beautiful face promised the rise of a whole new generation of hope in Iran: Samira Makhmalbaf, May 1998, when she premièred *The Apple* in Cannes was about thirteen. Samira's life was brutally shaken by this sudden loss. Four years later, I met Samira for the first time, in Tehran during the summer of 1997. By then, Mohsen had married his sister-in-law, and Samira was very comfortable with her aunt and stepmother Marziyeh. But a deep melancholy still hung over Samira. She was a silent listener as her father and I talked endlessly into the midnight hours at their home. Even when Mohsen showed me her short film *The Desert* (1995), she merely listened attentively as I said how much I liked its last scene, in which the frustrated young artist suddenly stands fully erect in a medium shot against the distant foliage of a tall and verdant tree. Less than a year later, when, at the age of eighteen, she became the youngest director ever to enter a film at Cannes, Samira and I must have promenaded the Boulevard Croissette a hundred times, this time without her father, and she now conversed in a sparkling and mature manner, a delightful laughter balancing her serious gaze.

From Cannes, that year, she, her father, her brother Meysam, and I were driven by a delegation from the mayor to Yssingeaux, a small town fifty miles south of Lyon, where the Iranian national soccer team was staying for the World Cup. By the end of Cannes Film Festival that year, Samira's face had appeared in the news all over the world, and France in particular. Every day, an army of newsmen and photographers besieged her hotel on the Boulevard Croissette. The MK2 press secretary had planned every minute of her day to maximum capacity. The result was the sudden explosion of Samira as a wunderkind all over Europe. In Yssingeaux, the mayor and a handful of local Iranians held a reception for Samira and Mohsen. After spending a night in Yssingeaux, we were driven to Paris the following day where we spent two weeks. From Paris, Mohsen, Samira, and her brother returned to Tehran, and I flew to New York. In the following autumn, Samira, on a world tour to promote *The Apple*, came to New York and stayed with me for six weeks. On 21 May 2000, she called me from Cannes in excitement to say that she had won the Jury Prize, and to tell me what she was going to say in her acceptance speech. It was for almost three years, from July 1997 to May 2000, that I had witnessed the blossoming of an artist who still has much to offer the world.

Samira opted for home schooling very soon during her secondary school years. The mind-numbing ideological disposition of Islamic indoctrination has forced many parents to choose alternative modes of educating their children. Teaching his children and preparing them to be financially secure and independent has become the primary occupation of Mohsen Makhmalbaf over the last few years, at the expense of his own creative output. "Instead of making films, I decided to make filmmakers," he once told me in jest. Regular readings in Persian prose and poetry; courses in painting, photography, acting, directing, cinematography, and mise-en-scène; frame-by-frame analysis of masterpieces of world cinema; and field trips throughout Iran and precise recording of local music, customs, and other folklore have been among the staples of Samira and her siblings' education. During his prison years in the mid 1970s, Mohsen Makhmalbaf developed a penchant for simplification and systematicity in whatever he does, be it packing for a trip half-way around the globe or summarizing the main points of a book on the sociology of art. Reducing every complicated subject to its most basic principles and cultivating a minimalist spirit in himself and his children have been the hallmarks of his pedagogy. Samira Makhmalbaf was the first beneficiary of her father's prodigious care. Then Marziyeh Meshkini, Mohsen's second wife, Samira's stepmother and aunt, joined her in this free-ranging education. By the time Samira's *Blackboard* was acclaimed at Cannes, Marziyeh's *The Day I Became a Woman* (2000) was accepted for the Venice Film Festival. Meanwhile Mohsen was busy editing a behind-the-scenes documentary that his son Meysam had shot of Samira directing *Blackboard*.

But all has not been theoretical speculation in Samira's education. She and her siblings have accompanied their father on his sets. Most recently, they were all with him when he directed his short film *The Door* for *Kish Stories* (1999), and just before that, they had all gone to Dushanbe in Tajikistan to help Makhmalbaf shoot *The Silence*. While he was shooting *Safar-e Qandehar* ("*Kandehar*," 2001) in Afghanistan, Samira was with him, taking stunning photographs that were later exhibited at Cannes 2001, where *Kandehar* was premièred. In having abandoned formal schooling, and thus being more an exception than the rule, and yet precisely in being that exception, Samira Makhmalbaf stands for a generation of students who no longer represent their specific group interests and are an elite vanguard facing the harsh realities of the present. Her father's generation of students, however, from which Mohsen Makhmalbaf was also brutally cut off by his early political activity and subsequent incarceration, were mainly the crème de la crème of a middle-class bourgeoisie socially distinct from the lower classes,

While, of Mohsen Makhmalbaf's generation, about 100,000 high school grad-uates took the national university entrance examination every year and competed for about 10,000 places, in Samira's time, some thirty years later, about 3,000,000 high school graduates take the examination to compete for fewer than 250,000 places. While university capacity has increased by twenty-five-fold, less than 10 percent of students actually enter college. The 10,000 students who were lucky enough to get a higher education in Mohsen Makhmalbaf's generation were by and large socioeconomically isolated from the rest of society and yet assumed the moral responsibility of its revolutionary leadership. The 250,000 students who are lucky enough to get into the university system in Samira Makhmalbaf's generation, on the contrary, are far more representative of the population and in no mood to write ideological checks that the nation at large cannot cash. There is thus a theoretical discrepancy between the young Iranian professoriate who study the student movement today with analytical tools that are thirty years out of date, and the subject of their investigation.

The extraordinary love and devotion, experience, and erudition of her father notwithstanding, Samira is ultimately her own person. Blessed as she has been to grow up with a gifted and dedicated father, her creative disposition is entirely different from his. To understand her creative character, we must place her in the context of the immediate events of her generation. When she accepted the Jury Prize at Cannes in 2000, Samira, choking with emotion and having to pause and start again from the beginning, spoke of a dream: "On behalf of a new genera-tion of hope in my homeland, I accept this prize to honor the heroic efforts of all young Iranians who struggle for democracy and the promise of a better life in Iran." That dedication marks the generation that has come a long and arduous way to culminate in her eloquent voice and vision.

Mohsen Makhmalbaf commenced his filmmaking career as Islamic ideology reached a dead end in its failure to deliver what it had promised. Samira Makhmalbaf began her filmmaking career at the open-ended entrance of her gen-eration into a vision of reality with no claim to a monopoly on truth, an insistence on the particular, and no patience for the universal. Her generation was morally and materially fed on two complementary doses: first, the exaggerated claims of Islamic ideology, which were checked and balanced by, second, the rise of a mode of neorealism in Iranian cinema that achieved its most magnificent moments in the cinema of Bani-Etemad, Kiarostami, and Makhmalbaf, and which could easily trace its origin to another glorious achievement of Iranian cinema, Forough Farrokhzad's *The House Is Black* (1962).

Samira Makhmalbaf's generation of Iranian youth is post-ideological. The most emphatic expression of the death of ideology in Iranian political culture occurred in July 1999 when thousands of Iranian youth poured into the streets in support of President Khatami's reforms.[12] The singular feature of the July 1999 student uprising was its refusal to be part of any identifiable ideological movement. Scattered demonstrations against a severe press law that was intended to thwart the reform movement in anticipation of the February 2000 national election were brutally suppressed by armed vigilantes on the payroll of the religious right. Tehran University dormitories were ransacked and students were savagely beaten. Between 8 July and 12 July 2000, Iran was the scene of massive demonstrations against the abrogation of civil rights and the crackdown on the press.

Not a single ideological group, left or right, religious or secular, could claim this massive movement. Its grassroots force had long since abandoned any specific ideological claim. Two decades of empty ideological warfare had resulted in no tangible change in the status of youth. The revolution had run aground in both its moral and material bases. The 1979 revolution, for which Samira's father had fought and been jailed, and to whose ideological fortification he first devoted his creative talents, was the spectacular result of decades of ideological preparations that had woven the fabric of Iranian society into a massive millenarian expectation. Two decades of a tyrannical theocracy had extracted every ounce of hope and expectation from that ideology.

The presidential election of May 1997 was a spectacular upset that put Iran on an entirely unprecedented track. Mohammad Khatami, the former Minister of Culture, under whose auspices Iranian cinema had achieved much of its glory, won the election by such a large margin that there remained no doubt as to where the sympathy and hope of the postrevolutionary Iran lay. Samira Makhmalbaf was one among 20 million Iranians who voted for Khatami, some 65 percent of them like Samira in nature and disposition. They were fed up with ideological slogans and political demagoguery, the logic of their material need for change far exceeding their patience for ideological rhetoric.

In two crucial ways Samira represents the hope that is now invested in Khatami: in being young and in being a woman. Women and the young were the principal groups that overwhelmingly voted for Khatami. The reason is quite obvious: women have been the most disenfranchised segment of Iranian society, and the material needs of the Iranian youth have no time for exaggerated promises. Both of these critical themes entered into the defining moment of Samira's first film. If there is one counter-ideological statement that may serve as the manifesto of the generation that Samira best represents, it is in her first feature film, *The Apple*: "No one is to blame," it proclaims. Yet this film is unflinching in its diagnosis of what has gone wrong, what calamitous tyranny has been exercised over Samira and the rest of the population, women in particular, by the parental generation.

The Apple is based on the true story of an overprotective father, tyrannical in his custodial love, who kept his two daughters locked up at home since their birth. "It is the story of our nation," Mohsen told me when the news first broke towards the end of July 1997, as I was leaving Tehran some two months after Khatami was elected president. "We have all been kept in a cave by our fathers. We can't even look at the sun." But that is the parental judgment. Samira herself is far more forgiving, and yet far more clinical in her detailed analysis. *The Apple* chronicles the girls' liberation from their living burial and their restoration to life. Samira takes this story and works it into a simple but compelling account of society at large.

When the social worker assigned to help the newly liberated girls arrives, she first speaks with their father. He is seated behind the grill of his door and talks to the social worker through the barriers he has constructed. Suddenly, a ball comes over the courtyard wall, and the father says:

> Didn't I tell you, ma'am, that I have to lock the door. That's why. The boys in the street throw their ball into our court. Then they ring the bell, and when they don't hear any answer, they climb the wall and jump into our yard. Now, I ask you, if one of them were to do some harm to my girls, what am I to do?

As if to confirm his fear, a few particularly naughty-looking boys look over the top of the wall and ask the social worker to throw them their ball. "You know what the problem is, sir?" the social worker says. "The problem is that they are

Samira Makhmalbaf's *The Apple* turns the real-life story of the protective incarceration of two young girls by their father into an allegory of deliverance and redemption. Here she takes the story back a generation and tempts the mother of the two girls with an apple

From the proceeds of *The Apple* the two incarcerated young girls are schooled and socialized into a world with open-ended possibilities

girls. If they were boys they could have played outside. They could even climb people's walls." The father does not answer the social worker right away. He insists on referring to the authority of a book: the biblical terror of the written word. "Have you ever seen the book *Fathers' Advice*, ma'am?" She has not. "Do you know what it says about girls?" She does not. The father pulls a book from his pocket and hands it through the iron bars to the woman.

> Please, ma'am, study it and see what is written about young girls. It is written that a young girl is just like a flower, and the sun is like a man who is not related to her. Should the sun cast its light on the flower, the flower will wither. The story of man and woman is just like fire and cotton. Should fire come anywhere near cotton, it will burn it.

Samira does something magical with this metaphor of flower and sun. In the opening shot of the film, the hand of one of the two sisters reaches through the bars that have incarcerated her to gently water a lone flower in a pot. In that dilapidated prison house, that single shot brings water, flower, and sun into a singular celebration of life.

The Apple thus becomes a devastating condemnation of the mind-numbing oppression of women, not just in Iran, but anywhere. An allegory of global relevance, *The Apple* has particular force in Samira's own homeland where the hopes and aspirations of the young are bursting through all the historically received and ideologically reinforced injustices perpetrated against women. Indebted as Samira is to a gifted, caring, and dedicated father, it is more to her ancestral generations of spiritual mothers that she owes the power of her art. Simin Daneshvar in fiction; Rakhshan Bani-Etemad in cinema; Forough Farrokhzad in poetry: and then Parvin E'tesami, Qamar al-Moluk Vaziri, Taj al-Saltaneh, and, first and foremost, that glorious figure of the nineteenth century, Qorrat al-Ayn, stand behind Samira Makhmalbaf. It is not accidental that the first poem that comes to Samira's mind, when asked to recite her favorite stanza during an interview, is by Forough Farrokhzad:

> I speak of the depth of night,
> I
> of the depth of darkness
> Speak.

If you were to visit me,
bring me,
dearest,
a lamp,
and a crevice,
from which I could watch
the crowd in the happy street.[13]

BLACKBOARD (2000)

In *Blackboard*, Samira Makhmalbaf's camera becomes that very window that
Forough's poem demands. This film clarifies much in Samira's cinematic rebellion against her paralyzing culture. *Blackboard* is a film against culture and for
life. *Culture* here is personified by a band of jobless teachers, insurers of dead certainties, put out of work by brutal forces beyond their control. *Life* here parades
itself in the form of a band of children trying to make a living, while a group of
old men are in search of their death. Hovering between life and death, the two
factual realities of the evident, the teachers are hopelessly unemployed, unable to
persuade either the young or the old to learn how to read and write. Samira, the
high school dropout, is getting back at the system.

To condemn culture and celebrate life, Samira has to create the visual language of urgency. One sequence into *Blackboard*, she generates a succession of
negations and contradictions among characters fearing imminent attack by the
Iraqi army. In that tense atmosphere, she is ready to tell her story. First and foremost, the countercultural narrative establishes itself on a virtual ground, at once
particular and universal. We are not in Iran. We are not in Iraq. We are in Kurdestan, a nonstate. We are nowhere. We are everywhere. Visually conveying this
universality of the particular is an art that Samira has learned from watching her
father's latest work. No other Iranian filmmaker approaches Mohsen Makhmalbaf's ingenious ability to distill reality to its virtual signals.

Everything about *Blackboard* is familiarly particular, and yet that familiarity
leads to the making of a universal parable. The film seems almost like a documentary. It has only one professional actor; the rest are local people of the
Kurdestan province of Iran, children engaged in smuggling, old men returning

to their hometown of Halabcheh after an Iraqi gas attack, and teachers with no schools or students to teach. The teachers have on their backs, like black wings, their blackboards, which make them resemble strange, hopping birds, and we follow them as they negotiate their arduous way through the mountain passes. The result is a visual fable, where everything is familiar, and yet we sense the presence of something universal.

Samira puts a mommy-daddy-baby trinity at the center of the fable, as one of the wandering teachers, an insane unwed mother, and a bewildered, fatherless child are brought together. This is a family formed out of desperation, a parody of a family, brought together under duress. The mother seeks protection, the man craves a companion, and the child does not know what it needs. The result is a virtual family that is there but not there, that is dysfunctional, and gets placed at the center of a tale that is no longer just in Kurdestan. It is the visual evidence of humanity at large. This is Iranian cinema at its absolute best, where the Iranian particular is universalized without the slightest concession to that particularity or its universality. The culture collapses by dismantling its familial unit, de-Oedipalizing its sexual urgency, and erasing all its moral consequences.

The mise-en-scène of the marriage ceremony is ingenious. An old man presides. The blackboard stands right in the midst, the man on one side, the woman and her child on the other. While the man holds the blackboard erect, the woman supports the child as he urinates. Meanwhile the old man performs an impromptu marriage ceremony. "Do you take this man?" etc. For the groom, this is quite serious, but not for the bride. The event is as serious, or ludicrous, as her child's pissing in the air. She is, *ipso facto*, agreeing—is she not?—to yet another man's right to piss into her. She is consenting to this, as her son, the result of someone else's having pissed into her, is pissing in the air. The picture is perfect, brutal in its banality.

The marriage is never consummated. The man is desperate to make love to his wife. She couldn't care less. The child is always lingering nearby. The old men try to distract him so that the newlyweds can have a moment of privacy, but they fail. The woman calls her husband "Blackboard" after his occupation. For her, he is only his profession, the source of sustenance for her and her child. But now, his blackboard seems to be useless. It is turned into a shield to protect her and her child against the imminent attack, yet the protection it offers is fictitious. It can stop no bullet or bomb; it cannot even give them a moment of privacy. Its protection is only symbolic. The blackboard is the making of knowledge, black and blank, rarely anything written on it. The result is the accumulation of even more impetus to the intensity of this persistently dire narrative. The husband is desperate to fuck his newly wed wife, but he cannot. The cycle of desperation in *Blackboard* rises in a crescendo: young children urgently trying to get to their destination but lost in the mountains, old men helplessly trying to get to their village but trapped in the same landscape, teachers hopelessly trying to find students to teach, a mother sacrificing everything to protect her young child, a husband bent on cornering his wife. Samira draws all these pulsating tensions together in the figure of an old man who painfully tries to urinate but cannot. He is *Shash-band*, a clinically descriptive Persian term (literally, "piss-arrested").

Thus, everything is on the verge of happening in *Blackboard*; everything is in a critical moment of expectation. This is an odyssey of desperate expectations and impotence. One of the greatest achievements of *Blackboard* is the sustaining of this tension, this being on the verge. The constellation of these emotive urges, of expectation and urgency, accentuated by the imminent danger of an Iraqi gas attack, splits open the plaster of normalcy in the appearance of the real and pulls every aspect of the evident culture out for negotiation. The most critical moment Samira chooses for this negotiation is the pre-moment of *naming*, when *things* are still *things* and have no name. When the band of student-less teachers are wandering through the rugged mountains, desperate for students, we witness something more than Samira getting back at her teachers. In a brilliantly choreographed scene, a young woman who is milking a goat gives some milk to a teacher. He has finally persuaded a single boy to learn to write his name, and the boy takes in this knowledge as the teacher drinks his milk. In this epiphanic scene, the camera oscillates between the milk and the chalk, between a living white substance and dead white knowledge. The teacher takes in fresh life while he gives dead knowledge to the boy. Suddenly, the boy's head pops out from behind the blackboard, as he exclaims joyfully that he has finally learned to write his name, Ribwar. Instantly, a gunshot rings out and the boy falls dead. As the teacher is revived by his drink, the boy dies the moment he learns to write his name. The name thus becomes the death of the named. In Samira Makhmalbaf's received Qur'anic truth, God summons man, *before* his creation, and teaches him the names of all things. It is precisely that Qur'anic truth of the named things that is here erased, pulling the reality of things before they are culturally coded over and above that of their metaphysical codification.

Samira moves to redeem the teachers by instructing them how to teach unnamed truth. But first she has to release her alter ego, the woman in the midst of all these men. The wedding ceremony at the beginning of *Blackboard* is undone by the divorce ceremony at the end. The same blackboard stands erect between the husband and wife. The same old man who conducted the marriage ceremony presides. The man and woman take their places on either side of the blackboard. The old man raises his cane in his right hand and extends it to the woman, who grasps it. The old man gives his left hand to the seated husband, who grips it with his right hand and with his left holds onto the blackboard. A circle is thus formed from the woman's right hand to the wooden cane to the old man's right hand, through his body, to his left hand and on to the husband's right hand. He completes the circle with his left hand on the blackboard. Dead wood and living flesh welded together. The unconsummated marriage is annulled. The child remains immaculately conceived, the familial nucleus de-Oedipalized, the culture collapsed.

Blackboard ends as the teacher, now divorced and solitary, redeems himself by abandoning the teaching of dead certainties, and becoming a guide to unknown territories. He learns how to fabricate a signal truth, a different kind of *naming*. In the midst of the expected gas attack, the old men scream in fear that they want to die in their homeland. But there is no sign of any homeland, or any land at all. They seem to be suspended in midair, in a thick fog; no land is visible. In this moment that resembles the Day of Judgment, the teacher finally rises to the occasion, fabricating and authenticating a truth that matters. He raises his voice against the screams to proclaim that the land on which the old men are standing is holy. They *are* in their homeland. The teacher has used his privilege of *naming* and rendered this place their lost homeland. The old men prostrate themselves, ready to die in peace.

In the concluding scene Samira's camera stands still, as we watch the mother walk up a mountain path, finding her own way, with her son by her side, and the blackboard, the memory of a husband she never had, on her back. The blackboard remains as the reminder of a teacher who had finally learned how to teach. It is Samira's lesson to all the teachers she never had.

When Mohsen Makhmalbaf was seventeen years old he drew a knife to stab a policeman in order to launch a revolution to liberate his country. When his daughter Samira was seventeen years old, she borrowed her father's camera and shot a film to record the liberation of two young girls from their father's prison house. Mohsen Makhmalbaf failed to achieve his end and landed in jail. Samira Makhmalbaf succeeded in recording an emancipation and showed it to the world. She went on to make another film, anticipating a freedom no one can take away. Mohsen Makhmalbaf may have taught Samira Makhmalbaf how to make films, but she has taught her father how to liberate a nation.

WHITHER IRANIAN CINEMA?

While the old masters are waning in Tehran and in Cannes, the new ones are waxing in the creamiest of the Iranian puff surfaces, the United States. The principal venue for Iranian cinema in the United States is the New York Film Festival, whose programming director, Richard Peña, has introduced the best Iranian filmmakers over the last two decades. Commercial releases by New Yorker Films, Zeitgeist, Miramax, October Films, and the Shooting Gallery have made the treasures of the New York Film Festival more widely available. But the commercial success of films such as Majid Majidi's *Children of Heaven* or *The Color of Paradise* indicates that there is no critical apparatus to distinguish between a major Iranian film and a mediocre imitation. The fact that Iranians have produced three generations of first-rate filmmakers over the last half century does not mean that they have not produced popular entertainment of mind-numbing banality, as is true of any other great national cinema.

A common reading of Iranian cinema is predicated on the demagogic claim that many of the so-called auteur or art films which are internationally acclaimed are in fact locally irrelevant and inaccessible. This argument holds that the more accessible films that address common social issues—the oppression of women, the predicament of the youth—are far more locally relevant. Like all other such invidious claims, this position confuses the use of the cinema as occasional entertainment and Band-Aid collective therapy with the ability of art to imagine a culture otherwise. It is true that Samira Makhmalbaf's films, like those of a host of other great Iranian filmmakers, are viewed much more frequently internationally than domestically. It is equally true that popular films inside the country often address timely issues. But the timeliness of these latter films is precisely the recipe for their disastrous failure. By virtue of being timely, they are limited in their ability to imagine things otherwise than they are. They are too factually realistic to be effectively real. They are trapped in the surface of the real and can never bypass the immediacy of experience. As a result, they accept the status quo and cannot reconfigure the historical agency of their characters.

In contrast, what is taking place in the best of Iranian cinema is precisely that it is not *timely*. By not being timely, these films have been far more relevant. Iranian cinema at its best is the Copernican heliocentricism that has surpassed the geocentricism of Iranian politics. The problem is not that the best of Iranian filmmakers cannot see what is in front of them and are pursuing things irrelevant to their reality. On the contrary, it is the Iranian public intellectuals, the so-called reformists, who cannot see what is in front of them when they are faced with a Kiarostami or a Makhmalbaf, and are busy digging their own narrative grave.

The virtual realism of Samira Makhmalbaf, predicated on the work of her father, dismantles the instrumentality of reason with which we see, do, or make things such as a mountain, a marriage, or a revolution. Whereas her father had to learn to tear down the metaphysics of naming in order to reach for the pre-named thing itself through trial and error, to her it comes naturally. She does not have to unlearn her knowledge. She goes for the thing itself. She belongs to a post-ideological and pre-theoretical generation that has among its cultural heroes no grandiloquent ideologues like Jalal Al-e Ahmad or Ali Shari'ati. Cinema corresponds to the moral disposition of this generation, and thus the best of them are attracted to it. Cinema is predisposed to be post-ideological because its visuality subverts any trace of verbality, ideological or otherwise, that may have contaminated its delivery.

The reason that films such as *The Apple* and *Blackboard* are superior to an avalanche of socially and politically relevant films that address the plight of the poor, the oppression of women, or the calamities of the religious revolution is their constitutional defiance of the instrumentality at the core of the culture

From *The Apple*: without passing any judgement, Samira Makhmalbaf issues a damning indictment against Iranian patriarchal culture

which those films seek to subvert. The most debilitating aspect of journalistic writing about Iranian (or any other) film festival is precisely this aggressive reduction of a work of art to the kind of instrumental correspondence that journalists are quite naturally drawn to. "So this film is about women in Iran?" They ask, but really provide their own answer. "So here you are condemning Saddam Hossein's gassing of civilians in Halabcheh?" Any sane person is concerned about the oppression of women in Iran and much of the rest of the world, and categorically condemns Saddam Hossein's atrocities in Halabcheh and anywhere else. But this is not the way a work of art alerts, objects, condemns, or celebrates.

Like *The Apple* and *Blackboard*, a work of art must leave the material site of the real in order to reach for the moral venues of the possible. It will have to be momentarily unreasonable in order to be reasonably able to dream the real otherwise. The persistent objection of many viewers, Iranians or others, that these films are different and thus difficult to understand, is due precisely to the graceful resistance of these films to assimilation backward into immediately useful and usable statements. They persist in their alterity, and the measure of their success is gauged precisely in their ability to defy regressing into that same instrumental reason. By reaching for the thing of the world prior to and after its instrumental readings, such works of art, as things themselves, assemble the world, as Heidegger has demonstrated,[14] or, even more precisely, constantly reassemble it. In the act of reassembling the world, the thing is stripped of all its prior and future readings, absolving it of all its modes of signification, and teasing out its signaling presence.

Two decades and then two centuries into a brutal head-on collision with the impossibility of being modern without being colonized, Samira's generation has finally opted for visually theorizing the "thing-in-itself," with no need of its Kantian contradistinction to "thing-for-us." The reality of a colonial condition is so materially backbreaking that it is constitutionally desedimented toward its noumena. After a revolution that was to end all revolutions, Samira's generation is now de-experiencing every "thing-for-us" and taking it back to the "thing-in-itself." This revolution will thus end all revolutions, not by virtue of its political success, but by virtue of its ideological failure. Islamic ideology was no ordinary ideology. Muslim ideologues invested everything they had, their very stance in the world, their ancestral faith in their place of dignity. Thus, they exposed the ancient roots of their every claim to authenticity to the corrosive elements of Enlightenment modernity, instrumental rationalism, and the blind logic of a capitalism that would not compromise. Back to the "thing-in-itself" was no philosophical proposition in the coloniality of this condition. The "thing-for-us" had left us no possible choice. The "present-at-hand" of the colonial condition is the most common denominator of all possible things, the very materiality of our being-in-the-world. What is called Iranian neorealism is this uncanny ability to concentrate on the real in such a way that reveals its irreducible "round-about-us" nature,[15] its ready-at-hand quality, its refusal to heed the call to arms of any ideology, religion, or culture.

In an attempt to define philosophy, Heidegger once stated: "When we ask, 'What Is Philosophy?' then we are speaking *about* philosophy. By asking in this way we are obviously taking a stand above and, therefore, outside of philosophy. But the aim of our question is to enter *into* philosophy, to tarry in it, to conduct ourselves in its manner, that is, to 'philosophize.'"[16] In the case of Iranian cinema, the presence of visuality is constitutional to the deconditioning of the real, so that it can expose itself as no longer predicated on a basis, a ground, a frame of reference, a debilitating memory, a "culture." By framing the real *art*-ificially, the visual act deframes the real from all its conditional perceptions, receptions, and registers. To put art, the visual and performing arts in particular, consciously at the service of social and political causes ultimately and paradoxically ossifies and thus intensifies precisely those forces that have conditioned those causes. A far more radical and effective negation of those forces is to abandon the site of their authority on which the most politically subversive is mutated into its instrumental logic. That is why Kiarostami remains thus far the most political of all Iranian filmmakers despite the fact that he himself has never taken any political stance on anything.

In Iran, the old masters are indulging in self-reflection, and, in doing so take their ego for the world. In Cannes, the new masters are measuring themselves in and against the world. In Iran, the old masters are big fish in a small pond; at Cannes, the new masters are sizable fish in an ocean. The result is the end of the colossal correspondence between the large but empty egos of constitutionally inorganic intellectuals and their ideological wet-dreaming, yielding, as they must, to post-ideological organic visionaries and their ability to imagine themselves otherwise.

The new visionaries are creatures of an entirely different breed. They are yet to mutate their creative ego into a simulacrum of public persona because they are the children of a potential victory over both Persian monarchy and Islamic patriarchy, two deadly variations on the same theme. The older generation of public intellectuals were bound to have an expansive ego because they were the end, albeit negational, result of absolutist tyrannies. The greater the public perception of our cultural heroes, the closer they were to imitating the tyrannical totality of our dictators and their megalomania. It is the profoundest and saddest fact of our cultural life that our greatest and most valiant public intellectuals modulated their creative ego on a subconscious inflection of our most brutal tyrants. There is an affinity between Ahmad Shamlu and Ayatollah Khomeini that defines them both.

However rough, tough, and only modular in the making, even an Islamic Republic is a republic. These new masters are the children of a different future. They have seen the death and dissemination of their father figures in a historically miraculous scenario. They have heard from their parents that our modern history began with Reza Shah the Great, a tyrant father figure exiled from the country by the colonial power of an abstraction they know only as the Allied Forces. Reza Shah's son, Mohammad Reza Shah, was a feeble father figure, but he compensated for his inferiority by aggressive plans for a great civilization, aiming to become the Japan of the Middle East, and to have the highest dams, the biggest egos, and the longest history. But all this failed when the parents of these children sided with their grandfather to get rid of that passively aggressive father. The Shah they saw die in exile in Egypt and be buried with indignity in the al-Rifa'i Mosque in Cairo. As children, they saw their brothers and sisters sent by the millions to be killed on the battlefields of a brutal and barbaric war. The grandfather now sent his grandchildren to their death. Then they remember seeing that grandfather die also, and they well remember seeing the emergence of two figures to replace him, Khamen'i and Rafsanjani, one lacking his right arm and the other a beard. This was a wondrous semiotics of emancipation in which the father figure was split in half and metaphorically emasculated. Finally, when these children had a chance to choose between a stark Khomeini look-alike called Nateq Nuri and a man who was soft-spoken, gentle, smiling, and remarkably feminine in his facial features, Mohammad Khatami, they voted wholeheartedly for Khatami. Their father figure split and emasculated, they could finally vote for their mother. They are in very little danger of mutating their creative ego into the presumption of a public persona. The generation that preceded them crafted their creative ego out of opposition to tyrants. These children conform to an entirely different hope. They have seen the world celebrate and embrace their youthful dreams and deposit their fathers' overwrought works— now grandiloquent claims on our credulity—safely in the Museum of National Identity. Alterity is this generation's choice. A young woman from the southernmost part of the capital, a Kurd from the westernmost periphery of ethnic minorities, and then a filmmaker with enough courage and imagination to make a young Afghan refugee from the easternmost land of migratory laborers the center of his narrative are the new cultural heroes. This generation has been in the making for two hundred years. The generation that preceded them took their selves for the other. But they were not. Qobadi, Makhmalbaf, and Yekta-panah are not the same. They are the other.

The new filmmakers are immune from actively mutating their creative ego into a public persona because they are the children of a revolution, a war, and then of a democratic uprising. In the revolution they have seen the "father" of their country die with indignity, in the war they have seen their "grandfather" send their brothers and sisters to perish in millions, and in their glorious democratic uprising they are appealing to no other father figure, dead or alive. They have been born out of wedlock, of an immaculate conception: like Bashu and Baran, "they are the children and Heaven and Earth."

FILMOGRAPHY

Rakhshan Bani-Etemad

Farhang-e Masrafi (*"The Culture of Consumption,"* 1984).
Eshteghal-e Mohajerin Rustay'i dar Shahr (*"Occupations of Migrant Peasants in the City,"* 1985).
Tadbirhaye Eghtesadi-e Jang (*"The War Economic Planning,"* 1986).
Kharej az Mahdudeh (*"Off Limits,"* 1987).
Tamarkoz (*"Centralization,"* 1987).
Zard-e Qanari (*"Canary Yellow,"* 1988).
Pul-e Khareji (*"Foreign Currency,"* 1989).
Nargess (1991).
Gozaresh-e 71 (*"The 1992 Report,"* 1992).
Bahar ta Bahar (*"Spring to Spring,"* 1993).
In film ha ra beh ki neshun midin? (*"To Whom Do You Show These Films, Anyway?,"* 1993).
Rusari Abi (*"The Blue-Veiled,"* 1994).
Akharin Didar Ba Iran Daftari (*"The Last Visit with Iran Daftari,"* 1995).
Zir-e Pust-e Shahr (*"Under the Skin of the City,"* 1996).
Banu-ye Ordibehesht (*"The May Lady,"* 1998).
Baran-o Bumi (*"Baran and the Native,"* 1999).
Zir-e Pust-e Shahr (*Under the Skin of the City,* 2000).

Bahram Beiza'i

Amu Sibilu (*"Uncle Mustache,"* 1970).
Ragbar (*"Thunder Shower,"* 1971).
Safar (*"The Journey,"* 1972).
Gharibeh va Meh (*"The Stranger and the Fog,"* 1974).
Kalagh (*"The Crow,"* 1977).
Cherikeh-ye Tara (*"The Ballad of Tara,"* 1978).
Marg-e Yazdgerd (*"The Death of Yazdgerd,"* 1983).
Bashu: Gharibeh-ye Kuchak (*"Bashu: the Little Stranger,"* 1986).
Shayad Vaqhti Digar (*"Perhaps Some Other Time,"* 1988).
Mosaferan (*"Travelers,"* 1992).
Sag-Koshi (*"Dog-Eat-Dog,"* 2001).

Ali Daryabeigi

Tufan-e Zendegi (*"The Tempest of Life,"* 1948).

Bahman Farmanara

Khaneh-ye Qamar Khanom (*"Qamar Khanom's House,"* 1972).
Shazdeh Ehtejab (*"Prince Ehtejab,"* 1974).
Sayeh-ha-ye Boland-e Bad (*"Tall Shadows of the Wind,"* 1978).
Bu-ye Kafur, Atr-e Yas (*"Smell of Camphor, Fragrance of Jasmine,"*) 2000.

Forough Farrokhzad

Khaneh Siyah Ast (*"The House Is Black,"* 1962).

Farrokh Ghaffari

Jonub-e Shahr (*"Downtown,"* 1958).
Shab-e Quzi (*"The Night of the Hunchback,"* 1964).

Ebrahim Golestan

Khesht va Ayeneh (*"The Brick and the Mirror,"* 1965).
Asrar-e Ganj-e Darreh-ye Jenni (*"The Secrets of the Jinn-Infested Valley,"* 1974).

Ardeshir Irani

Dokhtar-e Lor (*"The Lor Girl,"* 1933).

Ali Kasma'i

Ya'qub Layth Saffari (1957).

Parviz Khatibi

Dastkesh-e Sefid (*"The White Glove,"* 1951).

Abbas Kiarostami

Nan va Kucheh (*"Bread and the Alley,"* 1970).
Mosafer (*"The Traveler,"* 1972).
Zang-e Tafrih (*"Recess,"* 1972).
Tajrobeh (*"The Experience,"* 1973).
Manam Mitunam (*"So Can I,"* 1975).
Do Rah-e Hal bara-ye Yek Mas'aleh (*"Two Solutions for One Problem,"* 1975).
Lebosi bara-ye Arusi (*"Suit for a Wedding,"* 1976).
Rang-ha (*"Colors,"* 1976).
Gozaresh (*"The Report,"* 1977).
Rah-e Hal (*"The Solution,"* 1978).
Qaziyeh Shekl-e Avval, Qaziyeh Shekl-e Dovvum (*"The First Version, The Second Version,"* 1979).
Dandan-dard (*"Toothache,"* 1980).
Beh Tartib ya Bedun-e Tartib (*"With or Without Order,"* 1981).
Hamsarayan (*"The Chorus,"* 1982).
Hamshahri (*"Fellow Citizen,"* 1983).
Avvali-ha (*"First-Graders,"* 1985).
Khaneh-ye Dust Kojast (*"Where Is the Friend's House?,"* 1987).
Mashq-e Shab (*"Homework,"* 1990).
Nama-y Nazdik (*"Close-Up,"* 1990).
Zendegi va digar Hich/Va Zendegi Edameh Darad (*"Life and then Nothing/And Life Goes On,"* 1992).

Zir-e Derakhtan-e Zeytun (*"Through the Olive Trees,"* 1994).
Ta'm-e Gilas (*"Taste of Cherry,"* 1996).
Bad Ma ra ba Khod Khahad Bord (*"The Wind Will Carry Us Away,"* 1999).

Mas'ud Kimiya'i

Qeysar (*"Caesar,"* 1969).
Reza Motori (*"Reza, the Cyclist,"* 1970).
Dash Akol (1971).
Baluch (1972).
Khak ("The Earth," 1973).
Gavazn-ha (*"The Deer,"* 1975).
Ghazal (*"The Gazelle,"* 1976).
Safar-e Sang (*"The Journey of Stone,"* 1978).
Khat-e Qermez (*"The Red Line,"* 1982).
Shab-e Samur (*"The Night of Samur,"* 1984).
Tigh-o-Abrisham (*"The Blade and the Silk,"* 1986).
Dandan-e Mar (*"Fang,"* 1990).
E'teraz (*"Protest,"* 2000).

Esma'il Kushan

Zendani-ye Amir (*"The Prince's Prisoner,"* 1948).
The Tempest of Life (1948).
Contrite (1950).
Intoxicating Love (1951).
Madar ("Mother," 1952).
Kolah-Makhmali (*"Velvety-Hat,"* 1962).
Ebram dar Paris (*"Ebram in Paris,"* 1964).

Mohsen Makhmalbaf

Tobeh-ye Nasuh (*"Nasuh's Repentance,"* 1982).
Do Chashm-e Bi-Su (*"Two Sightless Eyes,"* 1983).
Este'azeh (*"Seeking Refuge,"* 1983).

Baykot ("*Boycott,*" 1985).
Dastforush ("*The Peddler,*" 1986).
Bicycle-ran ("*The Cyclist,*" 1987).
Arusi-ye Khuban ("*The Marriage of the Blessed,*" 1988).
Nobat-e Asheqi ("*A Time for Love,*" 1990).
Shabha-ye Zayandeh-rud ("*Zayandeh-rud Nights,*" 1990).
Naseroddin Shah, Actor-e Cinema ("*Once upon a Time, Cinema,*" 1991).
Honarpisheh ("*The Actor,*" 1992).
Gozideh Tasvir dar Duran-e Qajar ("*Painting of the Qajar Period,*" 1992).
Sang-o-Shisheh ("*The Stone and the Mirror,*" 1993).
Salam Cinema (1994).
Nun va Goldun ("*Bread and Flower-Pot*" or "*A Moment of Innocence,*" 1995).
Gabbeh (1995).
Madreseh-i keh Bad Bord ("*The School That Was Blown Away,*" 1997).
Sokut ("*The Silence,*" 1998).
Dar ("*The Door,*" 1999).
Test-e Demokrasi ("*Testing Democracy,*" 2000).
Safar-e Qandehar ("*Kandahar,*" 2001).

Samira Makhmalbaf

Sib ("*The Apple,*" 1998).
Takhteh-Siah ("*Blackboard,*" 2000).

Farhad Mehraufat

Cherikeh-ye Huram ("*The Ballad of Huram,*" 2000).

Daryush Mehrju'i

Almas 33 ("*Diamond 33,*" 1967).
Gav ("*The Cow,*" 1969).
Agha-ye Halu ("*Mr. Simpleton,*" 1970).
Postchi ("*The Mailman,*" 1972).
Dayereh-ye Mina ("*Mina Cycle,*" 1978).

Hayat-e Poshti-ye Madreseh-ye Adl-e Afagh/Madreseh'i keh Miraftim ("The Backyard
    of the School of Universal Justice/The School We Used To Go To," 1980).
Ejareh-Neshin-ha ("The Tenants," 1986).
Hamoun (1990).
Banu (1992).
Sara (1993).
Pari (1994).
Leila (1996).
Derakht-e Golabi ("The Pear Tree," 1998).
Mix (2000).
Dokhtar-da'i Gom Shodeh ("The Cousin Is Lost," 2000).

Majid Mohseni

Lat-e Javanmard ("The Valiant Vagabond," 1958).

Davud Mollapour

Shohar-e Ahu Khanom ("Ahu Khanom's Husband," 1968).[1]

Ebrahim Moradi

Enteqam-e Baradar ("The Brother's Revenge," 1931).
Bolhavas ("Rapacious," 1934).

Amir Naderi

Khoda-hafez Rafiq ("Farewell, My Friend," 1971).
Tangna ("Tight Spot," 1973).
Saz-dahani ("The Harmonica," 1973).
Tangsir (1973).
Marsiyeh ("The Eulogy," 1978).
Sakht-e Iran ("Made in Iran," 1979).
Josteju ("The Search," 1981).
Davandeh ("The Runner," 1985).
Ab, Bad, Khak ("Water, Wind, Dust," 1988).

Manhattan by Numbers (1993).
A, B, C . . . Manhattan (1997).

Avanes Oganians

Abi va Rabi ("*Abi and Rabi,*" 1930).
Haji Aqa, Actor-e Cinema ("*Haji Aqa, the Movie Star,*" 1932).

Bahman Qobadi

A Time for Drunken Horses (2000).

Fereydun Rahnema

Seyavash dar Takht-e Jamshid ("*Seyavash in Persepolis,*" 1967).

Parviz Sayyad

Bonbast ("*Dead End,*" 1977).

Abdolhossein Sepanta

Ferdowsi (1934).
Shirin va Farhad ("*Shirin and Farhad,*" 1934).
Chashman-e Siyah ("*The Dark Eyes,*" 1936).
Leili va Majnun ("*Leili and Majnun,*" 1937).

Sohrab Shahid Sales

Yek Ettefaq-e Sadeh ("*One Simple Incident,*" 1973).
Tabi'at-e Bi-Jan ("*Still Life,*" 1975).
Dar Ghorbat ("*In Exile,*" 1975).

Musheq Soruri

Shab-Neshin dar Jahannm ("*Banquet in Hell,*" 1957).

Shapur Yasami

Amir Arsalan-e Namdar ("Amir Arsalan the Famous," 1955).
Ganj-e Qarun ("Qarun's Treasure," 1965).

Hasan Yektapanah

Jom'eh (2000).

NOTES

I ON MODERNITY AND THE MAKING OF
A NATIONAL CINEMA

1. For a brief historical account of Iranian cinema, see Farrokh Gaffary, *Le cinéma en Iran*, Tehran: Le Conseil de la Culture et des Arts et Centre d'Étude et de la Co-ordination Culturelle, 1973, or Mohammad Ali Issari, *Cinema in Iran*, Metuchen, NJ, 1989.
2. Immanuel Kant, *Grounding for the Metaphysics of Morals*, Hackett Publishing, 1981, p. 30.
3. See M. Mehrabi, *Tarikh-e Cinema-ye Iran*, Tehran: Film Publications, 1984, pp. 22–3.
4. See Jamshid Akrami, "The Blighted Spring," in D. H. Downing (ed.), *Film and Politics in the Third World*, Autonomedia, 1987, p. 133.
5. For a concise articulation of the Islamic juridical, theological, and philosophical positions vis-à-vis the issue of visual representation, see Seyyed Mohammad Kazem Assar "Tasvir dar Islam," in *Ma'aref Islami*, no. 2, pp. 5–19. Seyyed Kazem Assar (1885–1974) was a prominent Muslim theologian and philosopher with a rare affinity for the European Enlightenment. He had studied both in Najaf and in Paris. His views on the question of visual representation in Islam are a model of precision by an enlightened Muslim thinker.
6. Kant, 1981, p. 30.
7. Mehrabi, 1984, p. 17.
8. J. Omid, *Farhang-e Film-ha-ye Cinema-ye Iran*, Negah Publishers, 1987, vol. I, p. 7.
9. Mehrabi, 1984, p. 42.

2 THE MAKING OF AN IRANIAN FILMMAKER: ABBAS KIAROSTAMI

1. See Mas'ud Mehrabi, *Tarikh-e Cinema-ye Iran*, Tehran: Film Publications, 1984, pp. 50–51.
2. Theodor W. Adorno, *Aesthetic Theory*, newly translated, edited, and with translator's introduction by Robert Hullot-Kentor, Minneapolis, MN: University of Minnesota Press, 1997, p. 6.
3. Mehrabi, 1984, p. 52.
4. Ibid., pp. 53–4.
5. Ibid., p. 56.
6. Ibid., p. 60.
7. Ibid., p. 74.
8. Mohammad Reza Shafi'i Kadkani, *Advar-e She'r-e Farsi*, Tehran: Tus Publishers, 1980, pp. 67–8.
9. Mehrabi, 1984, p. 109.
10. Ibid., p. 115.
11. Arbi Ovanessian had started directing *Ahu Khanom's Husband*. But some disagreements resulted in his abandoning the project.
12. Adorno, p. 6.
13. Ibid., p. 7.
14. See Sohrab Sepehri, *Hasht Ketab*, Tehran: Tahuri Publishers, 1984, pp. 342–4. My translation.
15. Adorno, p. 5.
16. See Gilles Deleuze, *Negotiations*, New York: Columbia University Press, 1990, p. 37.
17. From Morteza Kakhi (ed.), *Roshantar az Khamushi: Bargozideh She'r-e Emruz-e Iran*, Tehran: Agah, 1989, pp. 916–19.
18. Aristotle's *Metaphysics* quoted in Albert Hofstadter and Richard Kuhns (eds), *Philosophies of Art and Beauty: Selected Readings in Aesthetics from Plato to Heidegger*, Chicago: University of Chicago Press, 1964, p. 80.
19. See Christoph Menke, *The Sovereignty of Art: Aesthetic Negativity in Adorno and Derrida*, Cambridge, MA: MIT Press, 1998, p. 3.
20. I noticed this aspect of Ahmad's character when I read Iraj Karimi's review of *Where Is the Friend's House?* in *Khaneh-ye Dust Kojast: Script, Reviews, Etc.*, Tehran: Kanun-e Parvaresh Fekri Kudakan va Nojavanan, 1989, pp. 205–12.
21. For an excellent reading of *Close-Up*, see Gilberto Perez, *The Material Ghost: Films and Their Medium*, Baltimore, MD: The Johns Hopkins University Press, 1998, pp. 263–5 and 269–72.
22. Sohrab Sepehri, *Hasht Ketab*, Tehran: Tahuri, 1985, pp. 303–4. My translation of the first stanza of "The Traveler."

23. For a short version of this story from *The Shah-nameh*, see Vesta Sarkhosh Curtis, *Persian Myths*. The Legendary Past Series, London: British Museum Press, 1993, pp. 31–2.
24. Hans Blumenberg, *Work on Myth*, translated by Robert M. Wallace, Cambridge, MA: MIT Press, 1985, p. 3.
25. E. M. Cioran, *The Trouble with Being Born*, translated by Richard Howard, New York: Seaver Books, 1973, p. 4.
26. Ibid., p. 36.
27. Sepehri, 1985, pp. 304–6. My translation of the second stanza of "The Traveler."

3 THE SIGHT OF THE INVISIBLE WORLD: THE CINEMA OF BAHRAM BEIZA'I

1. Åke Hultkrantz, "An Ideological Dichotomy: Myth and Folk Beliefs among the Shoshoni," in Alan Dundes (ed.), *Sacred Narrative: Readings in the Theory of Myth*, Berkeley, CA: University of California Press, 1984, p. 165.
2. On the quantitatively reducible number of variations on a single myth see, for example, the astonishing discoveries of Anna Birgitta Rooth, professor of ethnology at the University of Uppsala, about the North American creation myths. All of the 300 myths that she had collected could be assigned to no more than eight archetypes. See Anna Birgitta Rooth, "The Creation Myth of the North American Indians," in Dundes, 1984, pp. 166–81.
3. Shahla Lahiji, *Sima-ye Zan dar Athar-e Bahram Beiza'i: Filmsaz va Film-nameh-nevis*, Tehran: Roshangaran Publishers, 1993, p. 49.
4. See, for example, G. S. Kirk's "On Defining Myths," in Dundes, 1984, pp. 53–61, as an articulation of such choices.
5. Roland Barthes, *Mythologies*, selected and translated from the French by Annette Lavers, New York: Hill and Wang, 1972, p. 28.
6. Ibid., p. 28.
7. In one way or another most readers of Beiza'i fall into this trap. For good examples, see Lahiji, 1993, pp. 48–60; Baqer Parham, "Negahi beh Film-ha-ye Bahram Beiza'i," in *21 Sal: Az Amu Sibilu ta Mosaferan. Moruri bar Athar-e Bahram Beiza'i beh Bahaneh-ye Jashnvareh-ye Vinnale*, Vienna: Markaz-e Esha'eh-ye Iranshenasi, 1995, pp. 38–48; Zhaleh Amuzegar, "Raz-ha-ye Ostureh dar "Mosaferan," in Qukasian, 1992, pp. 29–33. The unexamined binary opposition between myth and history is central to all these diverse readings of Beiza'i. In the absence of a critical attention to the place and function of the mythical in Beiza'i's cinema, Parham, for example, comes to the outlandish conclusion that *Bashu* is "parenthetical" to Beiza'i's cinema! See Parham, 1995, p. 39.

8. Georges Bataille, *The Absence of Myth: Writings on Surrealism*, translated and with an introduction by Michael Richardson, London: Verso, 1994, p. 48.

9. See Lahiji, 1993, pp. 54–60. Lahiji has a similarly "motherly" reading of *Perhaps Some Other Time*, p. 66. In both these cases, Lahiji's laudable social concern for the condition of Iranian mothers dulls her critical reading of Beiza'i's film.

10. These are motifs A625 and A625.1 in Stith Thompson's *Motif-Index of Folk-Literature*, six volumes, Bloomington and Indiana, IN: Indiana University Press, 1955.

11. See Alan Dundes' editorial note in Dundes, 1984, p. 182.

12. For the full version of Professor Numazawa, see K. Numazawa, *Die Weltanfänge in der japanischen Mythologie*, Paris–Lucerne, 1946. For a short version of it, see Dundes, 1984, pp. 182–92.

13. K. Numazawa, "The Cultural-Historical Background of Myths on the Separation of Sky and Earth," in Dundes, 1984, p. 191.

14. Ibid., p. 191.

15. Ibid., p. 192.

16. Ibid., p. 192.

17. Dundes, 1984, p. 183.

18. Th. P. van Baaren, "The Flexibility of Myth," in Dundes, 1984, p. 222.

6 IN THE SPECULUM OF THE OTHER: THE FEMININE FIGURE OF MODERNITY

1. See Peter Smith, *The Babi and Baha'i Religions: From Messianic Shi'ism to a World Religion*, Cambridge: Cambridge University Press, 1987, pp. 16–17. This is an excellent source of information about the early Babi movement, and yet is marred by a deeply devout and panegyric reading of Baha'ism.

2. Ibid., p. 22.

3. Ibid., pp. 22, 36.

4. Ibid., p. 47.

5. There are two critical editions of this tract. One is by Hasan Javadi, Manizheh Mar'ashi, and Simin Shekarlu, *Ruya Ru'i Zan va Mard dar Asr e Qajar: Do Resaleh-ye Ta'dib al-Neswan va Ma'ayeb al-Rejal*, Bethesda, MD: Jahan Books, 1992; the other is by Afsaneh Najmabadi, in Bibi Khanom Astarabadi, *Ma'ayeb al-Rijal*, edited by Afsaneh Najmabadi, Chicago: Midland Press, 1992.

6. Javadi et al., 1992, p. 102.

7. For an essay on Taj al-Saltaneh's autobiography see Afsaneh Najmabadi, "A Different Voice: Taj al-Saltaneh," in Afsaneh Najmabadi (ed.), *Women's Autobiography in Contemporary Iran*, Cambridge, MA: Harvard Middle Eastern Monographs, 1990.

8. Taj al-Saltana, *Growing Anguish: Memoirs of a Persian Princess from the Harem to*

Modernity, edited with introduction and notes by Abbas Amanat, translated by Ana Vanzan and Amin Neshati, Washington, DC: Mage Publishers, 1993, p. 286.

9. By far the best available study of these poets is Ahmad Karimi-Hakkak's *Recasting Persian Poetry: Scenarios of Poetic Modernity in Iran*, Salt Lake City, UT: University of Utah Press, 1995.

10. Ibid., p. 300.

11. Ibid., pp. 300–301.

12. See Hamid Zarrinkub, *Chashm-andaz-e She'r-e Nu-e Farsi*, Tehran: Entesharat-e Tus, 1979, p. 44.

13. For a pathological example of this, see the review of *The May Lady* by Mihan Bahrami, "A Few Thousand Years of Wandering," in *Gozaresh-e Film*, vol. 9, no. 117, 15 Azar 1377/6 December 1998, pp. 71, 74. Ms. Bahrami is terribly incensed, and her sentimentality deeply offended, that Forough Kia is so entangled in the web of her social boundaries that she finds her love affair with Amir Rahbar rather ridiculous and socially irrelevant. She has the unbelievable audacity to accuse a filmmaker who has spent the last three decades of her life documenting the most brutal realities of Iranian society of being socially unconscious!

14. For an excellent reading of these films, see Sheila Whitaker, "Rakhshan Bani-Etemad," in Rose Issa and Sheila Whitaker (eds), *Life and Art: The New Iranian Cinema*, London: National Film Theatre, 1999, pp. 66–73.

15. To be distinguished from a feature film with the same title that Bani-Etemad directed in 2000.

16. This is the critical summation and the best compliment that Michel Foucault could give to Gilles Deleuze and Félix Guattari's *Anti-Oedipus: Capitalism and Schizophrenia*, Minneapolis: University of Minnesota Press, 1983, p. xiii.

17. Ibid., pp. 51–6.

18. Ibid., p. 51.

19. Ibid., p. 51.

20. Kristeva calls this stage "semiotic." See Julia Kristeva, "Revolution in Poetic Language," in Kelly Oliver (ed.), *The Portable Kristeva*, New York: Columbia University Press, 1997, pp. 32–4.

21. Ibid., pp. 32–9.

7 WHITHER IRANIAN CINEMA? THE PERILS AND PROMISES OF GLOBALIZATION

1. See Houshang Golmakani, "Sar Maqaleh," in *Mahnameh-ye Cinema'i Film*, February–March, 2000, vol. 18, no. 249, p. 7.

2. On the difference between *sign* and *signification* and my principal argument against

the Husserlian collapse of the two, see my "In the Absence of the Face," *Social Research*, vol. 67, no. 1, Spring 2000, pp. 127–85.

3. See Jalal Al-e Ahmad, *Gharb-zadegi* ("Westoxication"), Tehran: Ravaq Publishers, 1962. For an English translation, see Jalal Al-e Ahmad, *Occidentosis: A Plague from the West*, translated by R. Campbell, edited by Hamid Algar, Berkeley, CA: Mizan Press, 1984.

4. *National Geographic*, vol. 196, no. 1, July 1999.

5. Catherine A. Lutz and Jane L. Collins, *Reading "National Geographic,"* Chicago: The University of Chicago Press, 1993.

6. Lest we think that these developments at Cannes are completely extraterritorial to Iran, we need to pay a quick visit to Sanandaj in Kurdestan, not only far from Cannes, but even further from Tehran, one in miles and kilometers, the other in mores and mind-sets. Right after the conclusion of the Cannes Film Festival there was a conference on Kurdish culture and folklore in Sanandaj, from 7 to 9 June 2000, in which both Bahman Qobadi's *A Time for Drunken Horses* and Samira Makhmalbaf's *Blackboard* were screened. A third Kurdish film by Farhad Mehranfar, *The Ballad of Huram*, however, was the most acclaimed by the audience. See *Bahar*, vol. 1, no. 26, 11 June 2000.

7. Following René Char, "pulverized poem" (*poeme pulverisé*) or "archipelagic speech" (*parole en archipel*) are terms used by Reiner Schürmann in his *Heidegger: On Being and Acting from Principles to Anarchy*, Bloomington and Indianapolis, IN: Indiana University Press, 1987, p. 6, to designate the post-metaphysical collapse of the singular logos. I extend it here to mean the destruction of the creative ego in positive and poetic ways authorizing the voices of many while putting the creative ego and its proclivity to mutate into the presumption of the collective will into the museum.

8. See his interview in *Mahnameh-ye Cinema'i Film*, vol. 18, no. 249, pp. 30–31.

9. See Bahman Qobadi's interview in *Fasl-nameh-ye Cinema'i Film*, vol. 18, no. 249, pp. 32–3.

10. Ibid., p. 33.

11. Ibid., p. 33.

12. For a reading of the death of ideology in the post-Islamic revolution period, see my "The End of Islamic Ideology," in *Social Research*, vol. 67, no. 2, Summer 2000, pp. 475–519.

13. See Samira Makhmalbaf, *The Apple: International Press Reviews and Screenplay*, translated by Minou Moshiri, compiled by Zahra Kamalian, Tehran: Rowzaneh Kar, 2000, conversation with Mohammad Reza Sharifi-nia, p. 11.

14. See Martin Heidegger, *What Is a Thing?*, translated by W. B. Barton, Jr. and Vera Deutsch, analysis by Eugene T. Gendlin, South Bend, IN: Regnery/Gateway, 1967, p. 5.

15. Ibid., p. 7.
16. Martin Heidegger, *What Is Philosophy?* Plymouth: Vision Press, 1963, p. 21.

FILMOGRAPHY

1. Arbi Ovanesian began directing this film. But after shooting one sequence, Davud Mollapour took over.

ACKNOWLEDGMENTS

Almost a decade ago I began offering a course on cinema at Columbia University, where I teach. From that beginning my friend and colleague Richard Peña has been a constant source of support and encouragement. I sincerely thank him for our years of friendship and for the matchless contribution he has made in making Iranian cinema visible in the United States. Some of my other colleagues at the School of the Arts—Dan Kleinman, Annette Insdorf, James Schamus, Andrei Serban—have helped me shape my thoughts in ways known and unbeknownst to them. I thank them all. Through Richard Peña and Dan Kleinman, I made the acquaintance of another colleague, Gilberto Perez, whose knowledge and interest in Iranian cinema has been a source of inspiration. Equally instrumental in my understanding of cinema have been two dear friends and colleagues: Ella Shohat and Bob Stam. I am grateful to both. My young colleague, Joseph Massad, has a piercing command of a critical intelligence for cinema from which he has never failed to teach me.

With my former student Kouros Esmaili, now a filmmaker of extraordinary promise, I have shared many wonderful hours of watching films and discussing them. The same is true of Farhad Zamani and Ramin Bahrani, two other former students both now on their way as emerging filmmakers. All of them have been my companions in many fruitful conversations about cinema and reliable sources of probing precision. Two of my graduate students, Bahbak Jason Mohaqhegh and Kamran Rastegar have been peerless in their critical readings of my work and in helping me prepare this book for publication. An early version of the manuscript was copy-edited by Kamran Rastegar.

Knowledge about Iranian cinema in the United States would have been much poorer and entirely at the mercy of bewildered journalism had it not been for the patient contributions of three prominent scholars and film critics: Jamshid Akrami, Bahman Maqsudlou, and Hamid Naficy. I have been fortunate to benefit from their friendship and long-term contribution to our understanding of Iranian cinema.

The pioneering works of Iranian film critics are instrumental in any serious grasp of Iranian cinema. I have much benefited from the critical writings of Babak Ahmadi, Ahmad Amini, Jamshid Arjomand, Parviz Dava'i, Mas'ud Farasati, Gholam Heydari, Shahla Lahiji, Mas'ud Mehrabi, Jahanbakhsh Noura'i, Jamal Omid, Zaven Qukasian, Bahram Reypour, Omid Ruhani, Naqmeh Samini, Javad Tusi, and Mostafa Zamani-nia. Two distinguished expatriate filmmakers, Reza Allameh-zadeh and Parviz Sayyad, have written perceptively on the international reception of Iranian cinema. No legitimate understanding of Iranian cinema can ignore their critical judgments. The addition of Godfrey Cheshire, Jonathan Rosenbaum, David Kehr, Leslie Camhi, and Nancy Ramsey to the increasing number of insightful commentators has vastly enriched the field. I must here add the name of Azar Nafisi, the leading Iranian literary critic, as among my closest friends and interlocutors in matters of Iranian culture. Alissa and Sue Simon have been great supporters of Iranian cinema in the United States, as has been Merhanz Sa'id Vafa. Rarely has a national cinema benefited from such *esprit de corps*.

My most sincere thanks though must go to the subjects of my book themselves, the distinguished array of filmmakers I have come to know and honor. Rakhshan Bani-Etemad, Bahram Beiza'i, Bahman Farmanara, Abbas Kiarostami, Daryush Mehrju'i, Amir Naderi, and Ja'far Panahi have been particularly generous with their time and instrumental in my knowledge of Iranian cinema. I am particularly indebted to Amir Naderi for sharing his extraordinary knowledge and critical acumen with me. For hours on end he has taught me generously of the inner workings of Iranian cinema in the subterranean walkways of New York subway.

My love and admiration for Mohsen Makhmalbaf makes it difficult for me to thank him properly in the publicity of these pages. For years I have been privileged in his close friendship and the confidence with which he has kept me in his company. There has emerged a Cannes camaraderie around Mohsen that includes his distinguished daughter Samira, his wife Marziyeh Meshkini and his two younger children Meysam and Hana. I am honored to be counted among them.

In Tehran, the distinguished Iranian film critic, Houshang Golmakani, has been extremely helpful in facilitating my access to Persian sources. Mohammad Ateba'i and Reza Safiri helped me in securing still photos and in a number of other important details. Many other Iranian friends, among them Mohammad Beheshti, Mehdi Faridzadeh, Mohammad Aghajani, Jahangir Kosari, and Shirin Dibadj have been generous with their time and help in ways impossible to describe. In Paris, Mohammad Haghighat and Kazem Musavi, and the staff of the MK2, have been indispensable sources of support. In Cannes, I have benefited from the friendship and hospitality of Simin Mo'tamad Arya and Nasrin Medard de Chardon, two valiant souls championing the cause of Iranian cinema. Through Simin Mo'tamad Arya, I came to know Rose Issa in London and benefit from her long-standing support of Iranian cinema. In New York, the office of the New Yorker Films has been a central gathering place of the best of Iranian cinema. Dan and Toby Talbot, Jose Perez, Susan Knubel, and Sasha Breman have been great friends and generous sources of support. The wonderful staff of the New York Film Festival and MOMA make their labor of love the source of joy and inspiration for thousands. New York is also now irreversibly linked in my mind with the name of four wonderful artists: Shirin Neshat, Nicky Nodjumi, Nahid Haghighat, and Ardeshir Mohassess. I am privileged by their friendship. To Mohammad Ghaffari I owe an enduring friendship and great artistic sensibility. Sara Nodjumi and Robi Ghaffari are the standard-bearers of the next generation.

Finally at Verso, my sincere gratitude goes to Colin Robinson and his interest in my work. Varese Layzer did a splendid editorial reading of an earlier version of this book. But my profoundest thanks go to Amy Scholder who finally brought this book to light. In that light, how can I ever thank David Williams of The Running Head for the gift of his grace in magically metamorphosing my meandering musings into the quiet elegance of these pages? He saw through the final stages of production with maddening speed and a miraculous sensitivity to the sense and nonsense of my text.

I have never accumulated so much debt in the writing of a book. My joy in its completion pales in comparison to the gift of so many good friends I have made.

Hamid Dabashi
New York
Summer 2001